Wise and Discerning Hearts

Jill Y. Crainshaw

Wise
and Discerning Hearts

An Introduction to
Wisdom Liturgical Theology

A PUEBLO BOOK

The Liturgical Press Collegeville, Minnesota

BV
176
.C73
2000

A Pueblo Book published by The Liturgical Press.

Design by Frank Kacmarcik, Obl.S.B.

Library of Congress Cataloging-in-Publication Data

Crainshaw, Jill Y., 1962–
   Wise and discerning hearts : an introduction to wisdom liturgical theology /
Jill Y. Crainshaw.
     p. cm.
   "A Pueblo book."
   Includes bibliographical references and index.
   ISBN 0-8146-6182-3 (alk. paper).
   1. Liturgics—History.   I. Title.

BV176.C73   2000
264'.001—dc21   99-054882

Contents

Chapter 1

Introduction

A table, bread, water. Singing, washing, eating. These ordinary objects and common actions, painted onto a particular canvas in a particular time and place, become the colors, the shapes, the rituals of Christian worship. In the introduction to *Holy Things: A Liturgical Theology*, Gordon Lathrop discusses the ways in which Christian worship has focused around particular objects; the constitutive elements of liturgy, elements that over the years have gained so much theological baggage, are, in their most primary sense, ordinary everyday objects—bread, wine, water, and table. As objects of daily life, these things bring to the worship event layers of meaning that exist even before theological language and significance become a part of them.

Lathrop notes, for example, that for many people around the world "bread" represents the "earth and the rain, growing grains, sowing and reaping, milling and breaking, together with the mystery of yeast, all presented in a single object."[1] Bread is food, and a loaf of bread can be thought of as food for a group. As it reminds us of hunger, of nourishment, and of sharing with others, Lathrop says, the meaning of bread becomes much more expansive than its strict utilitarian value. The same might be said of water or wine. The elements of worship have meaning, both utilitarian and symbolic, prior to their use in liturgical form.

In worship, as these everyday objects are juxtaposed to one another and to words about the promises of God, the gathered community learns to "look at the world twice";[2] it discovers new meanings about

---

[1] Gordon Lathrop, *Holy Things: A Liturgical Theology* (Minneapolis: Fortress Press, 1993) 91.

[2] Barbara Brown Taylor, *The Preaching Life* (Boston: Cowley Publications, 1993) 38–50.

the world and about God's presence in the world. Such is the power of worship's metaphorical process, of what some theologians call the Church's imaginative act. Two concepts, "two ideas are struck together and sparks leap through the air between them, revealing familiar notions in a new light."[3] In worship it becomes possible to envision a new world; in worship it is possible to envision the world redeemed.

Because of the transformative potential of its juxtapositions of daily life with the mysteries of God's presence, the structure of early Christian worship was accepted by those faith communities as the primary matrix or locus of knowledge; worship was where theology, or that journey in search of knowledge of God, began. In fact, the worship of the early faith community became a tapestry onto which the social, communal, political, and personal threads of a believer's life could be woven, through God's gift of grace, into a picture of hope for the future.

For those first believers, to acquire wisdom or knowledge of God was to gain insight into the complexities of life and to discover healing and hope in the midst of brokenness. It meant finding God's presence in both the mundane and difficult realities of human living. In their gatherings, as they broke bread that had been baked by ordinary human hands, Christ was made present among them.[4] When ordinary grapes grown in their own vineyards were made into wine and shared with other believers around a common table, the community remembered Jesus and continued to discover its own story within the gospel story.[5]

[3] Ibid.

[4] Lathrop, *Holy Things*, 43–4. Similar discussions of the way in which liturgical meaning or patterns occurred in the early Church can be found in Nathan Mitchell, *Cult and Controversy: The Worship of the Eucharist Outside Mass* (New York: Pueblo, 1974) 10–39; and James White, *A Brief History of Christian Worship* (Nashville: Abingdon Press, 1993) 13–39.

[5] Communal "remembering" or anamnesis, as it has been examined within the liturgical movement, means more than a mere reenactment of past events. The relationship of remembered events to the present is central to current ecumenical dialogue as scholars from various theological perspectives seek to overcome differences of eucharistic practice and understanding.

First, remembered events become a matrix of meaning in the present by being narrated. As David Power suggests in *Eucharistic Mystery: Revitalizing the Tradition* (New York: Crossroad, 1995), it is language that gives "past events the power to change the horizon of existence and offer future generations new possibilities of being" (304). Language structures shape our experiences and understanding of life in this world; of central importance to the

In the worship patterns of those earliest communities, all of the details of people's everyday existence were gathered together with God's Word, and new insights, new understandings, were made possible. The worship of the faith community became a matrix of redemption for all of the diverse aspects of human living. In its earliest conception, then, knowledge of God, or theology, was that primordial aspect of knowing that has ultimate value or life-determining significance. It was a knowledge mediated through the ordo or patterns of worship.[6]

In the past twenty-five years, scholarship within the liturgical movement has been vigorous in its exploration of the ordo as it can be discovered within the practices of early Christian communities. Much of this work has been done in response to contemporary challenges to the adequacy of Christian worship for providing meaning for the lives of people today. There are multiple questions driving the liturgical movement. How can the Church, in its worship, maintain its distinctiveness within the Judeo-Christian tradition and at the same time dialogue meaningfully with the world? To put it a different way, how can traditional patterns be renewed or reconstructed without diminishing the enduring truths they mediate? How has the epistemological framework of the Enlightenment determined the current relationship between liturgy and theology, and how has that relationship contributed to the bifurcation of worship forms and their content? In this contemporary situation, how are we to conceive the relationship between the faith community's ritual practice and its cultural context?[7]

Church's continued dialogue with the world is the way in which the Word of God is narrated and embodied by the community through liturgy.

Second, the "past" contains more than has been given authoritative status. For transformation to occur in the present, retrieval of those forgotten or overlooked elements of tradition is essential. See Marjorie Proctor-Smith, *In Her Own Rite: Constructing Feminist Liturgical Tradition* (Nashville: Abingdon Press, 1990).

[6] As Lathrop asserts in *Holy Things*, "To inquire into the structure of the ordo is to inquire into the way meaning occurs in Christian worship. . . . Meaning occurs through structure, by one thing set next to another. The scheduling of the ordo, the setting of one liturgical thing next to another in the shape of the liturgy, evokes and replicates the deep structure of biblical language, the use of the old to say the new by means of juxtaposition" (33–4).

[7] As Kevin Irwin outlines in *Liturgical Theology: A Primer* (Collegeville: The Liturgical Press, 1990), the phrase ascribed to Prosper of Aquitaine, *legem*

Liturgical theologians have engaged these questions from various perspectives, providing paradigmatic insights for the renewal of the Church and its worship forms; however, in order to continue to dialogue meaningfully and dynamically with this contemporary age, liturgical theology must constantly seek to be self-critical. While the liturgical movement has reminded Christian communities of the ways in which liturgical symbols and the primary patterns of the ordo respond to human need in this era, there are several areas of concern within the movement that require further critique and reflection. Two of these areas for critique constitute the parameters of this discussion and are outlined in a preliminary way here.

The first area of critique is related to a challenge of contemporary society not adequately addressed by the liturgical movement. Contemporary culture boldly asks whether there are any realities at all behind the languages and practices of the Christian faith; as the liturgical movement seeks to recover worship's basic mediating structures, this question of the validity of truth claims mediated by these structures must be addressed.

---

credendi lex statuat supplicandi, has become a theme statement for much of contemporary liturgical theology. It represents concerns to clarify the relationship between liturgy and theology. Central to many theologians' concerns is the argument that it was worship that served as the generative force behind the various creeds, doctrines, and institutions of the Church rather than the reverse.

The current liturgical movement is a part of the modern ecumenical movement, dated by many from the Edinburgh Conference of 1910, which led to the establishment of the International Missionary Council. The work of the Edinburgh Conference prepared the soil out of which grew the Universal Christian Conference on Life and Work in 1925 and the first World Conference on Faith and Order in Lausanne in 1927. These two bodies together became the World Council of Churches in 1948.

In addition, Vatican II sparked a spate of theological dialogue among the major Christian traditions. The groundbreaking work of the liturgical movement that grew out of these dialogues is a primary resource of this manuscript for several reasons: (1) the resulting scholarship includes work by scholars from a multiplicity of backgrounds and perspectives and thus provides fertile soil for mutual correlation and critique; (2) the theologies developed within the movement engage concerns of this era from within a contemporary context and perspective; and (3) a goal of the methodology proposed in this manuscript is a continuation of ecumenical dialogue amidst increasing theological diversity, a goal which is central to the liturgical movement.

Several broad questions related to this will be engaged in the chapters that follow. Sociocultural influences have led to increasing fragmentation and lack of coherency in people's lives and in society as a whole. How can the Church exist within this fragmentation and continue to offer patterns of meaningfulness and coherency? What are the implications of the contemporary diminishment of society's traditional deep symbols or organizing metaphors for a liturgical movement that seeks primarily to recover the liturgical symbols of the Church's past?

The second area of critique is connected to the first and centers on the liturgical movement's dependence on redemption history as the central biblical matrix of its methodologies. The liturgical movement has sought to create liturgies that are adequate to the needs of this contemporary age but that are also in continuity with the richness of tradition. One insightful critique of liturgy provided by the movement is that liturgical forms, throughout the Church's institutional history, have often developed out of doctrinal debate rather than out of the community's actual encounters with Christ. In their efforts to reform and restore the authenticity of liturgy as rooted in the faith community's experience of God's presence, liturgical theologians have looked primarily to events in redemption history and the way these events have been remembered liturgically by ancient communities in order to discern the constitutive meanings and structure of Christian worship. Two issues emerge.

First, one result of the epistemological shift of the modern age is that the Church's historical assumption that it can make an authoritative claim on the basis of redemption history has been undermined. In addition, in recovering the liturgical patterns of the Church's history, the extent to which past and present liturgical forms impede or foster a sense of community and common Christian identity has not been adequately addressed. How can liturgy mediate truth so that the community is challenged more nearly to correlate its divine immanent essence? How can dialogue between contemporary concerns and tradition guard against hegemonic forms that perpetuate oppression? What biblical methodological center presupposes liturgical forms within which a liberating dialectical movement between contemporary concerns and tradition is possible?

The aim of this discussion is to advance a wisdom methodology for liturgical theology that addresses both of these areas of critique and begins to answer the related questions. The wisdom methodology for

liturgical theology proposed here involves a three-way dialogue between (1) liturgical theology within the liturgical movement of the last
twenty-five to thirty years, (2) practical theology, primarily as it is conceived within the philosophical perspective of Edward Farley, and (3)
wisdom theology as its dialogical movement between contemporary
concerns and tradition can be sketched in Proverbs 1–9 and Job. More
distinct parameters for this dialogue will be outlined in the remainder
of these introductory pages. The argument to be developed in this
book can be given this initial statement:

A liturgical theological method grounded in the dialogical movement
between the horizons of everyday reality and tradition found in the
structural forms of Proverbs 1–9 and Job contributes to the ongoing
work of the liturgical movement by (1) providing a theological foundation for renewal of liturgical forms that engages the question of the
validity of truth claims mediated by those forms, (2) maintaining a
rootedness in the Judeo-Christian biblical tradition that is methodologically centered on cosmology and anthropology rather than solely
on redemption history, and (3) implying within its hermeneutical
framework an ongoing process of self-critique.

It is important to signal at this point a presupposition that will be
developed later in this introduction—namely, the assumption by contemporary Old Testament scholars that Old Testament theology
should be both descriptive and constructive. This presupposition
underlies the project's thesis statement.[8] What this means, as several
practical theologians have also argued, is that interpretation of Old
Testament texts is a conversation that is shaped by practical questions
about application of the texts' wisdom to present concrete concerns.[9]
With this understanding of Old Testament theology as a foundation,
I propose that liturgical theology should also be both descriptive and
constructive; I also contend that the fusion of horizons between tradition and contemporary culture finds its generative source in ecclesial

[8] Leo Perdue, *The Collapse of History: Reconstructing Old Testament Theology*
(Minneapolis: Fortress Press, 1994); Mary Catherine Hilkert, *Naming Grace:
Preaching and the Sacramental Imagination* (New York: Continuum, 1997). This
aspect of the thesis will be developed more fully in later chapters.
[9] See David Tracy, *Analogical Imagination* (New York: Crossroad, 1981); Don
Browning, *A Fundamental Practical Theology* (Minneapolis: Fortress Press, 1991).

presence, namely the liturgy. As practical theology and new developments in Old Testament theology are critically correlated, the question for liturgical renewal becomes how the critical-reflective interaction between present concerns and the wisdom of tradition, and in particular biblical tradition, is to be focused in the worship event.

To enter into dialogue with this question requires an integrative approach that is able to recognize the horizons of meaning that exist in both the historical and contemporary cultures; in other words, the purely descriptive and positivistic historical theology on which much liturgical theology is grounded is not adequate. This discussion can be thought of as creating an interdisciplinary dialogue that will imply a corrective to those liturgical theologies that have maintained too close an identification with and focus on positivistic appropriations of redemption history as the central biblical matrix of their methodologies.

The remainder of this introduction will offer a preliminary sketch of the two areas of critique stated above as they relate to the central thesis of the discussion.

A PRELIMINARY SKETCH OF THE FIRST PART OF THE PROBLEM

A theme common to contemporary liturgical scholarship is that there is an ordo or core structure to the Church's liturgical life. Often, this core structure becomes hidden beneath layers of interpretation or behind the written text and rubrics. The core structure of Christian worship, the most basic pattern, arose out of juxtapositions in the actual experiences of the early Church. Belief in the risen Lord became the focus of the early Church's gatherings to read Scriptures, to pray, and to share in a common meal. Eventually, the juxtapositions of belief in Christ with these ritual practices developed into patterns of worship particular to Christian believers.

In this contemporary era, the diminished significance of those deep symbols or patterns that historically provided a matrix of social and communal meaning has stirred a number of crucial questions for the community of faith. Edward Farley, a practical theologian working from the perspective of philosophical theology, sheds new light on some of these concerns, particularly as they relate to the liturgical renewal movement.

As Farley explains, we live in a society with increasing population, a growing sense of personal insecurity, disparities in economic classes, and festering ecological crises.[10] Farley's argument is that many of these problems are the result of a loss of society's deep symbols. It is a loss that has created a society cut off from past wisdom and one whose institutions have become disconnected from their sources of humanization.

Our society is experiencing, he says, a loss of its "words of power."[11] When words of power, or deep symbols, are intact, they provide society with a particular kind of knowledge that Farley says has two primary elements. On the one hand, the symbols are distinctly visible in society's sociology of knowledge. At the same time, the symbols are to some extent elusive because they arise out of the dimension of the "interhuman."[12] Within the dimension of the interhuman operates an

[10] Edward Farley, *Deep Symbols: Their Postmodern Effacement and Reclamation* (Valley Forge, Pa.: Trinity Press International, 1996) ix.

[11] Ibid. The phrase "words of power" is common to feminism, to interpretations of the Bible as literature, and to treatments of Native American religion. Farley uses this phrase and a parallel one, "god-terms," interchangeably. His linguistic framework for defining "words of power" provides an insightful perspective on sacramental theology, an issue I will address at length later in this project. Farley's treatment of the eschatological "vision" embodied in words of power or deep symbols is particularly intriguing in dialogue with eucharistic theology as it is conceived by Alexander Schmemann in his two works *The Eucharist: Sacrament of the Kingdom,* trans. Paul Kachur (Crestwood, N.Y.: St. Vladimir's Seminary Press, 1988) and *Introduction to Liturgical Theology,* trans. Asheleigh E. Moorhouse (Crestwood, N.Y.: St. Vladimir's Seminary Press, 1986).

Several questions will require further examination in this regard. In contemporary liturgical theologies that seek renewal of worship forms, how can scholars hold in tension the language of "enchantment," or of the paschal mystery, and society's demand for empirical data and objective explanation? How is the faith community to maintain the power of liturgy's symbols to point beyond the present moment to the mysteries of the world's createdness? How can the faith community maintain the eschatological power of its symbols to summon people as a community out of their brokenness to envision and to enact a better future?

[12] Farley defines the "interhuman" in *Deep Symbols,* 21–6. As he explains, words of power or god-terms are not created by institutions. God-terms originate in community, as humans exist in relation to one another in the sphere of the interhuman. This is a sphere of relatedness that is formed within individuals prior to the establishment of social organizations and institutions. Because god-terms originate in connection with this primordial sphere, they resist absolute or conceptual translation and are beyond the parameters of

irreducible element of human relatedness that coaxes individuals beyond self-centeredness to see the face of the "other" as a subject rather than as an object. In an ideal society, god-terms or deep symbols develop within the sphere of the interhuman and are the values by which individuals within a community relate to one another and to the rest of the world. The consciousness and integrity of those who are part of the community are shaped by its deep symbols.

What does all of this have to do with faith communities and their worship? Farley explains that because worship in traditional faith communities continues to be centered on words of power, there are significant numbers of persons for whom words of power are still functional and authoritative. Most faith communities, however, are made up of people who are entangled in the institutional structures, ethical norms, and brokenness of contemporary culture; ours is a society in which "compassion," "obligation," and "interrelation" have been replaced by faceless institutions and a media-dominated transferral of social knowledge. In addition, the deep symbols, or ordo, that were central for mediating meaning in the early Church have in large measure become lost or distorted in the quagmire of ideology, historical debate over interpretation, and dogmatism.

As a result, the truths the Church claims to mediate through its worship are no longer readily assumed to be valid or even relevant; worse, in its efforts to compete with a market-driven society, the Church has tended to "close in upon itself," seeking almost frantically to appeal to the individual needs of people in the community and failing to nurture an authentic sense of interrelatedness.[13]

A number of questions crucial to liturgical renewal emerge. In Western societies and faith traditions, what has happened to our words of power that historically enabled people to gather and enact a shared vision that contained both communal and public

---

empirical studies and of positivistic historical studies that examine only cause and effect.

[13] Alexander Schmemann, *For the Life of the World: Sacraments and Orthodoxy* (Crestwood, N.Y.: St. Vladimir's Press, 1973), is particularly concerned that the work of the Church is not primarily for the Church but rather for the redemption of the world. A cultic understanding perceives the Church as an institution which offers grace to individuals; a communal perspective sees the Church as a people renewed by participation in the life of Christ who gather for the primary purpose of envisioning a liberated world.

meaning? In this contemporary society, what is the place of traditional words of power such as "covenant," "agape," "sin," "salvation," and "redemption"?

Today, Lathrop notes, there is increasingly less certainty about the existence of moral and spiritual universals, about the possibility of a core structure that somehow holds together the multiplicity of liturgical expressions in our faith. People are more aware of the shaping power of popular culture, and as implied above, they carry much of this environment and its entanglements with them into the worship event. In light of this, it is vital for liturgical theologians to ask what actually happens in worship as the existential realities of the gathered community intersect with truth as it is mediated by tradition.

Lathrop and other liturgical scholars engage this question by examining the core structure of the ordo, by investigating how meaning occurs in worship. As Lathrop explains, the ordo is not only the written text—Scripture readings, rubrics, and prayers. It is also the presuppositions behind the text. Lathrop's argument is that meaning occurs through juxtaposition. This meaning is relational, abstract, and contextual; the meaning or "knowledge" people experience through liturgy cannot be extracted from their participation in that liturgy or from its implicit order and pattern.

Not unlike Farley's description of the knowledge mediated by a society's words of power, the knowledge mediated through liturgy is not empirical knowledge. In liturgy, habits of heart and mind are formed within the dialectical structure of the ordo. It might be said, as Lathrop argues, that to participate in the meaning of the liturgy, individuals not only think about or talk about what happens in liturgy but also enter into the juxtapositions themselves; ideally, they enter into the sphere of the interhuman in a more explicit and focused way.

By contrast, dominant theories of knowledge today are centered on empirical or technological models. In these models, truth is obtained by extracting some aspect of the experienced reality from its context and concentrating on one of its researchable aspects. Knowledge, in this paradigm, results from empirical research done within specialized disciplines whose isolated facts and theories are applied to particular problems.[14]

[14] Donald Schon, "The New Scholarship Requires a New Epistemology," *Change* (November/December 1995) 27–33, provides a summary and critique of the epistemology of the modern research university that developed after

The result of compartmentalizing human knowing in this way is that there currently appear to be no words of power or organizing metaphors sufficient to deal with the "bits and pieces" of people's lives. The contemporary situation reflects a collapse of society's overarching narratives that located people within a particular history and provided them with a point of reference for the future. As Barbara Brown Taylor describes it, today's society has become a veritable shopping mall of images, each promising to paint for us a picture of the real world and our place in it.[15] Images bombard us from everywhere—sports, the media, politics—and their primary function is not the mediation of a wisdom that will assist us in ordering our lives; rather, the main concern of these institutions is to achieve their own aims, usually for profit.[16]

The result? With so many options, with so many pictures scattered across the study desks of our hearts and minds, choosing what images will shape our thoughts, actions, and ideas has become a complex task.

In the midst of all this stands the Church and its images—the bread, the water, the table—confronted with an increasingly urgent challenge to their integrity. That time in our history is gone when the Church was the primary place where people sought answers for the existential questions of their lives, answers to help them understand who they are, who God is, and where they "fit" in this world.

---

the Civil War when American scholars borrowed from Germany the idea of the university as the place where research is done in order to contribute to "fundamental knowledge." The result of this epistemological model has been a radical separation between research and practice, a separation in which practice is seen as derivative.

The importance of this for theological concerns has been discussed in two works by Edward Farley: *The Fragility of Knowledge: Theological Education in the Church and University* (Philadelphia: Fortress Press, 1988) and *Theologia: The Fragmentation and Unity of Theological Education* (Philadelphia: Fortress Press, 1983).

[15] Taylor, *The Preaching Life*, 41–2.

[16] Edward Farley, "Re-thinking the God-terms—Tradition: The God-term of Social Remembering," *Toronto Journal of Theology* 9 (Spring 1993) 67–77, asserts that each of these secular institutions and its images becomes a "world" of its own with its own criteria for judging truth, determining morals, and dispensing knowledge. As a result, individuals are forced to struggle with life's existential questions, not with the tools of mediated wisdom but with whatever concerns and "knowledge" these institutions offer.

Instead, the Church has become only one of many stocks of knowledge or value systems that are offered in the vast world marketplace for shaping a person's world view. The Church now faces the challenge of articulating in a meaningful way to larger society what happens in our worship that provides answers to those difficult questions people ask as they struggle through the obstacle course of life.

In a world where the dominant institutions have become indifferent and traditionless, what does Christian tradition offer to those people who "almost didn't come to church today but something made me change my mind"?[17] What words in our hymns, prayers, and liturgies describe that "something," draw it in living shapes and colors on people's hearts and minds so that they want to be in its presence again? When people in this fragmented society glance through the window of God's house and see the community of faith gathered around its table, sharing the gospel story, singing, eating and drinking—what do they see in that glance that will appeal to their deep hungers for love, security, and joy? More particularly, what happens in worship in its multiplicity of places and forms that suggests to people that all things really do "cohere in Christ"[18] and that through Christ they can rediscover meaning in their lives?

A PRELIMINARY SKETCH OF THE
SECOND PART OF THE PROBLEM

In *Theologia: The Fragmentation and Unity of Theological Education*, Farley discusses the diminishment of tradition's words of power in light of the loss of theology as habitus.[19] In its earliest Christian conception, as discussed above, the term "theology" meant "knowledge of God." Theology or habitus was an episteme, a "cognitive disposition of the heart toward the things of God"—namely wisdom.[20] It stood at the center of all reality and was the prism through which the many colors of human existence were filtered and interpreted. Theology gave the multiplicity of human experiences a pattern or form.

The Enlightenment and the rise of the modern research university, however, spawned the understanding that theology, rather than being comprehensive, consisted of separate disciplines whose theoretical

[17] Taylor, *The Preaching Life*, 5–12.
[18] Col 1:17b.
[19] Farley, *Theologia*, 35.
[20] Ibid.

and factual gleanings were to be applied in ministerial practice. The notion of theology itself as a "practice" rooted historically and socially in the faith community was lost.

To summarize a much larger argument, the faith community's words of power, or ordo, are no longer recognized as the primary pattern or habitus within which knowledge of the world, science, or ethics develops. Constantly shifting historical and scientific understandings have drawn into question the certainties historically provided by the Church and its interpretations of redemption history, and contemporary culture questions whether there are any realities at all behind the languages and practices of the Christian faith.[21] A central question for worship thus arises: where can the actual "truth" or "wisdom" of faith be found today and what is the power of that truth for shaping a person's political, communal, and ethical character?[22]

[21] What this epistemological shift means in terms of theological language is of central importance to liturgical concerns and is outlined by Langdon Gilkey, *Naming the Whirlwind: The Renewal of God-Language* (New York: Bobbs-Merrill Company, 1969). In contemporary culture, the question is not whether language about God is valid; a pluralistic society such as ours allows for much diversity in what one believes "by faith." The question today is whether language about God has any "ultimate" meaning for us in our experience as far as making a discernible difference in our world. According to Gilkey, when we say that certain concepts are meaningless, we are actually saying that they do not intersect with human experience and therefore are not adequate modes for understanding experience.

[22] Mircea Eliade discusses at length the differences between religious experiences and "profane" experiences in *The Sacred and the Profane: The Nature of Religion: The Significance of Religious Myth, Symbolism and Ritual within Life and Culture* (New York: Harper and Row, 1957) 11. Eliade suggests that periodically we become aware of "realities" that do not belong to this world. This awareness is mediated to us through objects that are part of our "profane" world. One problem faced by people today is that the world has become desacralized; reality is no longer equated with the sacred.

Important to this project in this regard is Schmemann's insistence that the Church does not exist to provide a place of isolation from a profane world. The mission of the faith community is not the conversion of worldly or profane people to the religious life. This perspective, Schmemann argues, deprives the secular life of any ultimate meaning in itself. In liturgy, it is the juxtaposition of secular life in all of its many dimensions with words about the promises of God that enables us to envision a redeemed world; especially in the sacraments we are reminded that in Christ all of life is filled with meaning and purpose.

Farley attempts to answer this question, as noted earlier, by talking about the faith community's words of power or deep symbols. As he explains, there is a powerful reality of faith that stands beyond any human shaping of it. It is a primordial and pre-reflective reality that originates in the sphere of the interhuman. It is a reality that refuses to be carried in the vessels of human language or action but that at the same time does not become cognitively audible or visible outside of those forms; it is a reality that stands at both the beginning and end of most human journeying; it is a reality that is rooted in the deep affections of the human spirit and in the deep structures of creation that are hidden from the eyes of the world but that in a mysterious way animate our being in the world.

The role of the faith community in its worship is to provide a matrix within which this pre-reflective intuition of God and salvation can find some form of expression. In our world, people are shaped by competing ideologies ranging from abusive families to professional football to corporate bureaucracies; worship may be the only place where those primordial deep affections of thanksgiving, joy, love, fear, and sorrow can be embodied in ways that unify and transform communities and individuals. However, Farley insists, if the Church is to continue to "make sense," if it is to continue to provide organizing metaphors that offer coherence in the midst of fragmentation, theology as habitus must be restored.

This concern for a renewal of the understanding of theology as integrative and for a return to a focus on theology as being rooted in the faith community has been articulated by a number of practical theologians, in particular by liturgical theologians. Mark Searle, for example, in assessing the liturgical movement, writes that "there is hardly any serious theological issue that does not surface, in one way or another, in the liturgy: theological epistemology, God-language, theological anthropology, ecclesiology, salvation history, even the issues of critical theology, shaped as they are by particular cultural contexts."[23]

While contemporary liturgical theologians have offered insight into renewal of worship forms, most of their theologies maintain the traditional focus on redemption history as the central biblical matrix of their methodologies. What is needed, in light of contemporary challenges to the validity of the Church's truth claims, to its institutional

[23] Mark Searle, "Renewing the Liturgy—Again," *Commonweal* 115 (18 November 1988) 622.

integrity, to the Judeo-Christian "grand narrative," and to theological epistemology, is a methodological center or turning point that is a more direct correlate to theology as habitus.

I contend that wisdom theology offers a corrective to that contemporary liturgical theology which has maintained the traditional focus on redemption history. There are several particular reasons why wisdom provides a biblical correlate to the concept of theology as habitus. In his discussion of the place and role of wisdom in the Old Testament, for example, Leo Perdue notes that particular contemporary crises— "the threat of nuclear holocaust, the deterioration of the biosphere, ethnic cleansings, racism, and patriarchy"—have spawned recent interests in anthropology and cosmology.[24] While Scripture addresses these issues from various perspectives, the dominant view in Old Testament theology has been that the theme of redemption history is primary to biblical faith, while creation is secondary.[25] The wisdom corpus suggests a corrective to this view in several ways.[26]

[24] Leo Perdue, *Wisdom and Creation: The Theology of Wisdom Literature* (Nashville: Abingdon Press, 1994) 341. It is important to note here that David Power, in *Unsearchable Riches: The Symbolic Nature of Liturgy* (New York: Pueblo, 1984), offers insight into liturgical renewal by emphasizing how the liturgy functions within the larger society and in relation to the existential crises of this contemporary world. In *Context and Text: Method in Liturgical Theology* (Collegeville: The Liturgical Press, 1994) Kevin Irwin also focuses on the relationship between sociocultural contexts and liturgical forms. Neither of these works, however, suggests the wisdom corpus as a biblical correlate for their arguments.

[25] See Perdue, *The Collapse of History;* Robin Lovin and Frank Reynolds, eds. *Cosmogony and Ethical Order* (Chicago: University of Chicago Press, 1985); David Tracy and Nicholas Lash, eds., *Cosmology and Theology* (New York: Seabury Press, 1983); Samuel Terrien, *The Elusive Presence: Toward a New Biblical Theology* (New York: Harper and Row, 1978); James L. Crenshaw, "Method for Determining Wisdom Influence upon 'Historical Literature,'" *Journal of Biblical Literature* 88 (1969) 129–42.

[26] The focus on wisdom within Old Testament theology is rather recent. As Perdue discusses in *The Collapse of History,* renewed interest in the wisdom corpus emerged at about the same time as the biblical theology movement began to face serious criticisms. Before that, and particularly since World War II, history dominated methods of doing Old Testament theology. One reason that Old Testament study has been dominated by historical criticism is that it intersects with Enlightenment assumptions that value objectivity, positivism,

First, as Perdue argues, wisdom provides a delineation of biblical anthropology and cosmology. This is important for opening theological eyes and ears to how the biblical canon addresses contemporary issues of cosmological and anthropological import.

Second, while wisdom is centered on cosmological and anthropological concerns, it does not deny the purposefulness of redemption history. Setting redemption history next to biblical portraits of cosmology and anthropology actually substantiates a proper understanding of redemption history; as Perdue explains, "Israel's place in the cosmos and the relationship of the chosen people to the other nations are properly understood only by reference to the larger questions of the nature and character of the cosmos and humanity."[27]

Third, wisdom, with its focus on God as Creator, demonstrates that Israel's contemplative piety included an awareness of and deep respect for God's significance for all creation, particularly beyond the Hebrew cultic community.[28]

Finally, creation theology was at the center of the sages' understanding of God, humanity, and the world, making it universal in scope. Because of this, wisdom is a resource for reconstructing the faith and liturgical forms which remains grounded in the Judeo-Christian tradition but also contributes to efforts to express faith in ways that are more adequate to the needs and questions of this contemporary age.

One final reason that wisdom suggests a biblical correlate to theology as habitus is that, similar to Farley, the sages recognized that the most profound understandings of God and God's creative purpose are to be discovered in structures deeper than the human mind can fathom. In wisdom, these "deep structures" seek expression through metaphorical language, the same kind of language used in liturgical celebration. Through their experience of everyday things such as water, bread, and wine, and through ordinary actions such as eating,

---

and scientific precision in the study of texts. With the diminishing of history's dominance, new methods of Old Testament study have emerged that operate out of the hermeneutic perspective that theological interpretation is inherently constructive rather than descriptive. These newer approaches minimize the importance of facticity and focus on the ways in which the biblical text and tradition provide the material for various interpretations in different contexts.

[27] Ibid., 341.

[28] John F. Priest, "Where Is Wisdom to Be Placed?" *Studies in Ancient Israelite Wisdom*, ed. H. M. Orlinsky (New York: KTAV Publishing House, 1976) 281–8.

drinking and washing, the sages, using the metaphorical structure of wisdom sayings, were able to make connections to the deeper truths of the divine.[29]

MAPPING THE LANDSCAPE OF A WISDOM LITURGICAL METHOD

Questions facing the Church today are difficult ones; they are questions that liturgical theologians in most denominations struggle to answer as they search for those forms that will breathe new life into worship. In an era of rapid societal change, liturgical theology must constantly seek to be self-critical in order to maintain a dynamic and meaningful dialogue with the concerns of this contemporary age. There are several particular areas in which a wisdom methodological foundation can provide such a critique and further the ongoing process of liturgical reform.

The institutions that now compete to provide us with categories of meaning are consumer-driven and often depict ancient wisdom and tradition as lifeless relics of the past. In order to respond to this, those things claimed "by faith" to have life-determining value must be understood in terms of their impact on ordinary existence. This requires a theological method that constantly struggles with how the world is structured and with how things in the world are interrelated.[30]

---

[29] Claus Westermann, *Roots of Wisdom: The Oldest Proverbs of Israel and Other Peoples* (Louisville: Westminster/John Knox Press, 1990), states that underlying the wisdom statements in Proverbs is the human quest for knowledge of self, of God, and of the world: "'World' here is not to be interpreted as some abstract, general concept of the universe but strictly as the world of the person, insofar as it is accessible to his [sic] perception. In both realms—in his human existence and in the environment in which he lives . . . there is much for him to observe, to recognize, to understand . . . for humanity is on a journey of learning, observing and questioning" (6–9).

[30] Edward Farley, "Thinking Toward the World: A Case for Philosophical Pluralism in Theology," *American Journal of Theology and Philosophy* 14 (January 1993) 51–63, defines reality as those "things" (events, processes, objects, persons, societies and their actions) that we have to take into account as we engage in our daily activities. Theology, he argues, must always ask itself in what sense the things of faith are real. How are love, community, sin, and God a part of those "things" which make up our existence, and how do the "truths" that Christian tradition mediates to us transform the "tangled web of life" and society's power structures?

While a number of liturgical theologians have begun to examine more closely the relationship between the faith community and surrounding culture, a tension inevitably emerges between (1) how faith communities are to maintain their particularity without becoming exclusive and dogmatic and (2) how they can move in the direction of openness to and unity with differing traditions.[31] The following chapters will demonstrate that a wisdom perspective on liturgical practice provides a way for liturgical theology to maintain the integrity and richness of the Judeo-Christian tradition and at the same time address itself "toward the world."

First, the sages, with perhaps the exception of Koheleth, did not deal with the religious skepticism of their day at the level of dogmatic faith statements, but at the more foundational level of experience, primarily experience that begins in the faith community and then journeys out into the world. At this level, a community's distinctive beliefs are more open to dialogue with other knowledge claims.

Second, wisdom maintains a concern with how the objects, actions, and people within the world are connected to one another. To express it in Farley's terms, wisdom's moral world view is generated in the sphere of the interhuman.

Finally, the epistemological method of wisdom is to discover what is "real" by exploring how sin, and the believer's integrity in the face of sin, weakens or strengthens life. Wisdom is concerned with determining how its faith world view impacts ordinary existence in a transformative and life-shaping way.

Another area in which a wisdom methodological foundation can further the process of liturgical renewal is related to this. Farley expresses the concern that the epistemological model currently dominant in most theological institutions is rooted in the Enlightenment's critical principle and has resulted in the marginalization and fragmentation of theology. A question that needs to be addressed by liturgical theologians in light of this is how to restore to worship the ability to provide a matrix of redemption through which an integration of the personal, the political and the communal—in short, of knowledge—can occur.

Wisdom, because it has creation as its methodological center, offers an epistemological foundation within the Judeo-Christian tradition that understands theology to be integrative of the various dimensions of life, including anthropology, community, ethics, and politics.

[31] Langdon Gilkey, *Society and the Sacred* (New York: Crossroad, 1981) 42.

A wisdom methodological foundation provides one final corrective for current liturgical theologies. As suggested earlier, much of the liturgical movement has been concerned with recovering liturgical practices of the Church's past as a way to restore integrity to liturgy. As noted by Proctor-Smith in her work on constructing feminist liturgical tradition, this aspect of the movement is based on a recovery of historical norms and is led by clergy. As a result, it has neither adequately challenged the validity of the Church's tradition itself nor critiqued the extent to which past traditions were shaped by a patriarchal and oppressive Church and society. In other words, even though the liturgical movement has shifted the focus of liturgical action away from the ordained clergy to the faith community, it is important to note, as Proctor-Smith does, that its issues are still determined primarily "by those who already had access to legitimate authority and leadership."[32]

The question must then be asked, it seems, whether the liturgical movement has been adequately self-critical of its perspectives on its own traditions. We live in a world where people continue to be marginalized and where evils such as classism and racism are often legitimized on the basis of traditional or historical norms. It is therefore vital that the Church constantly examine whether its traditional liturgical forms distort or further illuminate the "divine immanent essence" they claim to mediate.

This discussion will examine how Old Testament wisdom provides an epistemological foundation for a liturgical theological method that answers these challenges in the following ways. First, a danger inherent in communal and institutional life is that the received vision of truth will develop into a "selective" vision that serves to perpetuate the mediating structures. The pedagogical form of Proverbs supports a wisdom that deals with this danger in that it requires "an intentional examination of the individual's and the community's own epistemological concerns, political/social influences, and historical roots."[33]

[32] Proctor-Smith, *In Her Own Rite*, 20–3.

[33] Alyce MacKenzie, "Different Strokes for Different Folks: America's Quintessential Postmodern Proverb," *Theology Today* (July 1996) 207. In Proverbs 10–31, some sayings appear to offer "contradictory" wisdom or knowledge, suggesting that shaping of character or virtue is not tied to any dogmatic moral rule or principle. The person of character, as part of the interpretive community, develops the wisdom to determine which saying is appropriate for a given context.

Proverbial wisdom's view of knowledge insists that human wisdom cannot be absolutized into inflexible doctrinal forms even for the purposes of preserving a particular tradition; rather, what we learn on the "journey" of life's experiences is intersubjective and therefore must remain dialogical.

Second, in later wisdom texts, such as Job, the traditional Hebrew faith world view is challenged and transformation of pedagogical forms is made possible. This discussion will argue that the structure of Job provides an avenue for critical commentary on institutions of faith (and thus on their liturgical forms) and how the truth claims they mediate often perpetuate oppression and injustice.

Liturgical renewal, understood and critiqued from the perspective of a methodology grounded in Old Testament wisdom, has the potential to reawaken contemporary faith communities to ways their liturgical forms can continue to "make sense," to mediate truths of life-determining significance and ultimate value in this contemporary culture.

CONCLUSION

This book attempts to delineate a wisdom perspective on liturgical theology. This means that the thesis, as it advances a wisdom method-ology, intends to be interpretive rather than instrumental as regards liturgical practice. The proposed outcome of the project, therefore, is not primarily to provide a model for worship or to hold up any particular tradition or style of worship as an example of a "wisdom" model.

Because the goal of this project is to develop what might be called a hermeneutical prolegomenon to a wisdom liturgical method, the dis-cussion will not answer questions such as "how do we translate this theory into actual practice." However, the question of "how" will be approached hermeneutically, to a degree, in the final implicatory stages of the project.

The wisdom methodology for liturgical theology proposed here involves a correlation of the general tenets of liturgical theology, wis-dom theology, and practical theology. The risk inherent in a project that seeks to bring three seemingly diverse fields into dialogue is that it is too wide-ranging and thus will lack focus. Because no correlation such as this one currently exists, the purpose of this project is to provide an initial sketching of the contours of a wisdom liturgical methodology as a foundation for later more focused work and appli-cation across the field of practical theology. The limit of this study is that its treatment of the literature in the three fields of concern is not exhaustive; the goal is to engage representatives from each of the fields for the purpose of creating a mutually critical dialogue that is necessary to the development of the proposed methodology.

The primary dialogue partner from the area of practical theology is Edward Farley. His methodological focus on the restoration of theology as habitus and his related understanding of redemptive ecclesial presence will be central to the defining and development of this thesis.

Discussions of wisdom will be limited to (1) the primary tenets of wisdom theology as they have been set forth in the secondary literature, (2) selected passages from Proverbs 1–9 that set forth the metaphorical movement and theme in early wisdom, and (3) the linguistic, theological, and structural framework of Job. While other traditional wisdom sayings within the Old Testament, the sapiential Psalms, Ecclesiastes, and the extra-canonical wisdom books are also valid conversation partners in this effort, the structural form and historical development of Proverbs 1–9 and Job suggest foundational elements for the purposes of this project.

In Proverbs 1–9, the basic tenets of Old Testament wisdom theology are explained in their most elemental form and the role of the community in shaping character is depicted. Job, particularly in its structural form, confronts the challenges of skepticism to the faith community's foundational beliefs and suggests a model for critical analysis and transformation of the community's traditional forms. This structural and historical development of Proverbs and Job models from within the biblical tradition the critical-reflective interaction between present concerns and the wisdom of tradition that I contend is central to a liturgical methodology adequate to this contemporary age.

Although wisdom literature has been a somewhat neglected subject until recently, a mastery of the secondary literature on the subject, much less of the actual biblical texts themselves, is impossible within the scope of this project. The aim of this discussion is to summarize the work of scholars in the field and invite them into an interdisciplinary dialogue with the liturgical movement and with representatives from the field of practical theology. A central concern in this process is that the voice of wisdom be heard with integrity on its own terms as a vital participant in conversations interested in liturgical renewal.

A number of scholars have argued that the liturgical movement began as early as the mid-1800s. For the purposes of this discussion with its focus on liturgical renewal in this contemporary era, I will limit my dialogue partners primarily to those liturgical scholars within the liturgical movement who have written following the publication of the term "liturgical theology" by Alexander Schmemann.[34]

This project is a correlation of three distinct fields of inquiry. To account for different readers' familiarity with the literature and concepts discussed, this work uses longer footnotes to accompany shorter text. The text concentrates on critical analysis in relation to the thesis. Footnotes provide definitions of concepts and explanations from within the respective fields.

[34] Schmemann, *Introduction to Liturgical Theology*, 14.

Chapter 2

Liturgical Theology at the Turn of the Century

Worship. *Leitourgia.* It is a mystery, a mystery of creation and transformation.[1] In worship, people from multiple places and situations journey to a common meeting space and through their experience of a word from God, ritual actions, and prayer, they become more than they were as individuals—a community of new life in Christ, the Church.

Even in the simple act of gathering, an act described by Don Saliers as a "slow inexorable dance by which we assemble in the name of and by invitation of Jesus," the creative mystery is present.[2] How can it be, Saliers asks, that the wrinkled hands of a grandfather, the weary fingers of a mother who has been awake all night with her sick child, the skilled hands of a musician, the reddened hands of the cook from the corner restaurant—how can all those different hands and people join together around an object as ordinary as a table and through the

---

[1] Don Saliers, *Worship as Theology: Foretaste of Glory Divine* (Nashville: Abingdon Press, 1994) 191–6, suggests that "to call something a 'mystery' in American culture is to invite misunderstanding from the outset." In the Christian tradition, the Eucharist is referred to as the "paschal mystery." What this focuses on is the "paradox of God's disclosure and hiddenness in Christ, and likewise, the hiddenness of human lives with Christ in God." The "mystery" of God's presence is revealed to the worshiping community in part through liturgical forms. The forms used in worship can draw the community into God's continuing redemptive presence, but liturgical forms may also subvert the mystery if they fail to remember the suffering of those who face injustices. As David Power suggests in *Eucharistic Mystery: Revitalizing the Tradition* (New York: Crossroad, 1995) 313, the question for the Church today is how the historical event of Christ's death and resurrection may be represented transformatively in a shattered and fragmented world such as ours.

[2] Saliers, *Worship as Theology,* 28.

sharing of a common meal be transformed into a unified whole? How can such diverse individuals gather together in the act of worship and discover a pattern of meaningfulness, the redemptive presence of God?

Even in an era when society challenges the transformative power of worship, Gordon Lathrop notes, the regular Sunday gatherings continue. The question arises: why? What is it about the age-old pattern of gathering, reading Scripture, singing, preaching, praying, and sharing a meal that offers meaning to people's lives today? What is the role of our traditional words, actions, and symbols in a contemporary marketplace flooded with competing images?

As noted in the previous chapter, a common theme in liturgical scholarship of the last twenty-five to thirty years is that there is a basic pattern to all Christian worship. The juxtapositions inherent in this pattern mediate ultimate truth and make possible transformation of human understandings of life and of God.[3] Within this theme, the question of "how" liturgy enables this transformation has become a central theme, particularly in light of the pressing questions of this contemporary era.

It is a concern focused on several primary issues: (1) the way in which liturgy embraces the struggle for meaning between humanity, God, and the world; (2) the extent to which the Church, through its liturgical practice, maintains patterns that correlate with what Farley calls its "immanent ideal essence";[4] (3) the problem of recovering liturgical practices of the Church's past as a means of restoring integrity to liturgy and enabling ecumenical dialogue; and (4) the problem of articulating a relationship between liturgy and doctrine that allows for dialogue and unity between multiple Christian traditions and practices.

The purpose of this chapter is twofold. First, scholarship in the field of liturgical theology which addresses the above issues from various perspectives will be examined. The second goal is to provide a critical analysis of existing perspectives and to demonstrate why another approach is needed. The critique will focus on the two areas suggested in Chapter 1 as constituting the parameters of this project. I will revisit them briefly here.

[3] Gordon Lathrop, *Holy Things: A Liturgical Theology* (Minneapolis: Fortress Press, 1993) 33–4.
[4] Edward Farley, *Ecclesial Reflection: An Anatomy of Theological Method* (Philadelphia: Fortress Press, 1982).

First, sociocultural and epistemological developments of this age pose serious questions to the reality constructs of the Church's language and practices. While liturgical theology has provided groundbreaking work toward renewal of worship forms, it has not dealt adequately with these questions.

The second area of critique is related to the first; it focuses on the liturgical movement's dependence on redemption history as the central biblical matrix of its methodologies.

The purpose of this chapter is to outline existing liturgical methodologies in relation to the above two critiques.

THE LITURGICAL LANDSCAPE TODAY

The title and content of a 1995 article by Donald Schon make a bold statement about education in this era: "The New Scholarship Requires a New Epistemology."[5] Schon argues in this article that there is a "knowledge" that cannot be captured or transmitted by a textbook, theoretical construction, or instruction in the classroom; there is a level of knowledge that is embedded in the intuitive actions of everyday living.

This tacit knowledge, or "knowing-in-action" as Schon terms it, constitutes most of what people know how to do in both personal and professional life; it is what enables people to negotiate the obstacle course of daily living. It is a knowledge that cannot be abstracted from its rootedness in particular concrete realities. Schon explains:

"When we go about the spontaneous, intuitive performance of the actions of everyday life, we show ourselves to be knowledgeable in a certain way. Often we cannot say what we know. When we try to describe it, we find ourselves at a loss or we produce descriptions that are obviously inadequate. Our knowing is ordinarily tacit, implicit in our patterns of action and in our feel for the stuff with which we dealing. It seems right to say that our knowledge is in our action."[6]

To discover what someone knows-in-action, it is necessary to observe the action, reflect on what we observe, describe the action, and reflect on the description.

[5] Donald Schon, "The New Scholarship Requires a New Epistemology," *Change* (November/December 1995) 27.
[6] Ibid., 29.

In contemporary scholarship, there is a growing respect for what people know intuitively, for that tacit wisdom or knowledge that enables them to "think on their feet" in difficult situations. This focus has developed in response to the dichotomy that exists in dominant models of scholarship between knowledge as research and knowledge as practice, a dichotomy that has emerged primarily as a result of the epistemological foundations of the modern research university.

In the pedagogical model of the modern university, research done in the university contributes to a corpus of fundamental knowledge. Within universities, and in professional schools that have emerged since 1964, "practice," has been seen primarily as the application of this fundamental knowledge to particular problems.

The critical eye of a contemporary age increasingly views this dominant paradigm with skepticism. Modern society has not achieved the understanding of society or humanity that the formal critical principle promised; poverty and tragic injustices are stark reminders that the receding era's technological advances have not brought affluence or equality to the whole world. People today, inheritors of an Enlightenment ethos that never lived up to its ideals, seek relevancy; they demand answers for the very real and painful exigencies of living in a chaotic world.

Schon argues that if research and scholarship are to provide appropriate wisdom and guidance for contemporary people, new models of learning are necessary that collapse the gap between research and practice that was created in the aftermath of the Enlightenment.[7]

In this "new scholarship," there are several primary understandings. These understandings operate on the basis of a different epistemological foundation than models that grew out of an Enlightenment metaphysics: (1) all knowledge, even scientific knowledge, is inter-subjective;[8] (2) there is knowledge embedded in our everyday actions;

[7] Donald Schon, *The Reflective Practitioner: How Professionals Think in Action* (New York: Basic Books, 1983) 21–69. For a similar treatment of this historical development from the perspective of theological education see Edward Farley, *Theologia: The Fragmentation and Unity of Theological Education* (Philadelphia: Fortress Press, 1983) and *The Fragility of Knowledge: Theological Education in the Church and University* (Philadelphia: Fortress Press, 1988); David H. Kelsey, *Between Athens and Berlin: The Theological Education Debate* (Grand Rapids, Mich.: Eerdmans, 1993).

[8] This theme is treated in terms of liturgical theology by Michael B. Aune, "Worship in an Age of Subjectivism Revisited," *Worship* 65 (May 1991) 224–38.

(3) practice is "the place both for the application of knowledge *and* for the generation of knowledge."[9]

The contemporary epistemological shift, this paradigmatic change in our understandings of "how we know what we know," is reflected in liturgical practices and scholarship of recent years. At the very least, theological education's working out of how theology is to be in conversation with culture, science, philosophy, and social sciences has influenced the way in which denominational leaders revise and understand liturgical texts, the way in which the Church envisions its relationship to culture, and the way in which the dialectic between liturgy and theology is conceived.[10]

In large measure due to society's disillusionment with the world that emerged during the modern era, the years from 1965 to 1995 witnessed unprecedented change in the understandings of worship in most North American traditions.[11] Much of that work was done in response to several primary questions. What does it mean for our

[9] Schon, "The New Scholarship Requires a New Epistemology," 28. Growing out of these understandings, the new scholarship will be a scholarship of "discovery" that integrates isolated facts, makes connections across disciplines, emphasizes the relatedness of context and learning, and creates a dialogical relationship between teacher and student.
Contemporary critical education theory raises an issue related to this. This body of scholarship argues that true liberation and restoration of world structures occurs when people within various institutional systems cease to be viewed as "objects," as mere recipients of the categories and principles propagated by the institution, and become subjects in a mutually transitive dialogue with those in authority. In general, critical educational theory reminds us that knowledge is not an "innocent" means to an end. Rather, it is shaped by a culture's dominant economic and social structures. See Paulo Freire, *Pedagogy of the Oppressed*, rev. ed. (New York: Continuum, 1995); Peter McLaren, *Life in Schools: An Introduction to Critical Pedagogy in the Foundations of Education* (Miami: Longman, 1989); Patti Lather, "Critical Theory, Curricular Transformation, and Feminist Mainstreaming," *Journal of Education* 166 (1982) 55–66.

[10] The various ways in which a more integrative scholarship has been configured in terms of theological education is outlined in the typology developed by James N. Poling and Donald E. Miller, *Foundations for a Practical Theology of Ministry* (Nashville: Abingdon Press, 1985).

[11] Power, *Eucharistic Mystery*, 9, notes that at its outset, with the Second Vatican Council, liturgical renewal generally accepted modern ideals and concepts and failed to note the skepticism that was already nibbling at the edges of modernity's constructs of meaning. Increasingly since the 1960s developments

worship, for example, that the modern era did not succeed in providing a coherent explanation of human reality? How does it affect liturgical practice that a human history now permeated by the evils of genocide and constant war destroys not only our perceptions of human potential but also of divine justice?

As White argues, the proliferation of revisions of traditional liturgical texts and the wide diversity of new styles of worship that have appeared on the scene during this era—feminist worship and the "woman church" movement, charismatic worship in mainline churches, and the Church growth movement—reflect the increasing plurality of ways that faith communities are reconstructing their cultural outlook and world view as they seek to answer these pressing questions.[12] Foundational to these recent developments is the unprecedented understanding that theological study, liturgical activity, and the worshiping Church cannot be viewed in isolation from one another but must be held in balance.

A common theme in the scholarship related to this is a concern to establish more clearly the relationship between the Church's liturgy *(lex orandi)* and its theology *(lex credendi)*.[13] This theme is grounded in the understanding that the faith community provides a fusion of horizons between tradition and contemporary culture that finds its generative source in ecclesial presence, namely the liturgy. Just how the relationship between liturgy and theology operates to make transformation of human lives possible has been configured in various ways by scholars, some granting primacy to theology over liturgy, others insisting on liturgy as primary to theology, and others seeking to characterize the relationship between liturgy and theology as a mutually informing dialectic.[14]

In *What Is Liturgical Theology? A Study in Methodology*, David Fagerberg distinguishes four understandings of the relationship between

---

within the liturgical movement have been more sensitive to the tragic destruction of peoples, such as in the Holocaust, and to cultural pluralism.

[12] James White, *Christian Worship in North America—A Retrospective: 1955–1995* (Collegeville: The Liturgical Press, 1997) vii.

[13] Kevin Irwin, *Context and Text: Method in Liturgical Theology* (Collegeville: The Liturgical Press, 1994) 3–32, provides a historical summary of the delineation of *"ut legem credendi lex statuat supplicandi"* ("The law of prayer grounds the law of belief").

[14] Ibid.

liturgy and theology as it has been delineated within the liturgical movement. The labels he assigns to these four approaches are (1) theology *of* worship, (2) theology *from* worship, (3) liturgical theology as he specifically defines it, and (4) the study of the third approach. I will use a revised form of Fagerberg's typology as a guide for defining the parameters of liturgical theology as it exists today.[15] Because the growing edges for both the third and fourth approaches overlap to some degree, I will not provide a separate treatment of each. More particular reasons for this departure from Fagerberg's typology will be made explicit as the chapter proceeds.

Clearly, individual theological treatments of worship and liturgy each offer helpful insights and have furthered the process of liturgical renewal; Fagerberg has demonstrated this in his discussion of the four "types" and corresponding representative theologians. The purpose of this chapter is to provide an overview of both the strengths and inadequacies of current liturgical theologies as a whole and to suggest areas for further growth within each type.

THEOLOGIES OF WORSHIP

The term "liturgical theology" has been variously demarcated by liturgical scholars in recent years. One aim of this discussion is to sketch the contours of a "liturgical theology" that will effectively correlate and dialogue with the epistemological shifts described above; to accomplish that task it is necessary to examine the layers of meaning the term has acquired since its publication by Schmemann.

Fagerberg calls one "family" of liturgical scholarship that defines the relationship between liturgy and theology "theologies of

---

[15] It is important to note that the defining parameters I establish here are not to be seen as dogmatic. Rather, because of the diversity of contexts and presuppositions from which liturgical theologies are conceived, guiding parameters must be seen as porous, representing only boundary markers for a very differentiated field of study. For a more complete cross-section of historical developments within the liturgical movement from varying perspectives see Kevin Irwin, *Liturgical Theology: A Primer* (Collegeville: The Liturgical Press, 1990); Mary Collins, *Worship: Renewal to Practice* (Washington, D.C.: Pastoral Press, 1987); Mark Searle, "Renewing the Liturgy—Again," *Commonweal* 18 (November 1988) 617–22; John Baldovin, *Worship: City, Church, and Renewal* (Washington, D.C.: Pastoral Press, 1991); White, *Christian Worship in North America.*

worship."[16] In general, these theologies treat liturgy as one among other sources for theology; liturgical forms are seen as expressions of an underlying theology or dogma which provides critical norms for the overall theme of worship.

Theologies of worship view the primary task of theology as delineating God's action in Jesus Christ. To the extent that worship is a human response to divine action and reflects something about the relationship between people and God, it is the focus of a theology of worship.

Scholars operating out of this perspective might be said to examine the "theme of worship" by looking through the lens or window of theology.[17] Thus, particular details of a concrete liturgy or of a liturgical tradition are not the primary concern. Fagerberg suggests, for example, that when a theology of worship describes the role of prayer, it does not distinguish between specific prayers as they have developed in historical texts and have been appropriated in the concrete practices of various faith communities.

As Fagerberg argues, this ability to "abstract from the particulars in order to speak about the theme of worship" is a strength of theologies of worship.[18]

Theologies of worship are important in that they are concerned to reconnect the second order theology of the academy to the worship of the faith community. They also expand our understanding of worship by thematizing the various practices of liturgy. Theologies of worship remind us that most important to what happens in every liturgical act is how it invites the community into the paschal mystery, how it ritually remembers God's saving action through Christ.[19]

[16] David Fagerberg cites the work of Regin Prenter and Vilmos Vajta as examples of theologies of worship. Other examples he cites within this category are Jean-Jacques von Allmen, *Worship: Its Theology and Practice* (New York: Oxford University Press, 1965); John Burkhart, *Worship* (Philadelphia: Westminster Press, 1982); Edward Schillebeeckx, *Christ the Sacrament of the Encounter with God* (New York: Sheed and Ward, 1963); and Herman Sasse, *This Is My Body* (Minneapolis: Augsburg Press, 1959). As stated earlier, these theologians exist to varying degrees under Fagerberg's rubric of "theologies of worship."

[17] David Fagerberg, *What Is Liturgical Theology? A Study in Methodology* (Collegeville: The Liturgical Press, 1992) 67.

[18] Ibid.

[19] Irwin, *Context and Text*, 46–9, defines "theology of liturgy" from a slightly different perspective. He suggests that "theology of liturgy" is one part of the

The major weaknesses of theologies of worship, in terms of their ability to address this contemporary age, arise from these strengths. For example, systematic theology and dogmatics often fail to consider what theologies of worship might call "the liturgical dimension." Recognizing this, liturgical scholars such as Burkhart emphasize what they believe to be a mutually influencing relationship between liturgy and theology. A weakness in most of these delineations of the relationship, however, is the implication that a critical norm must be provided to worship from the outside.

From the perspective of a theology of worship, *theologia secunda* provides the norms for liturgy's content and form; theology is foundational to liturgy and thus detachable from the liturgy for the purposes of critical examination. Two critiques are appropriate.

First, the thematizing efforts of most theologies of worship and their search for an underlying theological norm perpetuates the bifurcation of the academy and the faith community. In epistemologies growing out of the Enlightenment, the way to obtain empirical knowledge is to suspend the concreteness of the experienced reality and focus on one of its researchable aspects. This approach fails to acknowledge the "thickness" of reality and the contextuality of all knowledge, that aspect of our knowing that cannot be extracted from its rootedness in particular concrete realities.[20]

---

meaning of "liturgical theology." From his standpoint, the term "theology of worship" describes "what Christian liturgy is and what it does in terms of actualizing the reality of Christ's paschal mystery for the church. . . . Through the liturgy, contemporary believers are drawn into the paschal mystery and experience redemption through it." What Irwin includes as central to his definition is that liturgy is essentially "ecclesiological, a ritual expression of the community's self-understanding." To include this ecclesiological aspect suggests that the community's liturgical action, along with the academy's secondary reflections on and descriptions of that action, both provide the theological norms. See also Irwin, *Liturgical Theology: A Primer*, 64–6.

[20] The term "thick description" arises out of the field of anthropology and is defined by Clifford Geertz, "Thick Description: Toward an Interpretive Theory of Culture," *The Interpretation of Cultures: Selected Essays*, ed. Clifford Geertz (New York: Basic Books, 1973) 3–32. Tacit understandings develop through repetitive experiences of a practice (or in the case of worship, a particular ritual practice). Through critical reflection on these actions it is possible to make those understandings more explicit. "Thin description" seeks to describe a given action; "thick description" looks at the "stratified hierarchy

A similar critique can be directed toward theologies of worship to the extent that they search for a particular theological meaning or dogmatic principle that can be gleaned from or applied to the various actions of "the liturgy" as a whole. This kind of abstraction in liturgical study risks distorting reality because it overlooks the multidimensionality of "lived" liturgical events as they are experienced in particular communities and historical contexts.

The most profound theological meaning of liturgy is experienced as we participate in the assembly itself, as we hear God's Word, and as we gather around a common table with others. Truths of life-determining significance are inherent in the experienced worship event and cannot be extracted from their concrete frame of reference; to echo Schon, there is a knowledge or wisdom mediated *in* the action of individual liturgical rites. This knowledge cannot adequately be captured or transmitted by a theoretical construction or a dogmatic principle.[21]

David Power points to the multiplicity or "thickness" of meanings implicit in the celebration of a liturgical rite in a particular context. He argues that each liturgical celebration possesses a life of its own that reveals something unique about a given community's relationship with God in Christ.[22]

An enacted liturgical rite, he argues, contains at least three layers of meaning: (1) the meaning of the ritual as a historical text; (2) the meaning given to the ritual by a particular community as people bring to it the questions, moral categories, and philosophical constructs of their own worlds, and (3) the official meaning of the ritual provided by the clergy and the institution. As these spheres of meaning interact, each liturgical event mediates a distinct and unrepeatable knowledge and experience of God.[23]

Fagerberg's critique of theologies of worship is related to this. He argues that when

"the object of study is no longer the rite in motion, it is a theology in suspended animation. It can often be useful to make abstractions, such

---

of meaningful structures in terms of which actions are produced, perceived and interpreted."

[21] Schon, "The New Scholarship Requires a New Epistemology," 28.

[22] David Power, "People at Liturgy," *Twenty Years of Concilium—Retrospect and Prospect* (Edinburgh: T. & T. Clark, 1983) 8–9.

[23] Ibid.

as 'the liturgy' or 'worship,' in order to say what one wants to say, but notice should be taken of the category shift. A shift occurs when one speaks about 'the American' in order to generalize about the character of certain people, or about 'the college student' in order to generalize about the mind-set and activities of a certain student population, and a shift likewise occurs when one speaks about 'the liturgy' instead of liturgies."[24]

A risk inherent in theologies of worship is oversimplifying the relationship between theology and worship.

The second critique of theologies of worship is related to Farley's concern that contemporary society is experiencing a loss of its "words of power," those deep symbols that mediate the knowledge that shapes our consciousness and provides us with moral values by which we relate to one another and the rest of the world. As Farley argues, a particular knowledge is interwoven with our cultural ethos, with our ability to negotiate daily life, and with our communal relatedness. This knowledge cannot be dissociated from its existence in those spheres. Within these spheres of relatedness words of power, or god-terms, are generated.

Institutions, then, do not create words of power. Words of power "originate as human beings have to do with each other in the distinctive sphere of the interhuman."[25] In other words, words of power do not develop from creeds, dogma, or doctrine; instead, ideally, they should provide the foundation for such institutional forms.

With the Enlightenment's fragmentation of theology, Farley argues, theological institutions have gradually become separated from those deep symbols that are such an intrinsic part of communal existence and knowledge of God. Nathan Mitchell charts a similar development in the history of the Eucharist, an emergence of patterns in the celebration of the Eucharist that led to the separation of clergy and laity.

[24] Fagerberg, *What Is Liturgical Theology?* 68–9.

[25] Farley, *Deep Symbols,* 21, argues that the sphere of the interhuman is neither a collection of individuals nor an institutional structure. It is a relation between people, formed over many years, that cannot be defined in terms of either the psychological dynamics of the individuals in relationship or in terms of a social structure. "The interhuman," says Farley, "is already formed and in place by the time an infant or child becomes a self-conscious individual. And it is always, already there and in place when social organizations are created and human enterprises become institutionalized."

The Eucharist, Mitchell explains, gradually shifted from being an event engaging the whole community to being a static rite performed by the clergy and only observed by the assembly.[26] This shift was one of the stepping stones along the path to the current rift between theology and practice.

First, a change took place within the New Testament era from understanding the Eucharist as a communal meal to experiencing its elements as "sacred food." Liturgical focus was eventually drawn away from communal symbols to allegorical drama. As a result, the Eucharist was no longer understood as a transformative event participated in by the community here and now; it became instead a drama watched by the laity as the clergy enacted a remembrance from the sacred past.

The outcome can be traced through the history of the Church and parallels the phenomenon described by Farley. The norms for the practice and understanding of worship gradually became disconnected from the sphere of relatedness, from the people of the worshiping community. When this happens, when the sphere of relatedness is pushed to the margins so that it functions only as a faint background for the workings of the institution, then words of power, the faith community's constitutive images and metaphors, become shriveled, and their life-determining significance is diminished or forgotten.

Efforts by most theologies of worship to reunify liturgy and theology are commendable; voices within this "family" of liturgical theology have called for a necessary shift in focus, one that sees the theologian's function as that of "servant" to and with the community. Theologies of worship have also demonstrated the interrelationship of dogma and worship. The presupposition of theologies of worship in general, however, is that liturgical forms serve primarily to express particular preestablished theological norms. Such an understanding actually perpetuates the primacy of the academy over the worshiping community, of the institution over the sphere of relatedness.

Farley argues that the Church's words of power have not vanished in our era but have been effaced. They have become subject to institutional forms that are permeated by outmoded cosmologies, rigid hierarchies, ideological exclusivity, and pre-critical paradigms of authority.[27] In order for people in this technological society to be reawak-

[26] Nathan Mitchell, *Cult and Controversy: The Worship of the Eucharist Outside Mass* (New York: Pueblo Publishing Co., 1974) 56.

[27] Farley, *Deep Symbols*, 21–8.

ened to the significance of words of power and their juxtapositions in the worship event, at least three changes must occur: (1) the Church must recognize that neither words of power nor our institutional frameworks are the mystery itself; both require constant reflection and reinterpretation; (2) liturgical theology must recognize that perusing various liturgical rites in search of particular theological norms or truths is not the same as experiencing the paschal mystery as it is mediated by a particular community's *lex orandi*; and (3) if the Church's foremost sphere of relatedness is its *lex orandi* and its words of power originate in that sphere, then liturgical theology must find a way to articulate the relationship between *lex orandi* and *lex credendi* that grants primacy to the theologizing community. The growing edges for theologies of worship come at these three points. As the discussion continues, these three points will begin to form the foundation of a "wisdom liturgical theology" that provides both critique and continued development.

THEOLOGIES FROM WORSHIP

In his outline of the foundational elements of the "new scholarship," Schon describes what he calls the "dilemma of rigor or relevance" that currently plagues much professional practice.[28] On the one hand, he explains, there are "manageable" problems that can be solved through research-based study or technique. Other realities of living in a fragmented society, however, are "messier" problems that defy technical or empirical solution. Perhaps not surprisingly, those "messy" problems tend to be most prominent in daily human concerns.

The dilemma presents itself: Is the practitioner to continue doing the thing on which he/she bases the claim to technical rigor and academic expertise? Or is he/she to move outside the boundaries of academia as it is currently defined in search of more adequate answers to amorphous problems, problems that refuse to be delimited by any determinate zone of practice? Close on the heels of these questions appears another: Are rigor and relevance as mutually exclusive or separate as the dominant paradigm implies?

This so-called dilemma of rigor or relevance originates, Schon argues, in the epistemology built into the modern research university and in the tension that develops as people encounter ambiguities of life

---

[28] Schon, "The New Scholarship Requires a New Epistemology," 28.

which do not conform to the categories of that epistemology.[29] One resolution, discussed earlier, was offered in the 1960s as various professions (business, forestry, dentistry, social work, and engineering) were established as "schools" in the university; Schon refers to this particular solution to the dichotomy between theory and practice as "technical rationality."[30]

The model of technical rationality, Schon asserts, has greatly influenced the academy's current metaphysical outlook. According to this model, professional practice "is instrumental, consisting in adjusting technical means to ends that are clear, fixed, and internally consistent."[31] Researchers provide the theoretical knowledge; from this knowledge, practitioners derive techniques and principles for application to specific problems.

The hierarchical separation of research and practice resulting from technical rationality persists in theological education and in liturgical theology. In *Theologia*, Farley discusses this by describing a contemporary theological education process in which isolated disciplines lack any overarching philosophical or theological rubric. The result? Connections between specializations are unclear as is their importance for the "doing" of ministry "out there," in a world of violence, economic disparity, and ecological disaster. Theological education, Farley argues, has inherited problems similar to those of other academic disciplines that have failed to provide clearly relevant answers for the "messy" problems of life in a contemporary age.[32]

---

[29] Don Browning, *A Fundamental Practical Theology* (Minneapolis: Fortress Press, 1991), discusses this gap between practice and theory in terms of theological education and the Church. In his correlation of the categories of practical philosophy and theology, he suggests that the primary horizons of dialogue and change are at those points where the answers provided by tradition do not adequately address particular concerns of a given community. When solutions to problems of communal life cannot be found in traditional theological categories, the process of critical reflection begins; communities seek ways to appropriate inherited wisdom to meet current needs. The question of how this critical-reflective dialogue between the tradition and present concerns is focused in the worship event will be the subject of further discussion in this project.

[30] Schon, *The Reflective Practitioner*, 21–75.

[31] Schon, "The New Scholarship Requires a New Epistemology," 29.

[32] Farley, *Theologia*, 3–23, implies that the bifurcation of theory and practice occurs in theological schools. Theological schools historically have been

Worship is a discipline that traditionally has fallen within the area of study termed "ministerial practice." "Practice," or "applied theology" as it is defined within the prevailing theological paradigm, is "that aspect of clerical pedagogy addressed to the leadership practice of the clergy."[33]

An exciting aspect of liturgical study in recent decades is the way it confronts the dilemma of rigor or relevance described by Schon, seeking to restore the interrelationship of theory and practice in our understanding of liturgy. Theologies *of* worship, discussed above, represent one method for reuniting theory and practice in liturgical study. In the second "family" or type of liturgical theology outlined by Fagerberg, "theology from worship," the mutually transitive relationship between liturgy and theology becomes even more definitive.

Most theologies *from* worship focus on how doctrine is expressed in liturgical form as well as on how liturgy is rooted in doctrine. The method of these theologies, generally, functions to demonstrate how worship shaped and continues to shape doctrine and how the doctrines of the Church shape worship. Theologies from worship have contributed a number of valuable insights to the liturgical renewal

---

compared to the "professional" schools described by Schon as products of the technical rationality model.

[33] Ibid., 132. As Farley argues, practice was made "external to theology when *theologia* became an aggregate of four disciplines in which three are theory and the fourth is practice as ministerial responsibility." This fourfold pattern of theological education is well-documented in the literature; it is based on the foundation of Friederich Schleiermacher's *Brief Outline of Theological Study,* published in 1811. The phrase "clerical paradigm" is used by Farley and others to refer to how theological education has been configured since Schleiermacher—namely, the fourfold pattern.

The critique of that pattern is not intended to undermine the value of clergy education. It rather seeks to address the gap created by this paradigm between what happens in the academy and what happens in the local church. There is a rich texturing of voices in the ongoing debate over what constitutes a "good" theological school. See Kelsey, *Between Athens and Berlin;* David Kelsey, *To Understand God Truly: What's Theological about a Theological School* (Louisville: Westminster/John Knox Press, 1992); Farley, *The Fragility of Knowledge;* Joseph C. Hough Jr. and John B. Cobb Jr., *Christian Identity and Theological Education* (Chico, Calif.: Scholars Press, 1985); Barbara G. Wheeler and Edward Farley, eds., *Shifting Boundaries: Contextual Approaches to the Structure of Theological Education* (Louisville: Westminster/John Knox Press, 1991).

movement and to the question of how to balance rigor and relevance, theory and practice, in liturgical method.

First, theologies from worship or "theologies drawn from worship" are concerned with "how the words and symbols of liturgy can be utilized as a generative source in the church's systematization of her belief in theology"; these theologies aim to demonstrate how the actions, objects, and images of worship clarify or exemplify the themes of systematic theology.[34] The definition of systematic theology offered by at least one theologian working within this rubric reveals a closer dialectic between liturgy and theology than is witnessed in theologies of worship.

Geoffrey Wainwright, introducing a "systematic theology written from a liturgical perspective," states that "systematic theology" is an intellectual activity rooted in life, experience, and worship. For Wainwright, systematic theology is

"the articulation of a personal vision of faith which includes the insights of worship and carries ethical incidences. Logical argument continues to play a part in the coherent formulation of theology, but the total vision has other roots in life and experience. My own vision of faith is firmly shaped and strongly coloured by the Christian liturgy."[35]

Worship, argues Wainwright, is that event in which the Christian vision of reality discovers its sharpest focus.

Intellectual reflection on the worship event and its vision, he continues, falls under the rubric of "doctrine." Wainwright suggests several goals for intellectual reflection, goals that indicate his concern to be both rigorous and relevant in delineating what he believes to be a mutually influencing relationship between *lex orandi* and *lex credendi.*

First, through its explication of the worship event, doctrine seeks to systematize the Christian vision by providing "a coherent intellectual expression of that vision." Second, as Wainwright understands it, such an examination of liturgy from a doctrinal perspective enables the theologian both to learn from worship and to offer critique or suggestions for improvement. Finally, the task of systematic theology in this proc-

[34] Irwin, *Context and Text*, 66.
[35] Geoffrey Wainwright, *Doxology: The Praise of God in Worship, Doctrine, and Life* (New York: Oxford University Press, 1980) 3.

38

ess is to analyze how the "vision" in worship measures up to doctrinal norms and to propose "the most effective ways of allowing its vision to illuminate and transform reality to the advantage of all humanity."[36]

This accomplishment of theologies from worship, this effort to describe the mutual influence that doctrine and liturgy have had on one another historically and in the present, points to a second notable influence of this family of theologians on contemporary liturgical method. Most theologies from worship, loosely defined, establish liturgy as a starting point for doing theology and seek to set forth theological or doctrinal understandings of God, humanity, and the world by drawing on the resources of worship.[37] Because of their understanding that human words and acts in worship are doctrinal in that God uses them as vehicles of self-communication, theologies from worship contain a more detailed examination of the actual words and actions of liturgical rites than do theologies of worship.

Irwin sees this use of the actual historical data of liturgical rites to explicate the concepts of systematic theology as one of the valuable

[36] Ibid., 4. Wainwright's argument regarding historical precedent for doctrinal influence on worship forms is particularly insightful in relation to these several methodological focal points. In chapter 8 of his work he sketches doctrinal control over liturgy in the early Church and uses a scriptural basis to argue for the dialectic between dogma and liturgy today. He also offers the Reformation as a historical example of theological critique and correction of liturgical forms rife with political abuses and works righteousness.

In a similar vein, James White, *A Brief History of Christian Worship* (Nashville: Abingdon Press, 1993) 104–39, emphasizes that Luther broke with past worship forms whose scriptural and thus doctrinal foundation were in question but only made revisions to the extent that his critique of existing forms could be justified in Scripture. As such, Luther represents a rather unique combination of continuity with tradition and radical discontinuity with it; it is a tension that has characterized Protestant worship throughout its history and has spawned one of the central questions for liturgical renewal today: How are Christians to remain rooted in the tradition that provides for us our distinctiveness and at the same time appropriate that tradition meaningfully for contemporary culture?

[37] Historically, various starting points have been argued for doing theology by theologians working within different cultural eras, traditions, and presuppositions—for example, Scripture, morality, historical development, and tradition. That theologies drawn from worship begin from a liturgical point of view and set forth Christian doctrinal understandings from that perspective is paradigmatic.

contributions of theologies from worship. Not only does this method bind liturgical study more closely to actual texts and liturgical forms, but in looking to liturgy for clarification of our doctrines of God, Christ, and redemption, it recognizes liturgy as a place of convergence for otherwise separate and somewhat isolated disciplines such as christology, eschatology, or pneumatology.

To summarize, two primary emphases of theologies from worship are (1) to sharpen our awareness that worship practices provide concrete evidence or instances of dogma, and (2) to establish liturgy as a starting point for doing theology. This perspective has done much, as suggested above, to lessen the gap between the Church's *lex orandi* and *lex credendi*. It is at the point of these emphases, however, that the growing edge for theologies from worship emerges.

A presupposition of theologies from worship is that "one mode of expressing dogma or the Christian vision is doxology or liturgy or ritual," and that "a doctrine of worship can be mined from the practice of worship and made dogmatically explicit."[38] This is important to liturgical reform because it challenges us to examine more closely how liturgical rites image God, describe the Church, and reflect the work of Christ.[39] However, several issues present themselves as we consider the risk inherent in making any doctrine of worship dogmatically explicit, particularly when academic reflection on and perpetuation of that doctrine become ideological.

First, as already alluded to above, when the memory of Christ's death and resurrection is celebrated "in the midst of a dying ecclesiastical and ritual edifice" and when tragic events point to the sufferings imposed by ideological hegemony, it is vital that the Church critically examine how its liturgical forms either provide liberation from

[38] Fagerberg, *What Is Liturgical Theology?* 133, states that this is one agenda of theology from worship. Both Brunner and Wainwright, he argues, suppose that doctrine can be "quarried" from worship because worship is an expression of Christian dogma (Brunner) or the Christian vision (Wainwright).

[39] Irwin, *Liturgical Theology: A Primer,* 66–7, states that "theology drawn from the liturgy" seeks to "mine" the liturgy to discover how various rites treat formative aspects of theology. Irwin says that this approach can be helpful to the desired outcomes of liturgical reform; theologizing from the liturgy, for example, causes us to be more intentional in reflecting on the images of Christ that are found in the liturgy. The result of such reflection, he argues, is the discovery of "varied and pluriform images."

oppressive structures or tend to perpetuate them.[40] Several questions not adequately addressed by theologies from worship surface in this regard. How does liturgy's mediation of truth urge the faith community to grow closer to its divine immanent essence? Do current liturgical forms foster or impede a sense of community and common Christian identity?

In seeking answers to these questions, many theologies from worship recognize that the academic activity of theologians cannot be separated from their experiential matrix in communal worship. Wainwright, for example, makes explicit that his liturgical theology is written from "faith to faith." What this means is that the individual theologian operates within both the Christian community and the human community; as such he/she inherits both the faith community's language for articulating the Christian vision and the language of a wider cultural community to which the vision is being mediated. Wainwright's consequent recognition that our worship is provisionally valid and limited reminds us of the possibility of error in liturgical formulation.[41]

However, while Wainwright demonstrates an awareness that his work is an individual presentation of one version of the Christian vision, his method does not go far enough in examining how contextual and historical predispositions shape the doctrines which he argues are determinant for proper doxological expression. The result, in Wainwright's work and in other theologies from worship, is the notion that worship practices of the community do not achieve proper structure unless they are carved out of foundational doctrinal forms of secondary theology developed in the academy.[42] Theology and practice are pushed closer together in these theologies, but the role of the theologian as a sort of "guardian over worship" is maintained. As a result, this type retains barriers that see practice as external or subservient to theology. It also fails to ask the critical dialectical question of whether either the doctrinal *or* liturgical enterprise expresses the gospel in its fullest sense.[43]

---

[40] Power, *Eucharistic Mystery,* vii.

[41] Ibid., 2–3. Wainwright argues that the liturgical theologian uses "in a dialectical relationship both Christian language and the language of the wider human community which has not yet accepted the Christian vision but to which the vision is being commended."

[42] Fagerberg, *What Is Liturgical Theology?* 135.

[43] Ibid., viii.

Theologies from worship seek to articulate the mutually informative/corrective influence that doctrine and liturgy exert on one another. One reason that their articulation of the relationship between *lex orandi* and *lex credendi* is problematic surfaced in Walter Burghardt's keynote address to the Scottsdale Conference on American Liturgy in 1973.

The scholars gathered at the Scottsdale Conference were committed both to reaffirming the liturgical structures of tradition and to examining how tradition might be appropriated for the future. In that sense, the conference's implications for liturgical reform were and continue to be ground-breaking. However, at least one apprehension emerged in Burghardt's address that continues to challenge liturgical theologians in their work to date: the question of whether or not participating work groups adequately took up the challenge of examining their own presuppositions.

Burghardt's concern was that many scholars tend to work primarily within their own theological horizons. As reflected in his address, he saw this as both limiting and inadequate to the process of liturgical renewal:

"Whether you like it or not, at this moment you do have a style of historical thinking (perhaps unreflective); this style of historical thinking affects your theology of reform (perhaps unreflective); this reform theology dictates what you are ready or willing to change in today's liturgy, how far you are willing to go, where you believe you must say, 'This far and no farther.'"[44]

Liturgical reform that grows out of unreflective historical or theological thinking, argues Burghardt, does not result in transformation.[45]

---

[44] Walter J. Burghardt, "A Theologian's Challenge to Liturgy," *Theological Studies* 35 (June 1974) 233–48. This address was given at the Scottsdale Conference on the tenth anniversary of Vatican II's Constitution on the Sacred Liturgy. The conference dealt with the challenge of how worship is to reflect an ever-changing culture without becoming merely a mirror of it. Through its work, the foundations for the North American Academy of Liturgy were laid.

[45] J. W. O'Malley, "Reform, Historical Consciousness and Vatican II's Aggiornamento," *Theological Studies* 32 (1971) 573–601, suggests six types of reform—excision or suppression, addition or accretion, revival, accommodation, organic development, and transformation. Due in large measure to the work of scholars involved in the Scottsdale Conference, the 1970s witnessed much

A similar challenge can be directed to theologies from worship to the extent that they maintain the determinacy of doctrine for proper worship forms without also demonstrating an adequate awareness of the shaping power of pastoral, historical, and cultural horizons for their individual doctrinal perspectives. If liturgy is to continue to transmit a vision of reality that people can turn to for interpreting daily life, there must be a constant process of critical examination of all of the horizons that converge in the worship event.

Careful reflection on the symbols, images, and language of worship, their relation to doctrine, and the relation of both to pastoral, historical, theological, and cultural understandings is crucial for the Church today. Without such reflection, liturgical forms risk becoming too dependent on ecclesial or academic edifices that have not adequately addressed several crucial issues: (1) the world is permeated by contradictions and inequalities of power and privilege, contradictions which also permeate institutions; (2) organizational structures are arenas in which groups vie for power; without an intentional awareness of this, the Church risks reinforcing the dominance of an exclusive or oppressive minority; and (3) institutions such as churches are a matrix of institutional, personal, and social forces; these forces operate together to shape interpretations of the gospel and the worship forms used to mediate those interpretations.[46]

---

reform: a revival of those aspects of tradition that had been forgotten, a suppression of elements which historical research showed to be later additions to an originally simpler structure, an endorsement of additions of new elements to established liturgical rites, and proposals to accommodate traditional practices to new historical realities.

Collins, *Worship: Renewal to Practice,* 12, argues that "transformation" was not the central focus of the conference, although several groups probed issues in ways that were potentially transformative.

[46] These issues are addressed with regard to education in the work of critical education theorists. See Patti Lather, "Critical Theory, Curricular Transformation, and Feminist Mainstreaming." As Lather explains, hegemony "is a web of reciprocally confirming structures, activities, beliefs and ethics that interact to support the established order and the class, race, and gender interests that dominate." Transformation of hegemonic structures is possible, she says, when individuals become aware that the vision of reality provided by these structures is contradictory to daily experience. Such transformation rarely occurs because the dominant class secures hegemony by supplying symbols,

Two challenges arise from this that are of particular importance to this project. First, theologies from worship imply that academicians are the primary theologians. The recognition that the faith community itself, particularly in its worship, is the Church's foremost theological seedbed is more clearly reflected in those theologies that Fagerberg defines "liturgical theology"; this type will be the focus of the discussion in the next section.

Second, many of the outcomes of liturgical renewal in general, and of theologies from worship in particular, are rooted in a modern historical consciousness. For instance, as noted earlier, Wainwright grounds his theology on the dual claim that (1) the community has an existential impact on the theologian, and (2) in worship the faith vision of the community finds its most focused expression. The second part of this claim implies that the doctrinal canon is the lens through which the acts, words, and symbols of worship are filtered in order to further clarify the faith vision. A problem with this is that this doctrinal canon is founded on the crumbling norms of a modern historical consciousness.

In discussing *lex orandi*, for example, Wainwright raises several questions that are at issue when we examine the historical development of liturgy and doctrine. These questions themselves reflect his dependence on particular historical and doctrinal presuppositions:

"(a) What gives to the Church's worship any authority which it carries in matters of doctrine? (b) What is the relation between the doctrinal authority carried by worship and other instances of doctrinal authority in the Church? (c) Is the worship practice of the Church equally authoritative throughout, or are there rather internal gradations in its value as a doctrinal locus? (d) What is the role of worship in relation to the development of doctrine?"[47]

Wainwright highlights worship as *a* doctrinal locus but then seeks to establish by what criteria worship is allowed to influence doctrine and doctrine to influence worship.[48] The criteria his systematic theology

---

representations, and guidelines for moral practice in such a way that the true basis for authority remains hidden.

[47] Wainwright, *Doxology*, 240–1.

[48] Ibid, 218. In a historical treatment of the dictum *lex orandi, lex credendi,* Wainwright notes that it was the policy of the Reformers to establish doctrinal

offers are based on christological, pneumatological, ecclesiological understandings that are closely identified with positivistic appropriations of redemption history. For example, in his treatment of the "liturgical element" in the Old and New Testaments and in his argument for "the liturgy as hermeneutical continuum," Wainwright relies primarily on the discoveries and principles of the historical-critical biblical method.[49]

The problem with such a reliance is that modern historical categories, like the dominant theological education model critiqued earlier, grow out of the assumptions of an Enlightenment perspective. The biblical theology constructed within this perspective fails to shape a hermeneutic that addresses the challenges of this contemporary era.[50]

People face numerous problems that defy empirical solution; confronting these problems involves an integration of various skills and types of knowledge, an integration that does not always conform to the categories of objectivity, positivism, and scientific precision central to much theological study. As liturgical scholars seek the mediation of truth through worship forms, they must become attuned to the knowledge that is imbedded in the faith community in its individual acts of worship. They must also become more aware that this knowledge has

---

control over worship practices that they considered to be corrupt. The resulting primacy of doctrine over liturgy historically remained intact in Protestantism. On the other hand, Roman Catholics appeal to historical and current liturgical tradition for justification of doctrinal positions. One of the admirable goals of Wainwright's work is to respond to the "unevenness" in both of these traditions by restoring what he believes to be a "dynamic interplay between worship and doctrine."

[49] Ibid., 149–81. Wainwright examines some of the critical questions raised by modern biblical scholarship as they relate to liturgy. He notes the "uneven" use of the New Testament in worship. He emphasizes that the "variegated unity" of the Bible's treatment of liturgy serves as a sort of hermeneutical construct for interpreting Scripture. Wainwright's argument is limited by his reliance on the historical categories of modern biblical criticism. He states, for example, that "the liturgy is the pre-eminent place in which the Church ponders and applies the scriptures: it thus contributes creatively to the development of doctrine." How this hermeneutical understanding differs from a liturgical theology which sees the worshiping community as the generative source of doctrine will be treated in the next section.

[50] Leo Perdue, *The Collapse of History: Reconstructing Old Testament Theology* (Minneapolis: Fortress Press, 1994) xi.

both a historical origin and a connectedness to the contemporary horizon; it is thus both descriptive and constructive.

Worship theologies that fall under the rubric "liturgical theology" in Fagerberg's typology delineate how worship is the primary source of our knowledge of God and thus of doctrine. They have opened the door toward a greater recognition of how our study of liturgy and of liturgy's historical texts is itself constructive.

LITURGICAL THEOLOGY[51]

"Something" happens in worship; a particular knowledge is mediated through the worship forms of the gathered community, a knowledge that cannot be abstracted from its existential context. These two statements shed light on the relationship between liturgy as an act of gathered believers and theology as knowledge of God and the world.

What do these statements mean? More to the point, what does the liturgical assembly itself mean? A picture of a local worship event comes to mind. The worship space is a large open room in a nursing home. It is Sunday evening and members of the community gather for a celebration of word and table. The familiar words and notes of the "Doxology" draw the assembly into a time of worship. A prayer is voiced, inviting the people to experience and respond to the presence of God. A hymn is sung. Scriptures are read. A leader interprets the meaning of the texts and the assembly responds, once again with words familiar to many of them, the words of the Apostles' Creed. At the center of the room is a wooden table set with two items of food—a loaf of bread and a cup of wine. After a prayer of thanksgiving, the people share in this simple meal.

Gathered around the table in that nursing home are a diversity of persons—former housewives, doctors, farmers, college professors,

---

[51] For Fagerberg, a third type of worship theology is most properly defined by the term "liturgical theology." In his assessment of this type, he draws primarily on Schmemann's *Introduction to Liturgical Theology* and outlines a "topography of liturgical theology so defined." Fagerberg understands true "liturgical theology" to be "that theology which is found in the structure of a liturgical rite." It is theology inseparably connected to the worship event itself and not merely to be discovered in the written rubrics or texts. Fagerberg himself does not provide an explicit treatment of this fourth approach. Since my concern is to examine the adequacy of the secondary reflections and/or methodologies of the liturgical movement, my thesis also does not require a separate treatment of the fourth approach.

nurses, carpenters—people who for various reasons have reached a point in life when they are unable to live independently. Some are in wheelchairs. Others are unable to see; they depend on their senses of hearing, smelling, and tasting to experience the words and actions of the worship event. Others wrestle with dementia, a limited cognitive ability to grasp the meanings mediated in worship. The question of how or even whether faith "makes sense" of broken lives is at the heart of this particular worship gathering.

This description of a eucharistic meal reflects a pattern of worship common to the Christian tradition. However, as this ancient form and its symbols are set next to the particular social reality of a nursing home, the question asked at the beginning of this chapter emerges again. What is it about the pattern of worship that offers meaning within the pathos of this particular community's lived experience? How does the structure of words and actions in the Eucharist create a world of meaning for those who are no longer able to feed themselves or for those who cannot remember the names of their children? How are people who are victims of this world's tragedies enabled through liturgy to meet God in the midst of their sorrow and rediscover hope? When "incoherence and the absence of God seems the dominant pattern,"[52] how do the juxtapositions inherent in worship enable the mystery of God's presence, the mystery of transformation to break in upon us?

Liturgical theology, Fagerberg's third type, seeks to answer these questions in a way more directly parallel to the epistemological model of the "new scholarship" proposed by Schon.[53] As Fagerberg explains,

[52] Saliers, *Worship as Theology*, 22.

[53] In 1993 and 1994 the ATS Quality and Accreditation Project dealt with the contemporary epistemological crisis in relation to theological education. See Daniel Aleshire, "Introduction: The Good Theological School," *Theological Education* 30 (Spring 1994) 5–16. Religion, like the rest of society, has become increasingly pluralistic, making it difficult for any one form of religious expression and consequently any theological school realistically to claim superiority. Because of this, it seems impossible to think about theological education without juxtaposing it to the particular ministerial contexts for which it seeks to prepare people.

As it will become clear in the forthcoming critique of "liturgical theology," a similar recognition of the importance of context in the liturgy/theology relationship has emerged within liturgical scholarship. This recognition is summarized by Irwin's representative phrase "context is text—text shapes

the subject matter of liturgical theology is not liturgy; rather, it is God, humanity, and the world, and the horizon at which these three meet: liturgy. As a result, the primary goal of this method is to articulate the theology or knowledge revealed in and through liturgy, particularly in and through liturgies in their specific, unrepeatable contexts.

To accomplish this task, liturgical theology proceeds methodologically from the standpoint of two related understandings: (1) that the mystery of God is experienced through liturgical forms and (2) that the knowledge mediated through liturgies in their specific contexts cannot be contained solely in academia's didactic doctrinal explanations, in dogmatic principles, or even in the rubrics or written language of liturgical texts.

Because liturgical theology can be understood as an invitation to participate in the "meaning" of liturgy itself, the epistemological question, or the question of how we know what we know, becomes central. A further fleshing out of the issue from the standpoint of the new scholarship and theological education is needed, therefore, before setting forth a critique of that theology.

The epistemological subject area of this project has at least two overlapping levels. One level might usefully be described by the term "epistemology at the level of appropriation."[54] Vital to liturgical renewal is the recognition that all truth is mediated and thus subject to

---

context," *Context and Text*, 1. To state it briefly, Irwin believes that "for adequate liturgical theology, one must examine the component parts of liturgical rites—texts, symbols, actions and gestures—both in relation to each other and also in light of the times and places when and where communities were or are engaged in these rites" (54). The subsequent conclusion is like that established by the ATS project—that context is a source, or "text," for developing liturgical theology.

The questions raised by the ATS project enter into dialogue with liturgical theology at the point of liturgical theology's recognition that liturgy is the generative source for doing theology: what way of doing theology enables students to make explicit the theological horizon present within all learning? How does the combination of biblical studies, history and theology, preaching and worship, Christian education and pastoral care "form" theology students and enable them to be a ministerial presence in the communities they serve, effectively integrating intellectual pursuits with spiritual needs and understandings?

[54] James Loder, *Religious Pathology and the Christian Faith* (Philadelphia: Westminster Press, 1966).

the distortions of human interpretation and appropriation of that truth. It might be argued that the Church's official cosmology, ecclesiology, christology, Scripture principle, and liturgical texts/rites are a kind of epistemology at this level of appropriation.[55]

Phenomenological studies, such as the work done by Farley, challenge those structures that develop at this level of appropriation and dogmatically claim authoritative status. For example, Farley addresses contemporary challenges to the relevancy of the Christian faith by looking beyond the level of appropriation to another epistemological level; he constantly asks what it is that constitutes the "truth" in religion.

Farley argues that Christian theology "has often frozen into unrevisable doctrines and casuistries its cultural carriers of the wisdom of the enduring."[56] This move in the direction of dogmatism is one reason that the Church is now vulnerable to recent attacks on its "truth" claims. Thematic questions emerge throughout Farley's work to probe the issue of the "real" existence of God and to ask whether our structures of appropriation have enabled the fullest expression of that reality.[57]

A defining characteristic of liturgy is that it exists at the intersection of these two epistemological levels—the level of human appropriation or mediation and the level of the constitutive elements of the truth. Because the "cognitive territory surrounding faith's truth claims has undergone steady erosion," how we define and interpret the convergence of these two levels or horizons in the worship event is of major import both to liturgical renewal and to the future of the Church.

[55] See Farley, *Ecclesial Reflection*.

[56] Edward Farley, "Truth and the Wisdom of Enduring," *Phenomenology of the Truth Proper to Religion*, ed. Daniel Guerriere (Albany: State University of New York Press, 1990) 74. Farley argues that human beings exist as "complex biopsychological environments and in larger complex environments." Natural to all living entities, Farley continues, is the instinctive impulse to "endure." This requires a constant awareness of those factors that favorably impact continued human existence or that are possibly detrimental to it. What happens as a result of the impulse to endure is that human beings accumulate a kind of wisdom about their existential condition, a wisdom that (1) endures through its appropriation by later generations, (2) becomes a feature of how communities and cultures endure, and (3) shapes human transactions with the world.

[57] Irwin, *Context and Text*, 55. This second level of epistemological concern is not foreign to contemporary liturgical theologies that increasingly emphasize the nature of theology as "disclosive of the mystery of God, and not as defining or determining God's self-disclosure."

A premise of liturgical theology is that the worship of God in the faith community is theology in action. As Saliers insists, "worship in all its social-cultural idioms is a theological act."[58] Foundational to this premise is the understanding that an individual's or community's encounter with God precedes reflection upon that encounter; liturgy is primary theology.

In terms of secondary theologies that seek to describe and interpret this encounter and the theology implicit to it, two interconnected spheres of reflection that are directly related to the epistemological issues raised above present themselves: (1) liturgy as communal activity and (2) liturgical celebration as convergence of human pathos and divine mystery. The following treatment of these spheres is offered as a kind of topographical map of the territory that Schmemann termed "liturgical theology."

Leitourgia as Communal Activity

Schmemann asks a question that is at the heart of liturgical theology and that shapes the contours of one of the above "spheres of reflection" within "liturgical theology": "Of what life do we speak, what life do we preach, proclaim, announce when, as Christians, we confess that Christ died for the life of the world? What *life* is both motivation, and the beginning and the goal of Christian *mission*?"[59] The sphere of reflection connected to this question is constitutive of liturgical theology, namely that liturgy is communal theological activity done by the Church for the world.

Schmemann was a proponent of the understanding of liturgy as communal activity. His argument, that the Church does not exist to provide a place of isolation from a "profane" world but rather exists for the life of the world, is vital to liturgical renewal, particularly as it strives to respond to contemporary society's challenge to its integrity.

Schmemann's query emerges again: what does the faith community mean when it confesses that Christ died for the life of the world? Schmemann outlines several types of answers that have arisen historically in response to that question.

First, there are those for whom "life" for the world means "religious life," or life that is somehow isolated from the world. Within this

[58] Saliers, *Worship as Theology*, 15.
[59] Alexander Schmemann, *For the Life of the World: Sacraments and Orthodoxy* (New York: St. Vladimir's Seminary Press, 1973) 32.

viewpoint, the mission of the faith community is the conversion of the world "out there" to the "religious life." Schmemann's criticism of this view is that it conceptualizes Christianity as a religion of practices that exist under the rubric "sacred."

One problem with this, he says, is that it creates the impression that liturgy is an isolated sacred event. Liturgical rites are thus reduced to cultic categories and the world—its people, actions, and objects—is no longer viewed as permeated by God's presence. When this happens, the so-called "profane" world is not challenged by the sacred and liturgy is seen merely as a reenactment of something in the past rather than as participation in a present transforming reality.

Schmemann argues, by contrast, that the whole world "is an epiphany of God, a means of his [sic] revelation, presence and power." It is through the world's objects and events of history that humanity is able to know God; the gaining of such knowledge as it leads to communion with God is the whole purpose of worship.[60]

Second, Schmemann continues, there are those for whom the phrase "Christ died for the life of the world" more aptly means that Christ died for the betterment of the world. This perspective implies that the world is "lost" and must be recovered. When the Church operates out of this perspective, "worldly" people become the objects of Christian action and the faith community is challenged to step outside of its contemplative walls in an effort to impact or respond to the social, political, and economic issues of the world.[61]

A result of this second understanding, as it attempts to address itself to the crises of contemporary persons, has been the tendency to adapt liturgy to the tastes of people in a market-driven society. When this happens, Christian liturgy is no longer constitutive of persons; worship becomes something that is added to people's identity in order to improve their moral actions, emotional stability, or sense of well-being.[62]

[60] Ibid., 120.

[61] Ibid.

[62] Steeped in the Orthodox tradition, Alexander Schmemann, "Liturgy and Theology," *The Greek Orthodox Theological Review* 17 (1972) 86–100, condemns the individualism that has come to characterize liturgy, calling it the "Western captivity" of theology. What he means by this is similar to our earlier discussion of the fragmentation of theological education. As Schmemann emphasizes, Neo-Scholasticism felt threatened by modern philosophy and skepticism. To combat this, it isolated the content of faith not only from the modern world but also from the apologetics that served to present it to the world. The result

Schmemann contends that neither of these perspectives authentically reflects the Church's mission to the world. For him, operating out of the sociocultural perspective of the 1960s and 1970s, restoring the "organic" connection of theology to liturgy is the key to returning the Church to its generative and most essential mission. Several aspects of Schmemann's organic understanding are foundational to our grasp of the Church's praxis and to liturgical theology's perception of liturgy as communal theological activity.

In its most original sense, Schmemann explains, *leitourgia* meant an

"action by which a group of people became something corporately which they had not been as a mere collection of individuals—a whole greater than the sum of its parts. It meant also a function of 'ministry' of a man [*sic*] or a group on behalf of and in the interest of the whole community."[63]

When liturgy functions within this definition, the distinction between the sacred and the profane is abolished.

Reorienting the Church toward ritual practices that collapse the sacred/profane dichotomy is essential for liturgical renewal in a society increasingly preoccupied with cultic categories.[64] As Schmemann explains, in cultic categories a "cult" is required to make an object or action holy or sacred. The existence of a "cult" presupposes a radical distinction between the sacred realm and the profane realm. Rites within a cult are performed to establish a sort of contract between the community and God. Christian liturgy is not cultic, argues Schmemann, because through the sacraments people are reminded that all of life is filled with meaning and purpose.

Schmemann observes that liturgy has lost its transformative influence primarily because the faith community's comprehension of it has changed. In the modern consciousness, for example, the Church is viewed as a "cultic" institution and most of its activities—worship, education, mission—are directed at meeting the needs of its individ-

---

is reflected in the current theological crisis in which the formal institution of theology has become remote from the practical content of faith.

[63] Schmemann, *For the Life of the World*, 121.

[64] Alexander Schmemann, "Theology and Liturgical Tradition," *Worship in Scripture and Tradition*, ed. Massey Shepherd (New York: Oxford University Press, 1963).

ual members; liturgy, as a part of this configuration, is perceived as a group of individuals attending Church in order to satisfy personal needs rather than to fulfill the Church's mission.

An authentic and transformative understanding of liturgy, says Schmemann, challenges the notion that worship exists solely for the purpose of mediating individual salvation. Liturgy's most transformative element is that through its patterns a diversity of people come together to constitute the Church, to become "a new community with a new life." The purpose of this "coming together" is not simply to add a religious dimension to individual lives, but rather to embody Christ's vision of the world redeemed.[65]

In his summary of Schmemann's theology Fagerberg asks: "How did the church come to be seen as a sacred enclave in a profane environment where troubled individuals could go for help with their religious needs?"[66] The answer lies in the loss of our understanding of liturgy as a communal activity, of liturgy as the ontological condition of theology. It is a loss, Schmemann insists, of the understanding that "in Christ, life—life in all its totality—was returned to man [sic], given again as sacrament and communion, made Eucharist."[67]

Schmemann's insight that liturgy is the ontological condition of theology has provided fertile ground for most discussions of liturgical renewal following in its wake. By locating the roots of theological reflection in concrete rites of particular faith communities, his liturgical theology has also paved the way toward ecumenism in liturgical practice. At this current historical juncture, it is important to expand the parameters of this sphere of reflection, "liturgy as communal activity," at several important points.

Schmemann's work dialogues primarily with the epistemological structures of the modern era and its categorization of the sacred and profane. Phenomenological issues have reemerged in the last twenty-five years that challenge both modernity's claims and the relevancy of the Church. To make the most productive application of Schmemann's work to the current liturgical crisis, it is necessary to invite his insights into dialogue with these issues. Farley's recent work in the area of foundational theology and his appraisal of theological education

[65] Schmemann, *For the Life of the World,* 26.

[66] Fagerberg, *What Is Liturgical Theology?* 161.

[67] Alexander Schmemann, *Sacraments and Orthodoxy* (New York: Herder and Herder, 1965) 22–3.

parallel Schmemann's efforts in liturgical theology; it offers a potential arena for such a dialogue.

Farley argues that the categories of "sacred" and "profane," common to scholars such as Schmemann and Eliade in the mid-1900s, have become obsolete. The world has become desacralized; questions of ultimacy or truth are no longer immediately or even necessarily equated with religion, with the so-called "sacred." Farley argues that this is one of the crises of contemporary theology—that faith and the faith community are no longer recognized as the primary pattern or habitus within which knowledge of the world develops. Echoing Schmemann, Farley argues that religion no longer provides the primary organizing metaphors for life. It is now seen as only one of many options available to individuals seeking therapeutic help or emotional support in times of crisis. As noted earlier, Farley attributes this development to the diminishment of the power of religion's deep symbols.[68]

As Farley responds to contemporary questions aimed at the validity of faith's truth claims, he seeks renewal of a concept of theology that integrates theory and praxis—a restoration of theology as habitus. Expanding Schmemann's vision of the unity of the liturgical act and of all aspects of the Christian life, Farley argues that the believer's reflective life does not contain the sharp distinctions between science and practice (between the "sacred" and "profane") prevalent in dominant institutional structures and epistemological models. Instead, the contemplative life of the believer is a habitus, or hermeneutic orientation, that seeks to integrate and interpret the multiplicity of sights, sounds, issues, and circumstances that daily demand human response.[69]

[68] In *Deep Symbols*, 124, Farley discusses how in archaic societies, words of power or deep symbols are closely connected with "sacred" power. In so-called "postmodern" societies, such a link is at best sketchy. Within the current metaphysical structure, people tend to respond to words of power "on the basis of their apparent, intrinsic importance and use." Renewal of words of power demands the recognition that "no word of power is its own exhaustive self-referent, its own final justification, or properly evokes loyalty. All pretensions to completeness, autonomy, absolute importance, are undermined by the word of transcendence." Farley's challenge to push beyond the utilitarian sense of our words of power mirrors Schmemann's liturgical emphasis on the non-utilitarian, non-cultic essence of the Church's worship.

[69] The hermeneutical concern is central to the field of the phenomenology of religion. The task peculiar to phenomenology, says Guerriere (*Phenomenology of the Truth Proper to Religion*), "is not to treat religiousness as if it were a set

In this perspective, Farley argues, the Church becomes a matrix of redemption through which an integration of the personal, the political, and the communal can occur and through which persons' cognitive and affective disciplines can be shaped toward the things of God. This notion echoes Schmemann's understanding that authentic liturgy is

"an all-embracing vision of life, a power meant to judge, inform, and transform the whole of existence, a 'philosophy of life' shaping and challenging all our ideas, attitudes and actions, . . . an icon of that new life which is to challenge and renew the old life in us and around us."[70]

Of course, such an understanding inevitably raises again a question at the center of the liturgical movement: How is redemptive ecclesial presence, as it is shaped by liturgy, to exist in relation to the surrounding culture?

It is at this point that Farley's phenomenological treatment most clearly suggests an avenue for further development of Schmemann's method; efforts at joining Schmemann and Farley in a collaborative/ constructive dialogue will emerge in the next chapter.

Before turning to the other sphere of reflection present within secondary liturgical theology, one other area for further growth within the sphere of "liturgy as communal activity" will be touched on briefly here.

Bruce Morrill argues that from the standpoint of liberation, political, and feminist theologies, Schmemann's critique of modernity fails to make explicit how the Church is to confront systemic political and social realities. The ecclesiological strand of Schmemann's theology lacks, he says, a sufficient critical awareness of the social consequences of the Enlightenment.[71] Consequently, it also lacks an adequate internal framework for self-critique.

---

of propositions and then to inquire if these are 'true.'" The phenomenon of religion is not "a matter of propositions abstracted from life. It is a matter of concrete experience and its concomitant symbolization. The doctrinalization that is sometimes worked upon the symbols is secondary; doctrines are concrete experience become abstract, religiousness become proposition" (11). The questions that phenomenological philosophy asks, and that Schmemann insists liturgical theologians should be asking, concern the concrete phenomenon.

[70] Schmemann, "Liturgy and Theology," 51–2.

[71] Bruce T. Morrill, "Anamnesis as Dangerous Memory: A Dialogue between Political and Liberation Theology" (Ph.D. dissertation, Boston College, 1995) 126.

Since Schmemann, a number of liturgical theologians have become more attentive to the inadequacy of classical and modern approaches to liturgical theology, in particular sacramental theology. They have not, however, examined closely enough their own or Schmemann's continued theoretical reliance on a biblical theology rooted in classical metaphysics and modern historical awareness. The problem with this, noted by Morrill in relation to sacramental theology, is that "the metaphysics operative in classical theology is not only inadequate to the Enlightenment's recognition of history, but also unable to break the hold of middle class values on the promise of the Gospel."[72]

To his credit, Schmemann paves the way for dialogue with more constructive biblical theologies, theologies that offer a more even-handed treatment of Scripture's diverse corpus. For example, his arguments emphasizing the cosmological and eschatological dimensions of sacramentality urge that the New Testament does not supersede the Old Testament. He insists that it is impossible to understand the work of Christ separate from God's revelation in the Old Testament concerning creation, humanity, sin, and salvation.

The remaining chapters of this discussion will engage this issue and propose a prolegomenon to a liturgical method whose biblical foundation is less tied to classical metaphysical constructs.

X *Liturgical Celebration as Convergence of Human Pathos with Divine Ethos*
At the beginning of this section on liturgical theology, the following statement was made: "'something' happens in worship." In worship, people gather, bringing with them their daily celebrations of human living, those experiences of wonderment stirred up by watching a child at play or glimpsing a deer as it disappears into the woods. They also bring with them images of a world of despair and rage, a world of horrific and inhuman events, a world of political exploitation and ideological conquests imposed at the expense of innocent victims.

As Saliers suggests, the promise of authentic worship is that through the liturgical gathering, all of these things are drawn into a transforming encounter with God. Through this encounter, we are urged to new depths of being and offered a glimpse of that which is more "real" than any of the images on the surface of our worldly existence.[73] This creative intermingling of the varied textures of

[72] Ibid., 169–70.
[73] Saliers, *Worship as Theology*, 21–3.

human existence with the realities of God on the canvas of worship constitutes a second sphere of reflection in liturgical theology—liturgical celebration as convergence of human pathos and divine ethos.

In investigating the parameters of this sphere, several developments within liturgical theology become important. Of particular interest is the increased attention given to two facts: (1) that there is a mystery to God's revelation that defies human categories of conceptualization, description, and interpretation, and (2) that failure to confront honestly in liturgy the disparate features of human living results in skimming the surface of this divine mystery.

Saliers treats the first of these two realizations in his proposal to "rethink worship as an eschatological art." He seeks to make more explicit the metaphorical or aesthetic quality of liturgy, a quality that allows us to move beyond the discursive mode.[74]

One way to understand how the imaginative or metaphorical dimension in liturgy operates is to differentiate between what has been termed the "dialectical imagination" and the "analogical imagination."[75] While absolute distinctions cannot be made between the two, several defining characteristics of each can be established.

First, as Hilkert sets forth in her treatment of this dichotomy in preaching, the dialectical imagination emphasizes "the distance

---

[74] Marjorie Proctor-Smith, *In Her Own Rite: Constructing Feminist Liturgical Tradition* (Nashville: Abingdon Press, 1990) 54–5, states that this dimension of liturgy is often referred to as "mystery" or *mysterion*. Historically, the Church realized that God's mystery is revealed in celebrations of baptism and the Eucharist. As she explains, the Latin term *sacramentum* was used to translate the Greek *mysterion*. That is why we have come to call these events "sacraments." Efforts to define and institutionalize the sacraments have in most cases reduced the constitutive sense of the "mystery" to discursive explanations of God's revelation. In renewal of liturgical forms since Vatican II, much work has been done to restore to rites the imaginative dimension. Of course, care must be taken in using the term "imagination" in connection with the "truth" we seek to mediate through liturgy. Proctor-Smith argues that "imagination" implies a particular way of seeing; it is a mode of conceiving reality and of expressing reality that generates our vision of God, the world, others, and self.

[75] See Proctor-Smith, *In Her Own Rite*, 36–58; Sallie McFague, *Metaphorical Theology* (Philadelphia: Fortress Press, 1982); Mary Catherine Hilkert, *Naming Grace: Preaching and the Sacramental Imagination* (New York: Continuum, 1997); Paul Ricoeur, *Figuring the Sacred: Religion, Narrative, and the Imagination*, ed. Mark I. Wallace (Minneapolis: Augsburg Press, 1995).

between God and humanity, the hiddenness and absence of God, the need for grace as redemption and reconciliation, the limits and necessity for critique of any human project or institution including the church, and the not-yet character of the promise of the reign of God."[76] The analogical imagination, on the other hand, emphasizes

"the presence of God who is self-communicating love, the creation of human beings in the image of God (restless hearts seeking the divine), the mystery of the incarnation, grace as divinizing as well as forgiving, the mediating role of the church as sacrament of salvation in the world, and the 'foretaste' of the reign of God that is present in human community wherever God's reign of justice, peace and love is fostered."[77]

The more "authentic" and ecumenical liturgy sought by the liturgical movement requires a balance between dialectical imagination's insistence that the assembly gathers to be shaped by the text and analogical imagination's claim that the assembly is formed by liturgy. Current secondary reflections on liturgical theology attempt to achieve such a balance, interpreting liturgy as a meeting place where human passions and sufferings are transformed in light of Scripture's promise of the future reign of God.

Western Christianity historically has been dominated by the discursive and rationalistic patterns common to dialectical imagination;[78] as scholars continue to rethink worship, it is vital to renew our under-

---

[76] Hilkert, *Naming Grace*, 15.

[77] Ibid. Hilkert uses the term "sacramental imagination" as opposed to "analogical imagination." Her descriptions of these two modes, and particularly her emphasis on "sacramental imagination," is developed from a Roman Catholic perspective. From the standpoint of practical theology, David Tracy provides an overview of the defining characteristics of both the dialectical imagination and what he chooses to call the "analogical imagination." See David Tracy, "The Analogical Imagination in Catholic Theology," *Talking about God: Doing Theology in the Context of Modern Pluralism*, ed. David Tracy and John B. Cobb Jr. (New York: Seabury Press, 1983).

[78] This represents the Church's attempt, in response to specific historical eras or situations, to define in creedal and systematic form what it believes. Kavanagh's depiction of the contrasts between eastern and western Christian worship exemplifies how Western emphases have affected our conceptualization of how we know what we know; in some ways, these emphases have also inhibited our ability to participate in the juxtapositions of worship.

standing of how the metaphorical juxtapositions of worship—that unique constellation of word, bread, cup, song, and prayer—shape human perceptions, both cognitive and affective, toward the mystery of God's self-giving in Christ. To accomplish such a balance of the dialectical and analogical imaginations requires an examination of two related factors.

First, as noted earlier, continued liturgical renewal involves seeing theology as more than a transferral of knowledge. It requires seeing liturgy similar to the way Farley sees theological education. Theological treatments of existential phenomena are now emerging that are both integrative and contextual. These treatments understand theology to be an opening of people's minds to perceive the sacred in human experience. They also view the faith community as the matrix within which a "world-transforming integration of the personal, the political and the communal can occur."[79]

Within this understanding, Farley describes faith as the "way human beings live in and toward God under the impact of redemption"; as such, faith itself is a mode of knowing. The insights or knowledge of faith are, at their most elemental level, pre-reflective or pre-cognitive. In Farley's view, a process of critical reflection through which these pre-reflective insights are made self-conscious is implicit to faith. The knowledge that faith arrives at through this process is what he calls "*theologia.*"[80]

Theologia, as Farley defines it, is much like the knowledge or truth liturgical scholars argue is mediated through liturgy. It is not primarily

---

Western worship, Kavanagh explains, "tends to exploit meaning in such raw and aggressive quantity that congregations are often reduced to passivity, seated in pews with texts before them in order to give their full attention to the meaning purveyed in the service." In eastern practice, worship tends to be less cerebral and more open to movement, intuition, and contemplation. Through increased ecumenical dialogue, liturgical theologians from a Western perspective have become more aware that to expect worship to yield doctrinal certainty is incompatible with human living. See Aidan Kavanagh, *On Liturgical Theology* (New York: Pueblo Publishing Co., 1984) 4–5.

[79] Farley, *Ecclesial Man: A Social Phenomenology of Faith and Reality* (Philadelphia: Fortress Press, 1975). Saliers, *Worship as Theology,* 49–68, is representative of those liturgical scholars who have been more intentional in their treatment of contemporary epistemological issues. In particular, he is interested in the recovery of aesthetic modes of knowing.

[80] Farley, *Theologia,* 35.

descriptive but rather constructive; it is a reflective wisdom or knowledge. This approach to knowledge respects the quality of "mystery," the elusiveness of God's presence, that is inherent in liturgical forms. The importance of this epistemological perspective for liturgical theology will be developed in the next chapter. Its pedagogical relevance within the faith community is the subject of Chapter 6: "Creating a World: Proverbs and the Journey of Conversion."

The second important factor in establishing a balance between dialectical imagination and analogical imagination in liturgical theology relates to the structural patterns of liturgy. Dialectical imagination and analogical imagination converge in the literary structure of Proverbs and Job and in the way each dialogues with its own historical context; the dynamic of convergence reflected in their development suggests an unexpected biblical model for patterns of liturgical renewal, one that respects the mysterious aspect of God's presence.

Liturgical scholars emphasize that shifts in imagination are central to liturgical form. Such shifts occur in wisdom literature through the structural dynamic that Perdue calls "sapiential imagination," which is a metaphorical movement from orientation to disorientation to re-orientation.[81] I contend that authentic liturgical forms also reflect this movement as in the worship event people are drawn out of their cultural contexts into a new orientation of radical hope. This issue will be the theme of Chapters 4 and 5.

A second concern central to that sphere of reflection that sees liturgical celebration as convergence of human pathos and divine mystery emerges when dialectical imagination is emphasized in worship to the exclusion of analogical imagination—namely the risk of failing to confront honestly in liturgy the disparate features of human living. As Saliers explains, in worship people take their human condition before God and in the presence of God, through word and sacraments, they receive the gift of God's vision for the world. The danger is that the faith community will resist the invitation to experience the juxtaposi-

[81] This correlates with the dynamic of suffering and hope central both to Jewish piety and the Christian paschal mystery. This dynamic has been developed by Walter Brueggemann in two of his works: *The Prophetic Imagination* (Philadelphia: Fortress Press, 1978) and *Finally Comes the Poet* (Minneapolis: Fortress Press, 1989). Brueggemann argues that an act of imaginative construal to determine how the truths of God are to be discerned and practiced in our current situation is necessary for faithful proclamation of the word.

tion of the symbols and actions of thanksgiving with life's deepest realities.[82] When the full range of human hope, fear, and pain is not brought to the worship event or when it is excluded by liturgical patterns, then the truth mediated by liturgy's language and forms becomes distorted.

The human condition consists of daily struggles to make sense of the pieces of our lives. We live in a world in which our language and actions marginalize people and perpetuate oppression. In the context of worship, however, it is possible for redemptive discourse and action to disrupt evil and give hope to the concrete situations of peoples' lives.[83]

Of course, it is also characteristic of the human condition that we lack the honesty necessary to create such an authentic worship context. That is why liturgical theology must constantly seek a self-critical moment when it can ask itself vital questions about its internal coherence and integrity. The eschatological task of liturgy is to imagine the world whole; do our liturgies accomplish that? Do our liturgies take on the reality of injustice and its sources and ritually imagine an alternative? To what extent have we redemptively remembered the victims of the world's evil and oppressiveness?[84]

Proctor-Smith's development of a feminist liturgical theology is especially thought-provoking in this regard. She emphasizes that the androcentric nature of liturgical tradition causes the Church to provide only a partial "remembering" of the stories of women. Anamnesis, or what Proctor-Smith terms "embodied remembering"

---

[82] Saliers, *Worship as Theology*, 24–5.

[83] Edward Farley, "Toward a New Paradigm for Preaching," *Preaching as a Theological Task: World, Gospel, Scripture,* ed. Thomas G. Long and Edward Farley (Louisville: Westminster/John Knox Press, 1996) 165–75.

[84] Power, *Eucharistic Mystery,* 328–49. These questions are especially important when we take into consideration Farley's contention that suffering is never solely a neurological or physical stimulation but that it is at the same time an interpretive response. Through the centuries, society has institutionalized human experiences of suffering and given it enduring expression in basic metaphors and symbols. Thus, in our social worlds and institutions, suffering is understood or labeled as "heroic, trivial, meaningless, or repressed." Suffering also can become an instrument of political exploitation. How suffering is thematized in corporate memory and passed from generation to generation through various institutions is a vital issue for liturgical theology. See Edward Farley, *Good and Evil: Interpreting a Human Condition* (Minneapolis: Fortress Press, 1990) 59–60.

of the paschal mystery, is the constitutive element of liturgy. When the remembering of historical events in liturgy is faulty or incomplete, Christian identity suffers.

Proctor-Smith argues that liturgical tradition has preserved and ritualized patriarchal memory to the exclusion of the memories of women and other marginalized peoples. This androcentric bias is particularly evident in the Church's remembrance of constitutive events in redemption history. This project proposes a biblical matrix for liturgical methodology that challenges this androcentric bias and that insists on discovering God's presence in the midst of all the contingencies of life.

CONCLUSION

Traditional theological method fails to provide a treatment of human existence adequate to the questions and understandings of this contemporary culture. Although a number of liturgical theologians have productively dealt with this challenge by focusing on the way in which liturgy "creates a world," not enough attention has been given to the issue of "how" this happens in a desacralized world.

I propose that a wisdom perspective on liturgical practice establishes a method that continues the process of liturgical renewal by addressing the concerns raised in this chapter. As noted earlier, various scholars have dealt with one or more of these areas of critique individually, but no methodology has been advanced that addresses them in an integrated way. The next chapter continues to lay the groundwork for the proposed wisdom liturgical method by taking up these areas of critique as they have been dealt with in the field of practical theology, in particular in the work of Farley.

Saliers makes the point that the worship gathering itself is a metaphor; the meaning of the gathering is woven into the very fabric of its context.[85] This insight draws us back to the image of the nursing home that provided the entranceway into our discussion of liturgical theology.

The elders and I offered the bread and cup to each person gathered in the room that day. One woman who suffers with Alzheimer's disease took the cup in a trembling hand. She looked at it; then she smelled it. Finally, she drank and spoke: "It tastes so good." It is unclear to what extent the woman was able cognitively to grasp the doctrinal implications of that moment. Within the context of her

[85] Saliers, *Worship as Theology*, 28.

human suffering, however, as she saw, heard, and tasted, an aesthetic world of meaning was created. This is what Saliers intends when he says that "liturgy is a self-giving of God to us, the encounter whereby grace and glory find human form."[86] Liturgy, in all of its actions and symbols, says something true about God; thus, it also says something true about humanity and our world. In liturgy, meaning occurs.

[86] Ibid., 22.

Chapter 3

Liturgical Theology and Edward Farley in Dialogue

A Gallup poll reported in March 1997 that 96 percent of North Americans believe in God or a universal spirit. This is not a major change from similar polls dating a decade or two ago. The most significant development in recent years, it seems, is the way in which North Americans incorporate their spiritual beliefs into their daily lives.[1] Traditional formalized worship is one aspect of religious life that seems less important or even relevant to many people today as they integrate their spiritual beliefs and everyday activities.

Related to this, the importance of denominational distinctiveness is increasingly challenged as people express fewer ties to particular traditions and as the defining characteristics of those traditions become blurred. Much growth is seen now in nondenominational or interdenominational congregations that use marketing techniques similar to those of secular institutions to effect church growth. Some of these churches have such enormous size and range of services they tend toward institutional autonomy.

As it labors to restore worship as central to human living, the liturgical movement traverses this ever-changing landscape of American religious life. So far the results have been far-reaching as the movement, particularly since Vatican II, has succeeded in revising

---

[1] In a Gallup report entitled "Religious Faith Is Widespread but Many Skip Church: Little Change in Recent Years," Frank Newport and Lydia Saad state that a March 1997 poll indicates while two-thirds of North Americans maintain an affiliation with a church or synagogue, only about four in ten attend worship regularly.

traditional liturgical rites and in developing new ones that more directly intersect with the existential realities of this contemporary time.

However, even with the continued success of the movement's efforts at renewing liturgical forms and restoring the link between liturgy and theology, a daunting gap still exists between the Church's worship and the spirituality claimed by people in Western society.[2] Much work is yet to be done to restore liturgy as a primary beckoning voice that stands at the intersection of ultimate truth, the Church, and the marketplace.

As James Empereur notes, many within the liturgical movement continue to search for ways of bringing spirituality and liturgy together. One aspect of this search that necessitates further dialogue and investigation is the question of how the vision of truth mediated by denominational worship structures relates to the vision of truth that currently defines Western spirituality.

As seen in the preceding chapter, recent work in the study of North American religion and theological education indicates that one reason for the bifurcation of liturgy and spirituality in Western society is that liturgy has been too closely associated with and controlled by ideological institutional concerns rather than by communal concerns.[3] A result of this for many people is a perception of liturgy as antiquated ritual done behind the closed doors of a Church on the margins of society.[4] If there is any real contact with God, a "post-denominational"

[2] James Empereur, *Exploring the Sacred* (Washington, D.C.: Pastoral Press, 1987) vii–ix.

[3] Barbara G. Wheeler, "Uncharted Territory: Congregational Identity and Mainline Protestantism," *The Presbyterian Predicament: Six Perspectives,* ed. Milton J. Coalter, John M. Mulder, and Louis B. Weeks (Louisville: Westminster/John Knox Press, 1990) 67–89.

[4] J. Neil Alexander, "Individualism and the Body of Christ," *Time and Community,* ed. J. Neil Alexander (Washington, D.C.: Pastoral Press, 1990) 291–306, states that for many people today, "Life in the church is just one more activity performed alongside countless others, one more thing competing for their time, money and devotion and generally with little sense of integration with the totality of life." The result of this, he continues, is that the fragmentation people experience in daily life begins to permeate Church life. For instance, in a market economy the "successful" parish is the one that has "something for everyone." In this "shopping mall ecclesiology," argues Alexander, the Church is perceived by many only to be an option for entertainment, emotional support, or individual fulfillment; its truth claims are not seen to have any universal validity.

society insists to the contrary, it takes place in the private personal domain of individuals.

The first part of this chapter will address this crisis in Christian communal identity from the standpoint of primary themes in Edward Farley's philosophical theology. In particular, Farley's depiction of theology as habitus will be explicated as it intersects with understandings implicit to liturgy that God cannot be objectified, that God is the reality or truth that transcends all other reality, and that God cannot be adequately defined by empirical reasoning or rational forms.[5] In Farley's understanding, what is mediated within the faith community and its ritual forms is not an "object" but rather a horizon of truth in terms of which everything else in life is then interpreted and experienced.[6]

Focusing attention on this horizon of truth, on the validity of the truth claims mediated by liturgical forms at this horizon, and on the implications of this for communal identity paves the way for the dual concerns that will be treated in the second part of the chapter. First, Farley asserts, when theology is understood as a matrix through which all reality is seen in light of God, communal identity is shaped within a theocentric piety. This means that life is ordered by devotion to God and participation in the community of faith. Important to our discussion here will be a closer look at Farley's "nuanced interpretation of the historical, located, pluralistic, and incomplete character of truth" and the value of that interpretation for liturgical concerns.[7]

[5] Wendy Farley, "Eros and the Truth: Feminist Theory and the Claims of Reality," *Theology and the Interhuman,* ed. Robert R. Williams (Valley Forge, Pa.: Trinity Press International, 1995) 25.

[6] See Edward Farley, *Theologia: The Fragmentation and Unity of Theological Education* (Philadelphia: Fortress Press, 1983) 151; and James Empereur, *Exploring the Sacred* (Washington, D.C.: Pastoral Press, 1987) 23. Margaret Mary Kelleher, "Liturgical Theology: A Task and a Method," *Worship* 62 (January 1988) 2–24, argues that the horizon of meaning created in liturgical praxis is a dynamic horizon involving ongoing reflection on the significance or value of religion in society.

[7] Farley, "Eros and the Truth," 21. Vital to liturgical renewal is determining how to correlate Christian truth claims with the contemporary situation. Farley insists that all truth is mediated truth. Thus, our knowledge of truth is always "in process" as is the formation of our faith and moral world views. John Cobb, "Good and Evil in Process Perspective," *Theology and the Interhuman,* ed. Robert Williams (Valley Forge, Pa.: Trinity Press International, 1995) 3–20, examines this issue from the perspective of process theology.

Second, to adopt this stance toward theology in a way that is in keeping with the essence of Christianity and appropriate to contemporary challenges involves constant critical reflection. For Farley, this means thinking about theology from the standpoint of reflective ontology.[8] Reflective ontology challenges contemporary quantifications of reality that produce a one-dimensional knowledge that fails to respect the complexity of created beings. I will argue in this chapter that Farley's mode of ontology provides one piece of a critical-reflective structure that informs the liturgical movement as it becomes more intentionally self-critical.[9]

Paralleling these concerns, Farley warns that grasping the reality of faith cannot be reduced only to understanding or interpreting the Church's vehicles of duration, such as historical statements of belief, traditional texts, and official doctrines. To equate truth with its vehicles of mediation risks denying to particular faith communities their prophetic role in calling to account society's deepest corruptions and ideological hegemonies.

One reason the Church has ceded its prophetic calling is because the relationship between the Church's historical structures and the validity of the truth claims mediated by those structures has not been adequately delineated by historical theology. Farley's reconstrual of historical theology suggests an alternative to historical methods dominated by an Enlightenment epistemology. The relation of Farley's alternative, "theological portraiture," to liturgical method, his critique of Christianity's "house of authority," and a proposal for an alternate

---

[8] Edward Farley, *Good and Evil: Interpreting a Human Condition* (Minneapolis: Fortress Press, 1990) 1–2, is acutely aware of the fact that his work is ontological and that there is a "deep suspicion of ontological theology" in contemporary times. He responds to several critiques directed to ontological thinking: (1) that ontological thinking is unhistorical, (2) that deconstruction has displaced ontology, and (3) that an ontological approach tends to support the status quo rather than to promote change. These continue to be valid criticisms, but Farley's reflective ontology is rooted in phenomenology and practical wisdom. Contrary to most ontologies, therefore, his effort affirms the historicity of thought and supports the goals of justice and liberation in the face of oppression.

[9] David Power, *Eucharistic Mystery: Revitalizing the Tradition* (New York: Crossroad, 1995) 324–6, notes the limits of ontology for eucharistic theology but argues that "an ontology that retains modernity's unbending concern with the human subject, while stressing the negation and self-surrender of faith, is vital."

way in which Scripture and tradition can be seen as authoritative will be treated later in this chapter.[10]

The third part of this chapter will address the question of how the faith community is to address the moral ambiguities of our time. Saliers reminds us that Scripture "is a record of God's mighty acts; but it also records the struggle of a people to live according to a vision of the good believed to be given by God." In other words, communal life is intimately connected to ethics and to character formation.[11]

As Saliers argues, the shape of the Christian moral world view is directly connected to how Christians worship God. Communal praise, thanksgiving, confession, and prayer create a matrix that shapes human intentions and actions. However, like the gap between worship and the spirituality expressed by people in Western society, a disparity also exists between how people enact their worship and how they live their daily lives.

One reason for this is the influence on worship of a post-Enlightenment world view that focuses on the ontological priority of the individual. By contrast, post-Vatican II worship rites, texts, and books celebrate the ontological priority of the Church as an eschatological community elected by the free choice of God. This clearly sets up a dichotomy between the ethos of this technical and individualized era and the ethos of the Church. At least in part, the redemptive horizon in worship occurs as a result of the dialogue that seeks to lessen this gap. The goal is to enable the community of faith in its worship practices and in its daily life to envision the world as God intended it and to awaken the cultural ethos to the presence of God.

The redemptive horizon present in the faith community is one of the themes in Farley's *Good and Evil: Interpreting a Human Condition*. As he explains, redemption, if it is related to real exigencies of the world we inhabit, must exist as some form of "thinking toward the world," as some form of practice. Just what form this practice takes and how such practice is both constitutive of persons within the community and directed beyond the community has important implications for the eschatological dimension of liturgy.

Implications for the Church's understanding of conversion and for the relationship between conversion and worship also grow out of this

[10] Edward Farley, *Ecclesial Man: A Social Phenomenology of Faith and Reality* (Philadelphia: Fortress Press, 1975) 206–31.

[11] Don Saliers, *Worship as Theology: Foretaste of Glory Divine* (Nashville: Abingdon Press, 1994) 172–3.

understanding. To conclude this chapter, I will address several questions related to conversion that are central to a wisdom liturgical method: How are we to understand the biblical concept of a "conversion community" in terms of contemporary liturgy?[12] What does David Power mean when he discusses Christian conversion as conversion to the Christian horizon?[13] What is the primary aim of conversion and how does this relate to liturgy?[14] What is the role of biblical redemption history when conversion and communal identity are conceived in the way Farley suggests?[15]

THEOLOGY AND THE QUESTION OF TRUTH

In 1979, Russell Ackoff, working in the field of operations research, made an intriguing statement, one that echoes the discussion of the dilemma of rigor or relevance discussed in the previous chapter:

"Managers are not confronted with problems that are independent of each other, but with dynamic situations that consist of complex systems of changing problems that interact with each other. I call such situations messes. Problems are abstractions extracted from messes by analysis; they are to messes as atoms are to tables and charts. . . . Managers do not solve problems; they manage messes."[16]

What Ackoff means by this statement and how it might be related to liturgical concerns becomes clearer by looking briefly at Donald

[12] Empereur, *Exploring the Sacred*, 50.

[13] David Power, "Cult to Culture: The Liturgical Foundation of Theology," *Worship* 54 (November 1980) 482–94.

[14] Douglas Ottati, *Reforming Protestantism: Christian Commitment in Today's World* (Louisville: Westminster/John Knox Press, 1995) 41–2, emphasizes that "reforming piety strives for *metanoia*: not in the first place thinking about ourselves and our isolated groups, but being caught up in the messianic event of Jesus Christ—the person-for-others whose way in life is oriented by devotion to God, the Word who discloses the faithful God-for-others." Reforming piety challenges us to pursue true communion with God in community with others. Through God's grace, and in spite of sin's corruption of community, we are enabled to pursue this promise. Ottati's understanding of the Reformed tradition's theocentric piety intersects with Farley's treatment of redemptive ecclesial presence at points that both critique Farley's thesis and help to clarify it.

[15] Farley, *Ecclesial Man*, 164–80.

[16] Russell Ackoff, "The Future of Operational Research Is Past," *Journal of Operational Research Society* 30 (1979) 93–104.

Schon's exploration of professional practice in *The Reflective Practitioner: How Professionals Think in Action.*

Schon argues that the "professions" have become essential to the functioning of our society. People look to professionals as having a particular expertise in their respective fields of law, medicine, education, religion, or government.[17] Recently, however, we see a growing public skepticism toward professionals' claims to special knowledge. This is accompanied by a general loss of confidence in the ability of the professions to solve the actual problems of societal life.[18]

In particular, there are not a few worldwide problems that professional representatives of science, technology, or public policy seem unable to prevent or solve. Some critics even argue that national crises such as military involvement on foreign shores, deterioration of cities, pollution, decreased availability of energy resources, crises in the health care system, and growing violence appear to be rooted in the advances of technology gone awry.[19] Several causes for this can be suggested.

One common assessment is that professional knowledge "is mismatched to the changing character of the situations of practice—the

[17] Joseph C. Hough and John B. Cobb Jr., *Christian Identity and Theological Education* (Chico, Calif.: Scholars Press, 1985) 5–6, discuss this from the standpoint of theological education. In certain periods of American history, dominant ministerial "types" emerged to define the profession for that time period. These types were shaped by theological concepts that arose as a result of particular sociohistorical situations. Paradigmatic changes in the concept of ministry have emerged during those times when the theological bases for a particular type were challenged by social or intellectual changes within and outside the Church. Hough and Cobb describe several professional ministerial "types" that have dominated the practice of ministry historically.

[18] Many note the height of what has been called the "triumph of professionalism" with the publication of the Fall 1963 issue of *Daedalus,* the journal of the American Academy of Arts and Sciences. In this volume, dedicated to the professions, the expansion and visibility of the professions in almost all areas of American life is heralded. Much of the impetus for the flurry of scientific development in America came in the wake of World War II and in response to Soviet technological advances such as the launching of Sputnik. After 1963 and continuing to the present, there has been increasing awareness of the limitations of the professions to solve problems whose lines of demarcation are blurred and that do not fit prescribed empirical models.

[19] Donald Schon, *The Reflective Practitioner: How Professionals Think in Action* (New York: Basic Books, 1983) 3–9, focuses on the period between 1963 and 1981 and the various public events that have undermined belief in the competence

complexity, uncertainty, instability, uniqueness and value conflicts which are increasingly perceived as central to the world of professional practice."[20] Professionals find themselves facing problems which are not solved by applying certain technical skills; they are, as Ackoff termed them, "messes." They resist the purely empirical solutions of technical rationality.

As noted in the last chapter, while Schon agrees with this assessment, his own perspective adds an interesting twist that intersects with this project's focus on the relationship between the "practice" of ministry and theology. Schon suggests that successful professional practice has as much to do with finding the right problem to solve as it does with developing more accurate techniques or theories for solving the problem once it is found.

What Schon means by this is that application of specialized knowledge does not solve the complexity of problems that exist in contemporary life. In daily living and practice, problems do not present themselves in clearly defined packages. Instead, as practitioners face complex situations, they must decide what goals they hope to achieve and what means they will adopt to reach them. This task is what Schon calls "problem setting." Problem setting, he says, is "the process in which, interactively, we name the things to which we will attend and frame the context in which we will attend to them."[21]

Even professionals agree that there is an element to professional competence that defies established techniques or theories. The effective use of specialized knowledge gained in the academy, argues Schon, involves a "prior restructuring of complex situations." This aspect of professional practice consists of an "irreducible element of art," a pre-critical element not teachable by current models but still learnable as practitioners negotiate concrete situations.[22]

---

of the "knowledge industry." Particular national events in which professional effectiveness has drawn heavy criticism are the Vietnam War, the Bay of Pigs, and Three Mile Island. One of numerous scholarly and journalistic critiques of these so-called "professionally managed disasters" is David Halberstam, *The Best and the Brightest* (New York: Random House, 1972).

[20] Schon, *The Reflective Practitioner*, 14.

[21] Ibid., 40.

[22] Ibid., 18. Saliers, *Worship as Theology*, addresses that element of liturgy that is "art." Paralleling Farley, he explains that shaping human affections and dispositions toward God takes place liturgically in art forms—speaking, acting,

Farley addresses this question of knowledge from the standpoint of philosophical/constructive theology. He proposes a restructuring of theological education that is more integrative of *scientia* (empirical study) and *sapientia* (practical wisdom). At heart, his proposal of theology as a life-forming pursuit involves a rethinking of the entire problem of theological method. Farley's configuration of the problem of theological method for this post-Enlightenment age, his "setting of the problem," is what opens it to dialogue with current concerns for liturgical renewal.

The foundation is laid for Farley's constructive theology in *Ecclesial Man: A Social Phenomenology of Faith and Reality.* In this work, Farley addresses what he calls "the problem behind the problem of theological method." He notes that the historical development of traditional theology reflects a general consensus that faith points to certain "transcendent, human and historical realities." Methods that arose out of this historical consensus dominate theological method today. They are primarily concerned to explicate principles and theories for clarifying these transcendent truths or realities. Traditional theological method, argues Farley, is criteriology.[23]

---

singing, and seeing. Through these forms the mystery of God's presence and grace is revealed in the community in its most primary sense. See Rachel Reeder, "Art of Our Own Making," *The Landscape of Praise: Readings in Liturgical Renewal,* ed. Blair Gilmer Meeks (Valley Forge, Pa.: Trinity Press International, 1996) 11–13.

[23] Farley notes two major shifts in post-medieval Christianity that turned attention to theological method. The first was the Reformation and its disputes over the authority of Scripture and tradition. In this, Protestant reformers attacked the metaphysical element of Catholic scholasticism and allied themselves with the anti-metaphysical tradition of modern philosophy. See Edward Farley, "Truth and the Wisdom of Enduring," *Phenomenology of the Truth Proper to Religion,* ed. Daniel Guerriere (Albany: State University of New York Press, 1990) 61. The second major shift, according to Farley, occurred as a result of the emergence of the historical-critical method in the study of Scripture.

The ultimate outcome of historical criticism was the de-supernaturalization and relativization of classical authorities; this made theological method itself problematic as it became clear that neither Scripture nor tradition could be subject to historical origins and also contain those transcendent qualities that gave them authority as bearers of ultimate truth and reality. See Farley, *Ecclesial Man,* 3–6. For other discussions of how theological method has developed see Gordon D. Kaufman, *In the Face of Mystery: A Constructive Theology*

As noted previously, however, recent epistemological and cultural developments pose a direct challenge to traditional theological criteriology, questioning both the frameworks and principles of clarification (in other words the institutions and structures of mediation) and the realities mediated by those frameworks. This questioning of the reality-apprehensions of the faith, says Farley, exists prior to the traditional problem of theological method; it replaces traditional disputes over criteriology with the issue of whether or not "faith apprehends any realities at all."[24] Contemporary epistemological and religious pluralism draws this "problem" to the forefront of theological discussion. Because liturgy stands at the intersection of communal faith and public life, it is a problem aimed at liturgical method as well.

In reconfiguring the "problem" of theological method, Farley confronts this question of faith's reality-references. His impetus for pursuing theological method from this angle is the conviction that whether society's suspicion is confirmed that faith has no distinctive reality apprehensions or whether we discover that faith is in fact directed toward particular realities, theological method is affected. In Farley's own language, addressing the question of reality

"pushes traditional theological method (criteriology) back to the pre-criteria situation in which realities are immediately grasped. The description of this situation has priority over criteriological clarifications. Some may argue that, in theology, criteria (Scripture, tradition) replace all direct apprehensions. In our view, redemption itself involves direct apprehensions and falsifies this claim. Furthermore, the clues to the nature and function of the criteria lie in the pre-criteriological situation of faith. This is the only protection available against idolatrous and arbitrary manipulations of the authorities."[25]

In his formulation of the pre-critical problem of theological method, Farley argues that questions directed at the realities of faith are generated within the faith community. Therefore, theology must primarily address itself to the practices and existential questions of the community.

(Cambridge, Mass.: Harvard University Press, 1993); and George A. Lindbeck, *The Nature of Doctrine: Religion and Theology in a Postliberal Age* (Philadelphia: Westminster Press, 1984).

[24] Farley, *Ecclesial Man*, 8.
[25] Ibid.

It is at this point that Farley's "setting of the problem" of theological method intersects with methodological efforts within the liturgical movement. Several points of intersection are vital to our proposal of an alternative liturgical method.

First, phenomenological theology, in which Farley is grounded, insists that the task of philosophy is contrary to academic custom. Philosophical theology does not treat religion as a set of propositions and then examine whether these propositions are "true." The phenomenon of religion, Farley asserts, is not a set of propositions or doctrines to be separated out from the concreteness of life. Rather, doctrines develop secondarily, as concrete experiences are generalized into propositions.

In contrast to dominant discursive/rationalistic approaches, phenomenological theology, much like liturgical theology, directs its questions toward the concrete phenomenon of religion and religious experience. It asks particular types of questions that shape its method, questions not unlike those that currently bombard the Church: To what existential problem are religion and its practices a response? What is the meaning of "God" and how does it relate to human existence? How are religions true? How are the good and the true related to religion? How do language, symbol, and myth affect the status of truth in religion?[26]

As noted in Chapter 2, recent liturgical method has directed its efforts in an analogous way toward the pre-criteriological situation of faith by focusing on the worship of the faith community as the primary location of immediate apprehensions of God's presence. An awareness has also developed within the liturgical movement that the meaning mediated by liturgy cannot be isolated from the practice of ritual in its various contexts.

Within liturgical renewal efforts, then, there is a movement similar to that in Farley's philosophical approach. The liturgical movement, as it inquires into the ordo, pulls back the layers of traditional theological

[26] Guerriere, ed., *Phenomenology of the Truth Proper to Religion*, 10–12. A number of practical theologians have developed their methods from the perspective of foundational theology. Examples include: David Tracy, *Blessed Rage for Order: The New Pluralism in Theology* (New York: Seabury Press, 1975); John Cobb Jr., *The Structure of Christian Existence* (New York: Seabury Press, 1975); Langdon Gilkey, *Naming the Whirlwind: The Renewal of God-Language* (New York: Bobbs-Merrill Company, 1969); and Peter Hodgson, *New Birth of Freedom* (Philadelphia: Fortress Press, 1976).

inquiry, seeking out the pre-criteriological situation in which ultimate realities are most immediately grasped. It seeks truth about God that exists prior to both institutional and doctrinal shaping of that truth.

Specifically, to revisit Schmemann, the primary task of liturgical theology is to find the core structure of the Church's liturgical life. This structure of meaning exists prior to the written typicon and the unwritten rubrics—prior to the Church's objectified renderings of and secondary reflections on its worship. "Whatever else the Sunday assembly of Christians is intended to do," says Lathrop, echoing Schmemann, "there can be wide ecumenical agreement about this: The Sunday assembly means to say the truth about God."[27] To inquire into the structure of the ordo, he argues, is to inquire into the way meaning occurs in worship.

Of course, for Lathrop, there is a concern that worship forms be patterned so that they point beyond themselves toward the reality of God's presence. As Lathrop notes, in order to avoid distortions, the "truth" mediated in liturgy always involves "two words"; it requires juxtaposition because "in this world speaking about God with just one 'word'—one connected and logical discourse, for example—will almost inevitably mean speaking a distortion, even a lie."[28] To concretize theological truth in a particular doctrine or to attempt to abstract it from a liturgical form is to diminish the vitality of that truth.

Farley states the same concern. Faith, he argues, has always had a "reality-apprehending" aspect:

"Prior to the rise of such authorities as the New Testament canon or the crystallization of a doctrinal tradition, believers apprehended Jesus Christ, the power of evil, and the eschatological community in the redemptive shaping effected by participation in the community of faith. With the emergence of canon and tradition came a mode of

[27] Gordon Lathrop, "At Least Two Words: The Liturgy as Proclamation," *The Landscape of Praise: Readings in Liturgical Renewal,* ed. Blair Gilmer Meeks (Valley Forge, Pa.: Trinity Press International, 1996) 183–5.
[28] Ibid. As Collins (*Worship: Renewal to Practice* [Washington, D.C.: Pastoral Press, 1987] 57) notes, liturgical symbols and actions are elusive vehicles of meaning. They are not like public contracts and scientific inquiry which tend to focus on one word, one meaning. Rather, the symbolic language of liturgy embraces multiple points of reference and multiple meanings, "creating a veritable thicket of possible meanings."

engaging in disputation and interpretation which obscured the apprehensions concomitant with faith itself."[29]

The relation of this to liturgy becomes more apparent.

When the Church allows any part of worship to become only doctrinal or propositional speaking about God, it risks obscuring the mystery of God and instead draws attention to the object of mediation,
namely, human effort. Juxtapositions in the ordo—the placing of the
meal next to preaching, the joining together of singing and being
silent, of giving thanks and lamenting—these juxtapositions speak the
faith of the Church in a dynamic metaphorical fashion and draw
participants closer to the truth of God.

Lathrop looks to scriptural forms for the most authentic pattern of
the ordo in Christian worship. In biblical patterns, he suggests, the
basic juxtapositions of the ordo are the Sunday meeting next to the
seven day week and meal next to word. These basic juxtapositions,
along with others configured around these two poles, mediate to the
community a "vision" of God's grace in the past, present, and future.
This vision is not in the form of empirical truth. Rather, it is a horizon
of truth constantly shaped, clarified, and reinterpreted as people bring
the realities of their daily lives to participation in liturgy.

Paralleling Farley's insistence that the faith community is the matrix
of reality-givenness, Schmemann, Lathrop, and other liturgical theologians insist that the primary task of liturgical theology is to discover
the "living" norm that exists prior to the "rubrics" of worship. Central
to this process, again echoing Farley, is the understanding that the
canon did not create the Church but rather emerged to define what is
essential to the Church's structure. In the same way, the ordo does not
create or generate worship; it defines it.

[29] Farley, *Ecclesial Man*, 18–19. As Farley notes in a chapter on Husserlian
phenomenology, phenomenological theology is "that founding moment in
theological phenomenology which attends to faith's reality-directed apprehensions and their conditions, on which depends the second moment, theological method or criteriology" (24). Farley develops his phenomenological
approach by correlating the work of Edmund Husserl with his own theological perspective. See Edmund Husserl, *Ideas: General Introduction to Pure
Phenomenology* (London: Allen and Unwin, 1931); James G. Hart, "Divine
Truth in Husserl and Kant: Some Issues in Phenomenological Theology,"
Phenomenology of the Truth Proper to Religion, ed. Daniel Guerriere (Albany:
State University of New York Press, 1990) 221–46.

Efforts to uncover the ordo have been transformative for renewing the practice of worship, for addressing ecumenical concerns, and for lessening the gap between theory and practice in theology. It is my contention that Farley's particular approach to phenomenological theology challenges the liturgical movement to revisit an important question related to these accomplishments.

As noted in Chapter 2, the 1973 Scottsdale Conference on American Liturgy sought to reaffirm and expand traditional liturgical structures in an effort to appropriate them more effectively for the present and future. In Langdon Gilkey's address to the conference, some intriguing insights emerged that continue to challenge liturgical renewal.[30]

Gilkey argues that when contemporary culture asks about God, theological method is challenged with the task of justifying religious discourse as a whole. This is because recent Western epistemological and cultural shifts have moved to questioning the ultimate meaning of statements of faith. Gilkey argues that the current cultural situation requires that theological method must "set its problem" in a different way.

In his address, Gilkey connects this understanding of method to liturgical theology; he suggests that there are three levels or fundamental meanings of symbol in Christian theology. The primary meaning of symbol is that each created entity is a symbol of the presence of the Creator. Human beings, for example, embody the image of God; central to the faith journey is our seeking to reflect this image. This meaning of symbols is what provides the generative source for symbols in worship.

Because we live in a broken world, Gilkey argues, God, the authentic self, and the subjectivity of the "other" have been obscured. So, too, has the human ability to reflect the image of God in thoughts, language, and actions. In other words, the primary or essential meaning of symbol has become hidden. As a consequence, human awareness of God must be reawakened or renewed by a second level of symbols, by those "special manifestations of the sacred" that are mediated to us by "the privileged media of particular revelations."

The most basic Judeo-Christian symbols of special revelation are the history of the community of Israel and the person of Jesus Christ. These originating symbols or metaphors constitute the basic frame-

---

[30] Langdon Gilkey, "A Wayward Protestant's Shot at Liturgical Renewal," quoted in Collins, *Worship: Renewal to Practice*, 3–15.

work of Christianity's grand narrative of redemption history. The existence of sin requires this second level of symbol as a finite medium which embodies the essential nature of the true human community.

The third level of religious symbols consists of those human structures that point to the originating presence of the sacred in the symbols of the second level. Gilkey argues that these "tertiary" symbols include communal liturgical acts.

Much work has been done since the Scottsdale Conference both to affirm and dispute parts of Gilkey's argument. The thesis of Gilkey's address, however, continues to challenge the liturgical movement as it struggles to dialogue with contemporary society: unless tradition's symbols are more explicitly connected to the ultimacy that permeates created life, unless traditional symbols or words of power reawaken within us our role as sacraments of God, then there can be no experience of the divine in worship. Gilkey's argument suggests, as does Farley's, that the constitutive feature of faith is its reality-apprehending aspect, its pre-cognitive ability to recognize the presence of God in human existence. His concern is that as liturgical renewal has peeled back those layers of tradition that obscure the ultimate realities of faith, it has weighted its attention toward the third fundamental meaning of symbol and to a lesser degree on the second level. Gilkey considers the first level, centered on cosmology and anthropology, to be the level at which contemporary questions of meaning are directed. Although it is the primary level of symbol, it has not been adequately considered as a potential starting point for liturgical method.[31]

Farley's treatment of phenomenological theology suggests a corrective. As he explains, from Schleiermacher to the present, theology has struggled to overcome the affects of institutionalization on what is ultimate to faith.[32] Phenomenological theology stands with numerous

---

[31] Collins, *Worship: Renewal to Practice*, 3–15, outlines Gilkey's address to the conference and argues that "the liturgical renewal so recently begun will be achieved only when the celebration of the paschal mystery of salvation in Jesus Christ is adequately enculturated, that is, human grounded in the culture and in evangelical tension with it." It is this piece of liturgical renewal that Collins believes is critical as the movement continues to ask whether liturgy, in its deepest and most authentic sense, expresses the fullness of the gospel.

[32] Farley's indebtedness to Schleiermacher is clear throughout his work. In terms of the anti-formalist concern, Farley revisits Schleiermacher's attempt to

anti-formalist investigations that have appeared in response to Schleiermacher's work. Its primary purpose is "to locate and set forth the founding apprehensions of religious faith in the setting distinctive of that faith and with attention to the various strata of that setting."[33] Faith, Farley says, does not occur only in individual consciousness; it occurs communally as human beings participate in both a faith-world and a life-world that are interconnected.

Central to Farley's method is the assertion that faith itself is a particular kind of knowing, a particular way of perceiving and responding to the world. For Farley, faith is the mode of existence in which human beings live "in and toward God and the world under the impact of redemption."[34]

Faith, or life under the impact of redemption, shapes human thought and action in at least two important ways. On a secondary level, the faith-world consists of the images, doctrines, and structures of communal life. At its most elemental level, however, it is constituted by the realities mediated by these secondary vehicles. In other words, faith is inherently pre-reflective and shapes human understanding at a pre-cognitive level.

At the same time, people who live "by faith" also exist "in a particular social and historical situation."[35] This means that all theological knowing is tied to concrete situations in particular social places and historical times. The concrete situation, with all of its social, political, personal, and communal influences, also constitutes the matrix of theological understanding. As Farley says, even though theological knowing is pre-reflective, "there is simply no way of conducting theology above the grid of life itself. The dialectic of theological understanding is set in motion here, by the matters which evoke response and interpretation."[36]

More often than not, the lines of demarcation between the faith-world and the life-world are blurred. The two are interconnected such that one cannot be abstracted from the other without distorting our perception

---

locate religious acts in the immediate self-consciousness, as opposed to locating them in the cognitive and moral dimensions of consciousness. See Farley, *Ecclesial Man*, 52.

[33] Ibid., 54.
[34] Farley, *Theologia*, 156.
[35] Ibid., 165.
[36] Ibid.

of both. Because the faith-world and life-world are present in human existence in an ongoing dialectic, faith and theology cannot properly be conceived as separate entities, the one existing in the worshiping community and the other attached to the academic study of texts, doctrine, and systematics. Faith and theology do not exist in the linear or hierarchical relationship assumed by dominant educational models.

As an alternate model, Farley develops the notion of theology as a habitus—an enculturing or forming of dispositions of persons.[37] As outlined briefly in Chapter 1, Farley understands *theologia* to be more than the mere passing on of information or knowledge: it is a life-forming pursuit.[38]

David Kelsey summarizes Farley's concept of habitus in a concise and helpful way. As he explains, Farley characterizes *theologia* in two ways. In one sense, *theologia* is a believer's disposition to act certain ways in given situations. The classical name for such a disposition is habitus. In another related sense, *theologia* is a dialectical activity participated in by believers as they appropriate religious tradition for situations encountered in everyday life.[39]

The knowledge or faith resulting from this process, argues Farley, is not solely theoretical. It is "practical, salvation-oriented" knowledge "having the primary character of wisdom."[40] *Theologia*, particularly as Farley appropriates it, is both practical and theoretical.[41] It is a

---

[37] Farley's development of habitus is related to the classical conception of *paideia*. He appropriates this notion from the Greek idea of culture in which education "is the 'culturing' of a human being in *arete* or virtue." In Aristotelian anthropology, knowledge is a *hexis*, one of three states or characteristics of the soul. The school theologians translated *hexis* using the Latin term *habitus*, depicting knowledge as a habit, "an enduring orientation and dexterity of the soul." See Farley, *Theologia*, 35. As we shall see in our discussion of Proverbs, character formation, or shaping the dispositions of believers, is the primary function of the faith community as it is understood by the sages.

[38] Mary McClintock Fulkerson, "*Theologia* as a Liberation *Habitus*: Thoughts toward Christian Formation for Resistance," *Theology and the Interhuman*, ed. Robert R. Williams (Valley Forge, Pa.: Trinity Press International, 1995) 161. In this response to Farley's work Fulkerson discusses how the notion of *theologia* dialogues productively with liberation concerns.

[39] David Kelsey, *Between Athens and Berlin: The Theological Education Debate* (Grand Rapids, Mich.: Eerdmans, 1993) 103–4.

[40] Farley, *Theologia*, 39.

[41] Ibid., 29–44.

reflective wisdom that can be deepened by human study, reflection, and dialogue.

How is Farley's focus on habitus as an alternate model for theological education related to liturgical theology? Common ground can be found on several fronts. One obvious area of connection is Farley's and liturgical theology's shared concerns to lessen the gap between clergy and laity and to restore the faith community as the primary locus of theology.[42]

In advancing his understanding of theology as a habitus, Farley asserts that one fateful development in the Church was the restriction of theology primarily to the context of professional Church leadership. This restriction was unfortunate because it resulted in theology being defined almost solely as an enterprise of scholarship.

One contemporary consequence of isolating theology in this way is that the tasks of the clergy, such as preaching, presiding at worship, counseling, and teaching, are increasingly defined by sociological descriptions of the social/professional role of minister. In other words, following societal patterns for leadership, the Church in our era focuses on "routinized problem solving in the organization and management of their institutions as the chief locus of leadership effectiveness."[43]

Several problems are associated with this model's pattern for leadership: (1) it results in "professional" ministers trained to solve problems through application of empirical theory; (2) it produces leaders whose skills are not rooted in the memory and vision of Christ or grounded in self-reflection; and (3) it divests the faith community of its role in deepening corporate memory of God's creative presence through liturgical praxis.[44]

[42] As we saw in Chapter 2, liturgical theology has overcome the bifurcation of clergy and laity to varying degrees. For those methods designated by Fagerberg "theologies from worship," for example, there still exists an implied primacy of clergy/academy over the worshiping community. In addition, as Proctor-Smith indicates in her work, liturgical reform in general has been a clergy-dominated affair; as such, scholars risk working within their own theological horizons without critically examining them.

[43] Hough and Cobb, *Christian Identity and Theological Education*, 78. This particular pattern of ministerial leadership corresponds with the corporate or social image of professional "manager."

[44] Ibid., 83–4. Hough and Cobb argue that the most pressing requirements for contemporary Church leadership are: "first, a clear Christian identity; second, an extensive and reflective understanding of what constitutes that identity; third, self-consciousness as to how that Christian identity shapes

Farley's notion of habitus becomes particularly helpful at this point. As he argues, the transformative power of theology, and thus of liturgy, lies in its ability to integrate intellectual, spiritual, social, personal, and communal matrices of knowing. Such an integration orients the entirety of life to God's reign. This is what Farley means when he depicts theology as a habitus.

Theological understanding, in a habitus perspective, says Farley, is many things. It is, as Ottati similarly suggests, a "socially shaped and interactive orientation pregnant with implications for understanding God, the world and ourselves that issues in a particular practice."[45]

What this means is that theological knowledge is mediated by several different social matrices or contexts—the context of the believers within particular faith communities, the context of leadership in the Church, the context of inquiry and scholarship, and the context of the particular cultural and historical epoch. Each of these contexts has a distinctive mode of understanding that is vital to our knowledge of God.

Failing to recognize the interrelated character of these contexts, the clergy paradigm and technical rationality limit theology primarily to the context of the academy. The result is a diminishment of the faith community's role of offering in liturgy a horizon of meaning wherein all of these modes of knowing are integrated.

To be fair, liturgical theology has not overlooked this fundamental concern. Two examples emerge. In terms of leadership models, Lathrop examines how the clergy paradigm has resulted in unhealthy liturgical leadership. He argues that most people's memories of liturgical tradition are of rituals led primarily by seminary-trained male

---

perception of the present concrete world-historical situation; fourth, wise discernment of the implications of this Christian perception for action."

Ottati, *Reforming Protestantism*, ix, focuses on the distinctiveness of Protestantism as a voice of hope involved in a "multivalent relationship" with the world. He emphasizes the historical particularity of Protestantism and its role in "formation of affect, imagination, and responsibility that disposes persons and communities to interpret, engage, and order their environments in a certain way." The theme of Ottati's work, although he does not cite Farley, offers a working out of the concept of *habitus* from a theological foundation different from Farley's philosophical approach. However, his primary concern for the contemporary Church is not unlike Farley's—namely the Church's current struggle to "deliver theocentric sensibilities into all of life in the midst of our pluralistic and independent setting," 65.

[45] Ottati, *Reforming Protestantism*, 44.

clergy. In spite of contemporary discussions of diversity and inclusiveness, this image of a hierarchical social order within the Church often continues to be perpetuated at a practical level.[46]

Echoing Farley, Lathrop argues for a more authentic understanding of leadership, one in which leadership is subordinate to the structure of the ordo. This means that those ordained to Church leadership are not viewed as separate from the community or as functioning primarily to apply theories learned in isolation from the community.

Rather than standing in hierarchical superiority, says Lathrop, clergy are a dynamic part of the community's symbols, participating in the same interactions and juxtapositions that they do. When the minister enters fully into the structure of the ordo, both community and leadership can be formed in Christian identity. To conceive of clergy in a mutually dialectical relationship with the rest of the community is to recover a conception of theology as a habitus—a unified life process of (1) reflecting on the truth as it is mediated and shaped by tradition and by other social matrices, and (2) seeking to appropriate that truth for this contemporary situation.[47]

Another area of dialogue between Farley's notion of habitus and liturgical theology is related to the liturgical understanding that context influences how pre-reflective insights are mediated into consciousness. As set forth in Chapter 2, a defining characteristic of liturgy is that it stands at the intersection of two epistemological levels—the level of human appropriation or mediation and the level of the constitutive elements of the truth, elements that according to Farley are pre-reflective. If worship, in all of its particular sociocultural contexts, represents the primary horizon where these two levels converge, then how we define and interpret that horizon is of major import to liturgical renewal, particularly as it seeks to discover how meaning is created through liturgical forms.

One contemporary liturgical scholar, Margaret Mary Kelleher, develops the concept of worship as a public horizon of meaning. In her work on liturgical method, she dialogues extensively with Bernard Lonergan, also a phenomenological theologian. Basing her insights on Lonergan's work, Kelleher, like Farley, argues for a reunification of

---

[46] Mary Collins, *Worship: Renewal to Practice*, 12–13, echoes this sentiment in her discussion of how the Church continues to marginalize women in liturgy by denying to them leadership roles.

[47] Farley, *Theologia*, 164–5.

theological method by redefining method as a "framework for collab-
orative creativity." In her argument, Kelleher calls attention to the
common core of operations discoverable in the foundation of all
particular methods.[48]

Searching for this common core promotes interdisciplinary collabo-
ration, or in Farley's terms, a recognition of the interconnectedness of
the various social matrices of knowledge. It also suggests that theological method is a dynamic process as opposed to a normative set of
rules or directions to be followed.

Several implications for liturgical renewal present themselves. First,
as noted in Chapter 2, a critique of "theologies from worship" is that
they often seek to uncover theological meanings or principles that can
be extracted from or applied to the actions of the liturgy in general.
Kelleher insists that while liturgical method may be guided by certain
"immanent norms," its foremost aim is to reflect on liturgical praxis in
order to make explicit the redemptive horizon or world of meaning
made public in that praxis.[49]

To echo Farley, the public horizon mediated in liturgy is in fact a
habitus as it is constituted by an interconnection of horizons—the
horizons of meaning that individual members of the assembly bring
with them to the worship event, the horizons of meaning present to
the assembly because of its historical tradition, cultural horizons of
meaning, and the horizons of meaning identified in official texts. One
goal of liturgical method is to scrutinize these horizons in order to
clarify them and determine how they mutually influence one another.
As Lathrop says, liturgical theology attempts to explain what actually
happens in worship, in what he calls the "lived correlation," as the
questions and existential realities of people in this age intersect with
tradition and with the truths of the gospel.[50]

What is central to Lathrop's and Kelleher's liturgical understanding
is also foundational to Farley's thought: theological meaning or
knowledge is contextual and always incomplete, requiring constant
reinterpretation as traditional, societal, and personal insights meet the
challenges of each age. In authentic liturgy, when it exists as a habitus,
habits of heart and mind are formed within that liturgy's particular

[48] Kelleher, "Liturgical Theology," 2–24.

[49] Ibid., 2.

[50] Gordon Lathrop, *Holy Things: A Liturgical Theology* (Minneapolis: Fortress
Press, 1993) 33.

context and dialectical structure. Making this dialectical structure or public horizon explicit in liturgical method urges the faith community to distinguish between elements in its liturgical praxis that authentically mediate the Christian vision and those that distort it.[51]

Farley expands upon existing liturgical thought by defining "horizon" from within his own phenomenological perspective. He argues that there is a gap between the elemental human desires, which are our primary motivating inclinations, and their ultimate references. These desires seek a fulfillment that always alludes them.

For example, the passion for reality is a desire to understand the mystery of things in their full beauty. This passion, says Farley, has been the impetus for numerous artistic accomplishments and has challenged human history to heights of theoretical excellence. And yet, the knowledge, facts, and frameworks of meaning that emerge as a result of these human efforts cannot dispel the mystery of human reality.

Elemental human passions, Farley explains, always desire "past and through these things. They strive through what they actually experience, what is presented to them, and what momentarily fulfills them. . . . Because no finite resource fulfills the passions, their referent is an infinite resource, an eternal horizon." It is the human ability to desire "through our penultimate satisfactions" toward this indefinable eternal horizon that makes the notion of God meaningful.[52]

Saliers is particularly helpful in addressing the question of how liturgy shapes this affective life of a community. Reflecting Farley's philosophical concerns, he presses for liturgy that grounds "the formation and expression of human emotion in the deeper reaches of the symbols and ritual process of symbolization." As the deep affections, or elemental desires, of people are shaped by the symbols and actions of liturgy, the community draws ever closer to the mystery of God; people are also challenged to live and act a certain way.

In this, Saliers is careful to maintain that the mystery of God, to some extent, always remains a mystery. That is why liturgy, as it embodies God's pattern of self-giving in Christ, should compel the community beyond discursive or rationalistic certainties of belief and

[51] Kelleher, "Liturgical Theology," 22.

[52] See Farley, *Good and Evil*, 111–3; Walter Lowe, "Issues of *Good and Evil*," *Theology and the Interhuman*, ed. Robert Williams (Valley Forge, Pa.: Trinity Press International, 1995) 53–6.

action toward participation in a dynamic pattern of conversion, a conversion of the heart and mind.[53]

Liturgical methods that recognize the fragility and penultimate quality of the knowledge mediated by liturgical forms have the potential to renew liturgy such that it invites participation not only in secondary discourse but also in a horizon of meaning. In fact, for those operating within the type that Fagerberg calls "liturgical theology," liturgy itself is not an isolated "sacred" event; nor does liturgy mediate solely objective truth. Liturgical theology insists that the whole world—its people, objects, actions, and structures—is permeated by God's presence. The primary purpose of worship is to shape dispositions so that people can perceive God's presence in and through the world's objects and events of history.[54]

Farley insists that a constitutive feature of faith is its reality-apprehending aspect, its pre-reflective awareness of the presence of God in human existence. Liturgical renewal has made great strides toward critiquing modes of representation that have obscured this reality-apprehending potential of faith or that weaken the community's ability to shape pre-reflective insights into self-consciousness. In accomplishing this, however, attention has been weighted, as noted earlier, toward what Gilkey called "tertiary" religious symbols (communal acts, the elements of the sacraments, proclamation) and toward symbols of special revelation, namely the history of Israel and the person of Jesus Christ. For liturgical renewal, in an era of receding professional triumphalism and increasing religious skepticism, liturgical method must also seek renewal at the generative source of its symbols, at the ontological level of human experience and awareness of God's presence in all of life.

While liturgical theology recognizes liturgy as the ontological condition of theology, none of its adherents have made explicit in their methods a unifying factor that both holds in balance these three understandings of symbol and maintains an internal framework for

[53] Saliers, *Worship as Theology*, 174–6.

[54] Alexander Schmemann, *For the Life of the World: Sacraments and Orthodoxy* (New York: St. Vladimir's Seminary Press, 1973) 120. Ottati, *Reforming Protestantism*, 65, expresses this in a different way. His argument from a Reformed perspective echoes Schmemann's concern that all of the created world is "caught up in the intricate and encompassing web of divine power, presence and grace."

self-critique. The value of dialogue with Farley emerges again in this regard.

Farley departs from traditional criteriology to "set the problem" of theological method in a different way. His proposal of theology as habitus makes explicit a unifying factor but at the same time leaves space to acknowledge legitimate pluralism in liturgical praxis. To understand how the notion of habitus accomplishes this requires a closer look at the foundational elements of his theological proposal—namely, his appropriation of ontology for contemporary practical theology.

ONTOLOGY AND LITURGICAL RENEWAL

"The things around which we gather in church are matters of concern, events, objects put to use. They focus our meeting, itself a thing. Moreover, they propose to our imaginations that the world itself has a center. This may be a fiction from a scientific point of view, but we live by such fictions, sleep and rise and orient ourselves by them. . . . All the sacred connections of our central things . . . represent simply themselves and our culture. . . . Then, however, the ordo puts these symbols in motion, juxtaposes them to each other. The juxtaposition is meant to speak and sing Jesus Christ in our midst, God's presence of mercy."[55]

How the "things" of worship exist as meaningful public symbols is a question at the heart of liturgical renewal. It is related to another set of queries that have sparked much debate and theological discussion throughout the Church's history, particularly in connection to the sacraments.[56] How are the symbols of our worship connected to the sacred? How do they mediate God's presence and grace? In other words, how do they "speak and sing Jesus Christ in our midst?"

The Question of Ontology Revisited

Most traditions agree that the most enduring structure of Christian worship is the proclamation of God's Word and the sharing of a ritual

[55] Lathrop, *Holy Things*, 97.

[56] Gary Macy, *The Banquet's Wisdom: A Short History of the Theologies of the Lord's Supper* (New York: Paulist Press, 1983) 3, emphasizes that the Eucharist, which is heralded as the primary symbol of Christian unity, since the Reformation has also been the focus of much divisive theological debate. Much of this debate has revolved around questions of what it means to say and to believe that Christ is present to us in a real way in liturgical practice.

meal. Celebration of the Eucharist is an elemental communal action that has continued throughout the history of the Church in both Eastern and Western traditions. It is the Eucharist's juxtaposition of Word and table, says Gordon Lathrop, that provides the centerpiece, or the outline, for the rest of the actions of worship.[57]

Tracing the presence of what Lathrop calls the "word-table event" from New Testament communities to the present reveals how connected eucharistic practice and interpretation are to the cultural, political, and institutional situations in which they exist and which they seek to transform. A common inheritance of the Christian faith, the sacrament has at various times throughout the centuries been restructured, elaborated, and even diminished as it has been appropriated for a multiplicity of cultural situations.

In a wide-ranging and detailed reflection on eucharistic tradition, David Power demonstrates how the language and thought forms of culture throughout history have both opened the doors to renewal of eucharistic practice and been restrictive of its transformative potential. During some epochs of Christian history, for example, it is possible to glance through the windows of the church and see how the ordinary objects of bread, wine, and table have functioned transformatively; there have been times when the Eucharist has been "broadened in its power to include reality and unfold meaning."[58]

At other historical intersections, the picture is quite different as ideological power structures, doctrinal debate, or imposing cultural situations diminished the size of the table, both physically and symbolically, and limited both the expression and perception of the sacrament's meaning. It becomes clear in Power's treatment of the history of the sacrament that cultural categories of meaning influence how we understand and participate in the Eucharist.

As a part of his work on eucharistic theology, Power revisits the question of ontology. He highlights several fundamental ontological principles that are important for retrieving the word-table paradigm for the present cultural situation. This section of the chapter will (1) offer a synopsis of the current anti-ontological bias, (2) briefly outline Power's ontological argument, and (3) suggest how Farley's "reflective ontology" echoes Power's concerns but also expands upon them.

Farley argues that two primary claims have pushed ontology to the margins of accepted theological constructs. First, there is the claim

---

[57] Lathrop, *Holy Things*, 46–7.
[58] Power, *Eucharistic Mystery*, 283.

that ontology deprives reality of its concrete character, that it over-looks the historicality of all thought. Second, many scholars contend that anti-ontological modes of thought such as pragmatism, empirical-linguistic philosophy, and deconstructionism have emerged in contemporary times to displace ontological thinking.[59]

Both of these claims reflect the tendency of people in this cultural milieu to question any efforts to know "ultimate truth."[60] One result of this intensification of subjectivism in the contemporary era is the perception that the Church exists primarily as an institutional foundation for certain ethical understandings and practices rather than as a source of truth. The dilemma emerges again: How can the Church affirm the truth of the gospel in the face of this challenge and at the same time guard against allowing its mediation of that truth to become only a camouflaged claim to power?

A number of scholars conclude that a source of this dilemma is the Church's historical attempt to counter skepticism by turning to philosophy and its metaphysical efforts to prove the existence of God. One prominent voice in the critique against metaphysical approaches is that of Martin Heidegger.

Heidegger's primary critique is that a universal concept of Being such as that propounded by traditional Western metaphysics results in a reduction of reality and experience; because a universal concept of Being confers a meaning on reality before actual events occur, it silences the revelatory nature of experience and the questions raised by particular historical events.[61]

---

[59] Farley, *Good and Evil*, 1–26, responds to these two claims as he supports his appropriation of ontological theology for the purpose of "interpreting a human condition."

[60] Lesslie Newbigin, *Truth to Tell: The Gospel as Public Truth* (Grand Rapids, Mich.: Eerdmans, 1991) 1–4.

[61] The very limited perusal offered here of an entire epoch of philosophical thought clearly risks skewing our understanding of it. The argument for a "revised reflective ontology" offered in this manuscript grows out of Farley's orientation within the tradition of Continental philosophy. Farley locates himself primarily in the tradition of Edmund Husserl and Friederich Schleiermacher and interacts with literature ranging from Paul Tillich to Hans-Georg Gadamer to Emmanuel Levinas. See *Good and Evil*, xx.

These philosophical thinkers, in general, distinguish the moral/cultural sciences from natural sciences by providing the moral sciences with a unifying or fundamental philosophical foundation. Husserl, for example, advanced a

Similarly, the critique continues, metaphysics also deprives language of its power to shape meaning, since within its understanding words primarily have the functional status of classification. Heidegger argues against such a metaphysical construal of language, insisting that ultimate truth cannot be concretized in any linguistic form. In Heidegger's understanding, language is the "house of being";[62] it is a structure of mediation that allows Being to be self-disclosive.

To combat the use of language primarily as a tool of classification, Heidegger focuses in his later writings on poetic language. In poetic forms, creative juxtapositions of objects make new understandings of those objects possible while maintaining a sense of ultimate mystery.

This ongoing critique of metaphysics has a number of implications for liturgical theology. Lathrop, similar to Heidegger, highlights how the language used to name the objects of worship and the juxtapositions inherent in liturgical language break open meanings beyond the instrumental value of those objects. Water, for example, is an ordinary "thing" of daily human living. But the word "water" is laden with meaning. For some people, it awakens life-giving images of quiet ponds or gurgling mountain streams; for others, such as those whose homes have been washed away in floods, "water" stirs up destructive images.[63]

Used in worship, as these layers of meaning are juxtaposed to God's word, water invites people to participate in new meanings: adoption into God's family, hope, forgiveness, new life, and grace. It also invites participation in the paschal mystery, in the mystery of God's presence. Echoing Heidegger's interest in poetic language, Lathrop argues that

---

transcendental philosophy that sought to uncover the pre-reflective structures of meaning by setting aside or bracketing the presuppositions of the life-world. For a more extensive treatment of Husserl's thought, see Farley, *Ecclesial Man*.

Martin Heidegger and Gadamer challenged the metaphysical constructs of Husserl by arguing that it is impossible to set aside personal and contextual presuppositions in order to ascertain ultimate meaning. It is in the context of concrete reality, they insisted, that humanity must seek to discover meaning. See Don Browning, *A Fundamental Practical Theology* (Minneapolis: Fortress Press, 1991) 37–9; Power, *Eucharistic Mystery*, 277–8; Hans-Georg Gadamer, *Truth and Method* (New York: Crossroad, 1982).

[62] Martin Heidegger, "The Way Back into the Ground of Metaphysics," *Primary Readings in Philosophy for Understanding Theology*, ed. Diogenes Allen and Eric O. Springsted (Louisville: Westminster/John Knox Press, 1992) 248–62.

[63] Lathrop, *Holy Things*, 94–7.

the language of liturgy "unhesitatingly uses metaphors and images; it does not shrink from naming death and failure nor from unfeignedly expressing joy."[64] This demonstrates that the power of the language lies in it juxtapositions. Even as the words of liturgy elicit new meanings, however, the meanings are not such that they can be reproduced in a text or in a doctrinal statement. Rather, truths mediated by liturgical language cannot be abstracted from their particular and unrepeatable contexts. Meaning occurs within the entire pattern of juxtapositions, within the structure of the ordo.

What happens when such abstractions occur was discussed in Chapter 2 in relation to theologies of worship and theologies drawn from worship. As highlighted there and echoed in the above critique of ontology, attempts to abstract knowledge from its context establishes a preference for universals over particulars, thus creating a hierarchy of being that privileges the universal and relativizes actual historical events.[65]

Farley's defense of a "life-world universal" proposes a corrective for ontology at this critical point and attempts to retrieve ontology as valuable for dealing with the skepticism of this era. Before outlining the corrective itself, however, it is helpful to look more closely at how ontology is related to eucharistic theology.

A fundamental problem with a metaphysical approach to the sacraments is underlined by Power as he examines contemporary readings of the sacramental theology of Thomas Aquinas: "The defect in using metaphysics to explain sacraments comes from the use of the concepts of efficient and exemplarity causality to express God's action in the world, for grace is thus turned into an object that resembles objects purchased in markets or produced in factories."[66] In a Thomistic concept of instrumental causality "everything is thought of as having its

---

[64] Ibid.

[65] Robert R. Williams, "Tragedy, Totality and the Face," *Theology and the Interhuman*, ed. Robert R. Williams (Valley Forge, Pa.: Trinity Press International, 1995) 82–3.

[66] Power, *Eucharistic Mystery*, 279. In this critique of metaphysics, Power refers to how the eucharistic theology of Thomas Aquinas understands instrumental efficient causality. Aquinas speaks of God as primary cause; Christ's passion, the minister, and the sacrament itself are instrumental causes. Using the notion of "exemplarity," Aquinas suggests that in Christ's passion God's exemplary will or intention is revealed. By representing this exemplary intention in the sacraments, the Church mediates grace.

origin in everything else and is never respected in the sheer gratuity of its being there."[67] Power argues that Western sacramental theology has gone too far in expressing itself in terms of the metaphysical tradition that grew out of this concept. Scholars influenced by Heidegger oppose such philosophical efforts to express ultimate reality, arguing that such expressions are predisposed to categorize grace as a spiritual object or entity.[68]

Clearly, then, as the preceding critique of metaphysics indicates, there is a decided bias against ontology in recent literature. Still, Power suggests, several contemporary liturgical thinkers revisit the issues raised by the Heideggerian critique. These scholars conclude that an appropriate response to the critique cannot adequately be formulated in complete isolation from the metaphysical tradition.[69] There are aspects of sacramental understanding, these arguments insist, that are inherently ontological. Therefore, a retrieval of some facets of the metaphysical tradition are vital to liturgical theology.

From his dialogue with contemporary treatments of the sacramental thought of Aquinas, Power himself concludes that while there are obvious limits to metaphysical theories of causality,

"there are two fundamental principles [of ontology] that still orient celebration if well understood. The first affirms the total gratuity of finite being. The second speaks of humanity's inner orientation to seek the principle of all things, to find the source of life and being outside itself and its own making."[70]

---

[67] Ibid., 280. As noted in Wendy Farley's response to Edward Farley's work, the risk of objectifying reality in this way is that it results in ideological reduction of persons. A safeguard against this is to recognize that "all beings in themselves are beautiful, complex and plural." Such an awareness awakens the community both to truth and obligation. See Wendy Farley, "Eros and the Truth," 33.

Edward Farley's retrieval of ontology "not only targets quantifying reductions of human reality but exploitative social systems that would profit from obliviousness to the density and mystery of human beings." See Edward Farley, *Good and Evil*, 11.

[68] Power, *Eucharistic Mystery*, 281.

[69] Ibid., 269–90. Speaking from a Catholic perspective, Power highlights several contemporary retrievals of the theology of Aquinas: the work of Karl Rahner and Edward Schillebeeckx.

[70] Ibid., 324.

Ontological thinking does not have to objectify God's action, or in Farley's words, "freeze a changing and complex world into concepts and systems."[71]

Rather, Power suggests, ontology properly conceived can accomplish two things vital to eucharistic understanding. It can provide a mode for thinking about how God is ultimately unattainable to human thought; at the same time it can also offer insight into how God comes to us and is intimately present to us through the mystery of the Eucharist. When this is ontology's primary function, it provides insight into the mode of God's revelation and the mode of our human response to revelation. Rather than establishing God's revelation as an "object" or "instrument," it offers a focused method of critical inquiry into enduring patterns of human experience of God's presence, particularly as those patterns are formative of a community's tradition, discourse, and praxis.[72]

For ontological thinking to operate in this positive way entails a revision of its traditional approach to language. For example, the discursive logic of causality espoused by traditional Western metaphysics deprives grace of its ineffable quality. A renewed appreciation of metaphorical language, language that pushes beyond the constructs of philosophical language, helps to avoid this trap and complements the ontological foundation suggested above.[73] Such language is the focus of many contemporary eucharistic understandings.

[71] Farley, *Good and Evil*, 1.

[72] Browning, *A Fundamental Practical Theology*, 24–6, outlines the positive function of ontology from the perspective of practical theology. As he suggests, the reemergence of practical philosophy, particularly as influenced by Gadamer, makes explicit that our present concerns or situations determine the way we interpret the past. These philosophies, to varying degrees, hold in tension two poles of theological understanding: (1) that there is a hiddenness or ultimacy to the reality of God's presence that cannot be attained by human categories of thought or language, and (2) that efforts at describing, interpreting, or mediating that reality are inseparably linked to the contexts of our inquiries. These philosophies have made great strides toward maintaining an ontological foundation that does not abandon historicality. Browning argues in relation to this that the past, or tradition, does not exist only as an isolated entity to be remembered or reenacted. Rather, "the present is largely a product of the past. The past lives in the present whether we realize it or not."

[73] Hans-Georg Gadamer, "The Exemplary Significance of Legal Hermeneutics," *Primary Readings in Philosophy for Understanding Theology*, ed. Diogenes

As Power argues with regard to sacramental theology, for instance, "an ontology that retains modernity's unbending concern with the human subject, while stressing the negation and self-surrender of faith, is vital." This is because human language is unable adequately to express or "name" a reality that exists outside the boundaries of time; neither can the totality of Christ's gift to us be captured in the limiting symbols of a liturgical rite. That is why metaphorical language is so important.

In the Eucharist we seek to name or address God using the narrative language of memorial; through such metaphorical language we are invited not only into communion with God through Christ but also into the eschatological hope to which the juxtaposition of language and symbols points. Power insists that methodologies which too readily adopt the critique of Western metaphysics risk becoming so "enclosed in the text itself" that the mysterious aspect of God's truth, the eschatological dimension, is diminished.[74] However, when an awareness of the elusive nature of God's presence is maintained, then in "eschatological humility" the Church is able to retain "the importance of the intersubjective as testing ground of a truth and a love that frees."[75]

Individualistic manifestations of subjectivism in this age have led to a distortion of our conception of the Church as a "community" of interconnected persons. To utilize reflective ontology, as Farley does, to rethink the intersubjective nature of the faith community and its worship, helps us to look differently at how "meaning" is created in worship. Examined from the perspective of intersubjectivity, as we shall see later, "meaning" is not discovered in a particular linguistic "container." Instead, meaning occurs as the result of human interactions with the various spheres or horizons of living, such as environment, tradition, and cultural context.[76]

Allen and Eric O. Springsted (Louisville: Westminster/John Knox Press, 1992) 263–80. Gadamer, influenced by Heidegger, argues that interpretation of texts is never a matter of universal statements about what a text means. Instead, it involves dialogue with the historical tradition of the text. Understanding Scripture, he argues, "cannot simply be a scientific or scholarly exploration of its meaning." It also requires an examination of the presuppositions of the interpreter.

[74] Power, *Eucharistic Mystery*, 326.

[75] Ibid.

[76] Michael B. Aune, "Worship in an Age of Subjectivism Revisited," *Worship* 65 (May 1991) 224–6.

As a result of revisiting the ontological issue, Power suggests that three kinds of discourse are needed in eucharistic theology. First, there is the discourse of narrative, blessing, and memorial in which metaphorical language dominates. Second, there is ontological discourse, which is foundational for communicating the structure of creation and how it is related to the mystery of God. Ontological discourse also serves as a reminder of the distinction between ultimate reality and the shape given that reality when it is mediated through liturgical forms. The third form of discourse is what Power calls "institutional discourse." This is secondary theological discourse that attempts to describe or explain how persons within communities are related to one another and to tradition.

Power's argument regarding the Eucharist and ontology can be expanded to liturgical theology as a whole. It finds analogies in the wisdom tradition as it is developed in Proverbs 1–9 and Job. The "revised reflective ontology" that I will propose in the remaining chapters correlates liturgical theology's study of the ordo and Farley's reflective ontology. However, before examining Proverbs and Job in this light and establishing a "revised reflective ontology" as foundational to a "wisdom liturgical method," it is necessary to consider briefly how Farley's mode of reflective ontology provides one piece of a critical-reflective structure that can inform the liturgical movement.

Farley's Reflective Ontology

The stated purpose of Farley's *Good and Evil: Interpreting a Human Condition* is to explore the way "a portrayed paradigm of a religious faith and its determinate universals modify more general enduring features of human reality."[77] In other words, in this work Farley examines how a retrieved paradigm of a major world faith interprets a human condition; he analyzes how the history and symbolic world of an ancient faith tradition provide insight into what it means to be human and shape the way people today think about, make sense of, and act upon the realities of daily living. Specifically, he explores the sense in which the Judeo-Christian paradigm of good and evil meaningfully describes existential realities.

Liturgical theology also seeks to retrieve an ancient theological paradigm and demonstrate how its symbols enable people to "make sense" of contemporary living. Because of this, a dialogue with

[77] Farley, *Good and Evil*, xvi.

Farley's method is illuminating. In particular, Farley argues that there are constitutive features of the Judeo-Christian faith that endure to the present and are "true" in this pluralistic era. This conviction also stands at the heart of liturgical renewal. Farley uses "reflective ontology" as a mode of thought and discourse for retrieving these features so that they can be productively appropriated for the Church today.

The definition Farley offers for "reflective ontology" demonstrates his departure from more traditional ontologies that were critiqued earlier.[78] First, Farley explains that his work is "ontology" because it "is directed not to contingent events or discrete entities but to perduring features that constitute the being of something in its region or situation." As Power noted, this aspect of ontology is valuable for liturgical renewal in an age of skepticism and relativism; it increases awareness that the language and actions of liturgy point to an ultimate reality beyond themselves, a reality that stands outside of the expressive ability of these structures of mediation.

At the same time, Farley's style is "reflective" because it holds in tension with the above a recognition that any description of "ultimate reality" achieved by ontology is itself limited. Reality, he argues, is only partially grasped by empirical categories. Dialogical ways of thinking and learning "that embody modes of experience and practical interests" are also necessary.[79] In other words, Farley recognizes that our knowledge and understanding of truth are always in process.[80]

---

[78] Ibid., 2. Farley notes the connection of "reflective ontology" to "reflexive philosophy." Reflective ontology not only examines the structures of a particular condition but also examines how the philosopher's/theologian's presuppositions and context constitute one aspect of that condition. Both must be taken into consideration when describing a human condition. As discussed previously, liturgical scholars have also been challenged in the direction of more explicit awareness of how their own theological, geographical, and historical location effects efforts to renew liturgy.

[79] Ibid., xix.

[80] Cobb, "*Good and Evil* in Process Perspective," highlights the connection between Farley's work and that of process theologians. The major distinction between the two, Cobb argues, is that process thought aims toward a general ontology while Farley engages in what traditionally was called a "regional ontology." In responding to Cobb, Farley insists that the lines of distinction between his thought and process thought are less clear. See Edward Farley, "Response," *Theology and the Interhuman*, ed. Robert Williams (Valley Forge, Pa.: Trinity Press International, 1995) 247–62.

Farley's reflective ontology looks first at the pre-cognitive situation in which realities are grasped. This methodological starting point is akin to what Power suggests is necessary for an adequate reappropriation of ontology for eucharistic theology. Farley's work, however, expands upon Power's understanding. As Farley's reflective ontology describes a human condition, it overcomes many of the problems of traditional metaphysics while avoiding historical positivism.

Certain aspects of Farley's reflective ontology to be detailed in the following paragraphs bear mentioning in summary form here: (1) Farley orients his philosophy to time and history. As Cobb suggests, rather than abandon ontology as unhistorical, "Farley's ontology affirms the historicity of thought and reality and supports the goal of liberation."[81] (2) Farley attends to the historical realities of the human condition of suffering. This challenges temptations toward relativism prevalent in dominant epistemological models. As such his reflective ontology is soundly located in the concrete historical character of existence.[82] (3) Farley overcomes the contemporary tendency to quantify knowledge and reality. He insists on the concreteness of all beings and refocuses attention on the intersubjectivity of all reality.

IS REFLECTIVE ONTOLOGY UNHISTORICAL?[83]

In *Good and Evil,* Farley identifies what he calls "generic" or enduring features of human existence. The goal is to show how these features "are receptive to, and the bearers of, evil and redemption."[84] While those operating with the current anti-ontological bias have assumed that any such effort abandons historicality, Farley insists that the process of identifying constitutive or enduring features is not unhistorical but rather involves a different construal of what historical theology is or should be.

Farley's particular stance toward historical understandings is called "theological portraiture" and functions as one aspect of his proposed reordering of theological education. In general, the task of theological portraiture is to peruse the history of the Christian religion and ascer-

---

[81] Cobb, "*Good and Evil* in Process Perspective," 4.

[82] Wendy Farley, "Eros and the Truth," 21–2, develops this aspect of Edward Farley's theology in relation to feminist concerns.

[83] Farley, *Good and Evil,* 2.

[84] Ibid., 4.

tain those patterns that appear to have continuity.[85] An important difference between theological portraiture and more conventional approaches is that portraiture is not a purely critical pursuit of what traditional historical theology sometimes calls the "essence of Christianity." Nor is it an effort to recover every detail of the historical phenomenon we call the Church. Theological portraiture focuses on patterns and structures that recur over time, how they are interconnected, and how they function to shape the identity of the faith community.[86]

As noted earlier, Farley calls the type of corporate historical existence that embodies these enduring patterns "ecclesial existence." As he describes it, such existence is temporal and subject to temporal changes; therefore, the depiction of ecclesial existence is inherently historical.[87] In effect, the desired outcome of theological portraiture is to make explicit enduring features or patterns and to create a picture, albeit an abstract or incomplete one, of ecclesiality.[88]

One presupposition of Farley's argument related to this is what he terms a "commonsense conviction" that the activities and decisions of everyday living grow out of or are appropriations of continuing patterns

---

[85] Jack Forstman, "A Historical Theologian in Ed Farley's Court," *Theology and the Interhuman,* ed. Robert Williams (Valley Forge, Pa.: Trinity Press International, 1995) 138–9, offers several words of caution regarding Farley's historical perspective. He is concerned with Farley's apparent assumption that there is a unity of themes in earliest Christianity. It seems important, particularly as we turn to the New Testament witness for evidence of worship patterns, to be aware of the plurality of traditions that present themselves even within Christianity's earliest sources.

[86] Edward Farley, *Ecclesial Reflection: An Anatomy of Theological Method* (Philadelphia: Fortress Press, 1982) 190–6. Farley outlines "theological portraiture" in *Ecclesial Reflection* and then applies it to his description of a human condition in *Good and Evil.*

[87] Farley, *Ecclesial Reflection,* 205.

[88] Farley, *Ecclesial Man,* 128–9, distinguishes between transcendental existence and historical existence. Transcendental existence is portrayed in universal categories. The transcendental represents those constitutive features of humanity that endure over time. These features provide the structure within which acts, feelings, and activities occur through which human beings relate to the world. But the reality of human existence is that transcendental or constitutive structures combine with particular historical situations. As these two modes or horizons of existence "meet" in ecclesiality, redemption becomes possible.

of experiences, processes, events, or entities. He asserts, in response to accusations that his efforts are unhistorical, that his ontology "addresses what the commonsense convictions of philosophers and scientists take for granted, the world continuities at the root of ordinary discourse . . . . Reflecting on these continuities does not require the positing of unhistorical identities or transcendent universals."[89] Farley does not contend that the enduring features he uncovers are fixed entities or universals that stand beyond the reaches of temporality.

Farley instead uses reflective ontology to inquire into the spheres, patterns, and dimensions of human reality that have endured over time, seeking to uncover the human capacity to perpetuate good or evil. In this, he is critical of ontological thinking that suggests words or symbols as representative of realities that exist beyond the changing flow of historical events.

Reflective ontology, Farley maintains, does not attempt to extract enduring features from their participation in concrete existence in order to prove their existence empirically. In Farley's ontology and its partner theological portraiture, the enduring features of human existence are mutually influencing. Understanding of them can be achieved only through reflective inquiry. In other words, the human condition Farley describes is not a collection of disparate features of human existence; it is an enduring relational structure within which human beings interpret existential situations, make decisions, and determine actions.

Farley argues that as the faith community encounters the complexities of life, certain types of response and action are elicited. These patterns of action have endured over time even through some of the worst historical situations humanity has faced.[90] Describing these patterns departs from historical description common to dominant theological methods such as criteriology. Farley's project, unlike those methods, does not provide a positivistic analysis of Christianity's institutions or vehicles of mediation.

[89] Farley, *Ecclesial Reflection*, 9.

[90] Cobb, "*Good and Evil* in Process Perspective," 9, raises a critique of Farley's descriptive method. Farley's admitted connection to Continental philosophy of the last century risks limiting the argument to the parameters of the North American region. This requires exercising care in establishing Farley's description of a human condition as equally accurate of the condition of suffering of people in other sociocultural contexts.

Instead, theological portraiture, couched within the parameters of reflective ontology, insists that the truths of faith cannot be apprehended directly. Theology is a habitus—a "unified life process" of reflecting on the truth as it has been shaped by tradition and the various other social matrices or horizons.

Several links to liturgical concerns can be made. These connections, outlined in condensed form here, will function as thematic threads to be woven throughout the remainder of the study.

First, a recurring focus of this study is that epistemological shifts of this age demand a restructured approach to theological knowledge. Any restructuring that grows out of Farley's or Schon's critique of theological education requires an accompanying shift in our thinking about how the classic texts of the faith are to be recovered, interpreted, and appropriated for contemporary society. Reinterpretation and appropriation of historical/traditional texts is also central to liturgical theology. For example, Paul Bradshaw is representative of those efforts by liturgical scholars to examine the source documents of early Christian worship in an effort to uncover the deep structures or patterns that have endured over time.[91]

Important to continued development in this area are simultaneous developments in biblical theology. Shaking loose from the traditional grip of historical categories, recent biblical study has turned its attention to different starting points.[92] The liturgical movement is at the beginning stages of dialogue with these developments in biblical theology. The possible impact of this on liturgical theology as it continues its project of retrieving the elemental worship structures of the Judeo-Christian paradigm will be closely examined in the following chapters.

None of these efforts, if configured within the framework of Farley's reflective ontology, necessarily require an abandonment of historical-

---

[91] Paul Bradshaw, *The Search for the Origins of Christian Worship: Sources and Methods for the Study of Early Liturgy* (New York: Oxford University Press, 1992) 30–79.

[92] Leo Perdue, *The Collapse of History: Reconstructing Old Testament Theology* (Minneapolis: Fortress Press, 1994) viii. The traditional historical model enjoyed hegemonic control over how biblical study was to be done. Perdue argues that with the "collapse" of that method, broader representation of methods will emerge. These methods will exist in mutual dialogue rather than in competition with one another.

ity. They do, however, imply a shift in our understanding of redemption history as the central biblical matrix of liturgical method. Farley's reflective ontology and theological portraiture are valuable to this aspect of liturgical renewal for two reasons. First, Farley's theological project makes possible a revised perspective of redemption history that restores to it a balance with biblical cosmology and anthropology.

Second, the task of "picturing" urged by theological portraiture does not replace disciplines committed to the study of Church history, classic Christian texts, or systematic theology. Nor does it undercut recent breakthroughs in methodological pluralism.[93] Instead, it provides an opportunity for critical dialogue between these methods, the insights of so-called secular disciplines, and the complexities of human existence. It also provides a methodological framework for digging beneath the institutional topsoil of Christianity in order to cultivate it at the levels of its deep structures.

This focus on uncovering or describing the enduring features of the Christian faith represents a second link between Farley's reflective ontology and liturgical concerns. Schmemann makes clear that the purpose of liturgical theology is to determine the meaning of worship. To achieve this requires a particular method, a method within which an examination of the history of worship is not an end in itself. Sounding very similar to Farley, Schmemann argues that the purpose of historical analysis is to retrieve the basic structures of worship, the ordo, and elucidate how these structures recur over time, how they are interconnected, and how they function to shape communal identity.[94]

Farley's reflective ontology dialogues productively with liturgical theology at this point, challenging it to hold its efforts to describe the historical data in tension with the fact that this data is an interpretation-laden product of a particular culture. In other words, the pattern of the ordo, as it is discovered historically, is distinct from that truth which presupposes it and which it mediates.

Kavanagh expresses it well when he suggests that the work and discourse of the Church "is carried on by a vast interlocking series of transactions with reality, transactions consummated politically,

[93] This contribution of Farley's work is applauded by James Duke, "Farley's Prolegomena to Any Future Historical Theology," *Theology and the Interhuman*, ed. Robert Williams (Valley Forge, Pa.: Trinity Press International, 1995) 116–9.

[94] Alexander Schmemann, *Introduction to Liturgical Theology* (New York: St. Vladimir's Seminary Press, 1986) 10.

socially, philosophically, and morally in continuity with what went be-fore."[95] As Farley claims, there are elements constitutive of ecclesiality capable of enduring as a unity. These elements remain true to type even amidst changes over time. To have this ontological perspective as a starting point for interpreting the juxtapositions of the ordo both accomplishes Power's goal of reopening old lines of ontological thought and suggests necessary revisions in that thought.

This leads to a third link between Farley's reflective ontology and liturgical theology, one related to Power's elucidation of the three types of discourse vital to eucharistic theology. As noted earlier, a critique of metaphysics is that it deprives language of its ability to shape meaning, that it deprives language of its power to be disclosive of divine mystery. As the "new scholarship" of Schon and others insists, and as emphasized by Power in relation to the Eucharist, there is a knowledge that refuses to be contained within the parameters of discursive linguistic forms. To illuminate this truth, metaphorical lan-guage, or sacramental discourse, is vital.

Kavanagh suggests that what sacramental discourse does is "tran-scend and subordinate the discourse of academic theological reflection on the church, just as the law of worship transcends and subordinates the law of belief."[96] Human language about ultimate truth, life and death, and the Church necessarily becomes sacramental or metaphori-cal as it enters into transactions with reality that mere statements of fact cannot express.

How Farley's ontological thinking embraces this linguistic concern is laid out in some detail in *Ecclesial Man*.[97] First, Farley asserts that to exist as a faith community means having a certain collective memory, tradition, and ritual process, all of which are present in consciousness through symbolization. This linguistic aspect of a religious commu-nity, Farley continues, contains a constantly changing configuration of linguistic entities: "doctrines, myths, historical narratives, personal

[95] Aidan Kavanagh, *On Liturgical Theology* (New York: Pueblo, 1984) 42–3.
[96] Ibid., 46.
[97] Farley, *Ecclesial Man*, 112–3. Farley's hermeneutic in this argument grows out of Husserl's notion of intentionality in which a careful distinction is made between the object itself and the meaning that is grasped through that object. Farley develops this understanding and expands upon it in the face of con-temporary challenges to ontology by making clear how historical existence and transcendental existence are interrelated.

stories and autobiographies, images, theological arguments and concepts, and ceremonial expressions."

Because people carry their experiences of alienation and their entanglements in a broken world with them into their participation in the faith community, the language of the faith community can itself become a corrupt tool of ideology. The faith community has a language structure of its own, but it is a structure influenced by the various linguistic structures operative in its determinate social world.[98]

Farley combats this ideological tendency by adopting an approach to language that suggests that there are "constitutive images" which endure throughout the history of Christianity. These images, says Farley, do not originate in secondary reflection or discourse; nor is the linguistic mode of these images to be understood as a normative definition or concept. Instead, constitutive images are seen by Farley as generated within the everyday activities of the faith community. They are the "mode in which content is present [to the community] prior to its translation into definitions." These images, what liturgical theologians might call "deep structures" or "deep symbols," guide the everyday activities of the religious community.

The role of ontology is to retrieve these enduring images, suggest how they are related to the mystery of God, and examine how they have both shaped and been shaped by societal structures of meaning and discourse. This is one of the forms of discourse Power holds to be vital for eucharistic theology.

Farley is also concerned that these constitutive images and their linguistic representations not become the object of belief itself. That is why a connection with the first mode of discourse emphasized by Power, the mode of narrative, blessing, and memorial, is so important. In a later work Farley himself argues that it is through worship that the ideological nature of human discourse is transformed by juxtaposition with the redemptive discourse of the gospel.[99] In language not

[98] Ibid. As Farley insists, the language of the community of faith can be so dominated by theological accretions and cultic expression that the essence of its images might remain hidden.

[99] Edward Farley, "Toward a New Paradigm for Preaching," *Preaching as a Theological Task: World, Gospel, Scripture*, ed. Thomas G. Long and Edward Farley (Louisville: Westminster/John Knox Press, 1996) 165–75, insists that social and moral corruption are carried in the vessels of human discourse: "In and through language, we lie, deceive ourselves, insult, and reduce the beauty

unlike that of Heidegger, Farley suggests that redemptive discourse in worship challenges the faith community both to name the evils of the world and to offer the gospel's words, words that disrupt evil and offer hope in the concrete situations of people's lives.

Redemption, says Farley, is not just a way of doing but a way of speaking. For redemption to occur, human discourse must be altered. This requires a renewal of metaphorical language, a renewal of the patterns of relation emphasized by Lathrop and Power as inherent in the ordo. The structure of such language allows the stark realities of a broken world to be redeemed. This happens as those realities are juxtaposed to words about the ultimate reality of God's grace through the mystery of Christ's self-giving.

Worship, says Farley, provides an environment, or matrix, of redemption as participants listen for discourse that can disrupt the hold of evil and offer hope for change. Such a process of listening is an active stance in which persons place self, family, nation, environment, and relations before God. The environment of worship, Farley might say, is a habitus.[100]

THE FAITH COMMUNITY AS HORIZON OF REDEMPTION

In *Ecclesial Reflection,* Farley develops an understanding of the ecclesial community as the matrix of "reality-givenness." What he means by this is that the faith community provides structures through which the truth of the gospel is mediated. A central question of this contemporary age, says Farley, one that establishes the liturgical method proposed by this project, arises in relation to this. To what extent is the received vision of truth, mediated by the Church, actually a selective vision that serves either implicitly or explicitly to maintain the mediating structures? A corresponding question also emerges. How does the mediated vision of truth affect the Church's existence as a horizon of redemption?

Farley explores these questions in *Good and Evil* by examining how the mediating structures of faith, because they involve a "being-together" of individuals over time, have the potential to become manipulative and dehumanizing. Mediating structures can distort the truth, reducing individuals' powers of existence in the world; they can become oppressive and limiting.

---

and mystery of nature to what is utile. Sedimentations and prevailing metaphors of language give human evil an enduring and structural status."

[100] Ibid., 167.

However, if a community is what Farley calls a "community of redemption," even though it is "located in the spheres of human reality and thus will partake of the entanglements and mutual transcendings of those spheres," it will also be more aware of the intersubjectivity of communal existence and of the necessity of dialogue and interrelation between human spheres.[101] The question inevitably emerges: What is "intersubjectivity"?

The emphasis of a modern consciousness, generally speaking, has been on "subjectivity." Subjectivity, loosely defined, is that aspect of human activity that operates on the basis of principles of consciousness and intentionality. For example, when a person desires to reach a particular goal or acts to meet an emotional or physical need, a sense of agency is revealed.

What "agency" means here is that our participation in interpersonal relations and social institutions is not passive. How we act and react is determined by the things that we need or desire. As noted earlier, Farley calls those desires that structure the way we exist in the world "elemental passions." These elemental passions endure over time and are foundational to motives and actions.[102]

To recognize the "intersubjectivity" of all reality—of our actions, our relationships, even our consciousness—is to be aware of how our subjectivity, or our agency, influences and is influenced by the subjectivity of others. In effect, the notion of intersubjectivity challenges previous assumptions, set forth by the empirical sciences, that reality is disinterested. Instead, as the phenomenology of Husserl suggests, reality is a "plurality of subjectivity"; the conscious world of living beings is actually a symphony of physical, physiological, and emotional experiences. In other words, reality is intersubjective. The meanings, or "knowledge," we acquire are always part of a larger contextual whole. They are always "meanings-to-someone." Meaning is actually a web of interactions between persons and environment, culture and tradition.

Discussions of the intersubjectivity of communal existence, vital to Farley's depiction of authentic ecclesiality, are not absent from liturgical scholarship. Contemporary critiques of Western liturgical practice

[101] Farley, *Good and Evil*, 281–6.

[102] Ibid., 99–101. See also Don Browning, *A Fundamental Practical Theology* (Minneapolis: Fortress Press, 1991) 94–109, and his discussion of "tendencies, needs and premoral goods" and the "five dimensions of moral thinking."

point to the negative impact of cultural subjectivism on the worship life of the Church. These critiques suggest that one of the most detrimental consequences of the intensification of subjectivism has been an increase in individualistic understandings and interpretations of worship.

The tendency of the contemporary Church to adapt liturgy to the perceived needs and tastes of individual people in a market-driven society has been critiqued by Schmemann. Schmemann emphasizes, as noted in Chapter 2, that authentic liturgy does not exist solely for the purpose of mediating individual salvation or to add a religious dimension to individual lives.

The most transformative elements of worship, Schmemann insists, are that it (1) draws a diversity of individuals together to constitute the Church and (2) functions through its ritual actions and juxtapositions to embody Christ's eschatological vision of the world redeemed. At its root, worship is communal activity; the meaning created in worship is intersubjective, a distinctiveness overlooked by a contemporary society immersed in therapeutic and individualistic manifestations of subjectivism.

These contemporary insights into the negative influences of subjectivism on worship are paralleled by a renewed interest within the social sciences in how all meaning is actually intersubjective. In current scholarship, for instance, a task of cultural studies is to examine how contextual issues influence human expression and interpretation of events.[103]

One result of this for liturgical studies is a renewal of our awareness that those who worship are not separate or isolated entities. As Michael Aune puts it, the Church must be reawakened to the fact that "human expectations, thoughts, actions, interpretations, and feelings, are situated within an 'intersubjectivity,' within relationships or sets of

---

[103] Clifford Geertz, "Thick Description: Toward an Interpretive Theory of Culture," *The Interpretation of Cultures: Selected Essays,* ed. Clifford Geertz (New York: Basic Books, 1973) 3–32, is one of the voices in this realm of cultural studies who sees culture as semiotic. As he explains, humanity is "suspended in webs of significance he himself [sic] has spun." In light of this, the goal of ethnographic studies is not to "know" cultures other than our own but rather to "converse" with them in an effort to sort out the multiplicity of conceptual structures that exist both within the culture and within the descriptive efforts of the ethnographer.

relationships."[104] In short, the combined efforts of liturgical scholars, anthropologists, and philosophers have called into question traditional conceptions of autonomy and subjectivity, arguing that individuals fundamentally exist in spheres of relatedness to others, culture, and tradition.[105]

As a result, the question of how liturgical forms impede or foster a sense of community and common Christian identity has become central to many discussions of liturgical renewal, particularly as scholars become more aware of the intersubjectivity of communal existence. As seen in the above critique of liturgical theologies, most current liturgical methods lack an explicit framework for self-critique that enables them adequately to address this question.

Marjorie Proctor-Smith notes in her work, for example, that much of the liturgical movement is concerned with recovering early Christian liturgical practices. However, as noted earlier, because this effort is based on a recovery of historical norms and led by clergy, it overlooks the extent to which traditional practices were shaped by a patriarchal Church and society. The movement has not adequately responded to the challenge raised by Walter Burghardt at the Scottsdale Conference, namely that scholars more intentionally examine the effect of their own presuppositions on their historical thinking, analysis, and renewal efforts.

Tradition, as currently preserved, denies Church leadership and authority to some people and groups. This structure of limited authority, Proctor-Smith points out, becomes self-perpetuating when it is not taken into account that tradition is a process of remembering rather than an empirically pure account of what happened in the past. In other words, all tradition is constructed, and the dominant group within an institution or tradition often remembers only what is important for its own survival and identity.[106]

---

[104] Aune, "Worship in an Age of Subjectivism Revisited," 226.

[105] The restored focus on the intersubjectivity of human existence is central to feminist critique of ideological structures, especially structures that objectify created beings. These critiques point out that subjectivism, taken to its logical conclusion, diminishes the aesthetic and ethical dimensions of existence and creates the conditions for hegemony.

[106] Marjorie Proctor-Smith, *In Her Own Rite: Constructing Feminist Liturgical Tradition* (Nashville: Abingdon Press, 1990) 34. See also David Power, "Liturgical Praxis: New Consciousness at the Eye of Worship," *Worship* 61 (July 1987) 292–3.

Liturgical tradition, Proctor-Smith continues, is predominantly androcentric and patriarchal. The male sociocultural perspective provides its foundational norm. Because of this, it fails adequately to "remember" women's experiences or to respect them as equal voices in liturgical construction. To open up the more inclusive realms of the metaphorical, nonverbal, and visual requires an awareness that liturgical tradition is not in actuality based on a text but rather grows out of a community's intersubjective experience of God's presence. As the Church strives toward more inclusive historical remembering and works to establish broader participation in liturgical interpretation and dialogue, Farley's understanding of intersubjectivity and redemption becomes most helpful.

Farley identifies three interrelated spheres of human existence—the interhuman, the social, and the personal.[107] Each of these spheres has a corresponding elemental passion and vulnerability, characteristics that lead to the tragic structure of human existence. Farley argues that this tragic structure serves as the background for the Judeo-Christian paradigm of good and evil.[108]

As he explains, human reality is "not able to be content with oppressive socialities, fractured and alienated relationships, and imperiled subjectivity. . . . Finite being, in the sense of activity, can never exist in the mode of pure realization and hence embodies a gap between

---

[107] The parameters of this thesis do not allow for a full discussion of Farley's treatment of these three spheres. His own summary of them states that "the human life-form or human reality is distributed over three interrelated and overlapping spheres, each of which is a necessary condition of the other two: the interhuman, the social, and individual agents"; Farley, *Good and Evil*, 29.

[108] In "Tragedy, Totality, and the Face" (*Theology and the Interhuman*, ed. Robert Williams [Valley Forge, Pa.: Trinity Press International, 1995] 80–104), Robert Williams critiques Farley's understanding of the tragic. Williams raises the concern that strands of Farley's thought in this area tend toward nihilism, particularly as Farley introduces the theme of chaos. On the one hand, Farley depicts chaos as the seeming meaninglessness of life, a situation most intolerable to human beings. Williams suggests that this depiction grows out of the "continental" influence. At the same time, Farley also defends the essential goodness of being, reflecting the influence of pragmatism on his thought. Williams argues that Farley does not satisfactorily resolve these two concepts. The revised reflective ontology that emerges when biblical wisdom is invited into this dialogue provides a way of resolving this tension.

realization and any projected ideality."[109] A motivating factor of human existence is thus the desire for fulfillment of the elemental passions. However, a tension develops between what human desire pursues and what it actually obtains. Humanity wages a constant struggle against those conditions of life that prevent fulfillment of the elemental passions.

What makes this structure tragic, Farley continues, is not the struggle itself, but the fact that the struggle takes place in environments that both promote and oppose fulfillment. In other words, the tragic characteristic of humanity is that conditions of well-being can also be conditions of limitation and suffering; there is an "inescapable interconnection between suffering and satisfaction, between goods obtained and prices paid."[110] What is determinative is human response to such conditions.

As humanity aspires to resolve the tension between the fulfillment of our desires and resistance to that fulfillment, two types of responses develop. On the "resistance" side, Farley asserts, we cultivate actions and strategies for dealing with everyday obstacles. To live means to encounter situations that offer "resistance" to our existence. Certain situations "present us with what must be picked, gathered, cooked, shaped into a tool or weapon, built, avoided, thought about, escaped, learned, climbed, uncovered, composed, tracked down, and hidden."[111] The actions we take in these situations are motivated by all sorts of tendencies, needs, wishes, and interests; in effect, our actions are motivated by the desire to overcome resistance.

On the "desire" side, actions and attitudes are shaped for attaining those things that we desire.[112] The human tendency is to insist that worldly objects can overcome resistance and fulfill desires. Such a tendency creates false optimism regarding finite goods, causing us to relate to those goods as though they were the eternal horizon. When

[109] Farley, "Response," 249.
[110] Farley, *Good and Evil*, 96.
[111] Ibid., 98.
[112] Ibid., 172–3. "Desire" is a recurring theme in ancient Greek anthropologies. Scholars such as Goethe, Kierkegaard, and Jonathan Edwards have argued that the passions are needed to orient reason's function. As Farley says, "Things like justice, loyalty, and loving-kindness are engendered not by reason but from interests and desires. When reason loses its connection with these things, it loses what makes it important and useful." Technology offers research tools for creating marketable fulfillments of desire, but even with these advancements humanity senses a deeper desire.

we insist on substituting something finite for the eternal, idolatry occurs. Because finite goods are always limited and fragile, it is inevitable that the idolatrous substitute eventually encounters circumstances in which it fails to meet our expectations. Betrayed by what we thought was trustworthy, we experience despair.

The essential meaning of redemption in Farley's thought grows out of this understanding of the tragic structure of human existence. The core of his argument can be summarized in the following way.

The inability of human beings to live with the uncertainties of existence results in the corruption of the elemental passions. It is the "elemental" or enduring character of these constitutive passions, says Farley, that makes them tragic. As noted above, even though these passions determine our deepest inclinations and motivate our actions, they cannot be fulfilled by worldly goods. As Farley says, "their drive is always beyond their present realizations."[113] In addition, as noted above, conditions of fulfillment and well-being coexist with situations of limitation and suffering. What permeates human existence, then, is a constant dynamic of hope and despair.[114]

In his work on good and evil, Farley details how this dynamic operates within each of the spheres of human existence. There are within each sphere—the interhuman, personal, and social—both elements of corruption (evil) and the possibility of openness to transformation (good). Human evil and good appear in these spheres, Farley argues, as "idolatry and being-founded," "alienation and communion," and "subjugation and theonomous sociality."[115]

Farley's understanding of redemption departs most radically at this point from traditional understandings that grow out of a focus on redemption history. In traditional conceptions, evil is thought to be derived from sin; so too is the tragic. Farley's reflective ontology diverges from this understanding as he suggests that the tragic structure of human existence serves as the environment or background for sin. In this conception, sin and human corruption are seen not as objective universals but as responses to and resistance against this tragic structure, responses that result in idolatry.

[113] Farley, *Good and Evil*, 100.

[114] Walter Brueggemann, "Hope and Despair as Seasons of Faith," *The Landscape of Praise: Readings in Liturgical Renewal*, ed. Blair Gilmer Meeks (Valley Forge, Pa.: Trinity Press International, 1996) 172–9.

[115] Farley, *Good and Evil*, 119–53.

Redemption, within this understanding, occurs as within this tragic structure human response is shaped toward freedom, obligation, and communion. Such shaping of dispositions happens as persons participate in ecclesial existence, that dimension of sociality that is caught up in what Farley calls "modification of disruptive existence toward redemption."[116]

In existence modified toward redemption, the "power of self-serving," or the tendency toward idolatrous responses to the tragic nature of human living, is broken. Using language appropriated from Tillich, Farley argues that what replaces "idolatrous self-founding" is "being-founded," the power to live in the condition of tragic vulnerability without insisting upon absolute self-securing.

Within the faith community, "being-founded" is a condition of historical freedom and courage. As Farley argues, being-founded has a double function. On the one hand it breaks the hold of idolatry; it establishes a condition of freedom. At the same time, it also provides a way of existing in the midst of the tragedies of the world. This aspect of being-founded, says Farley, is related to a stance of courage.

When the dynamics of evil are broken, new possibilities are apprehended, possibilities founded on the historical reality of the Christ-event. A community of redemption courageously pushes past the tragic toward these new possibilities, toward reconciliation with God.[117] What happens in this process, liturgically understood, is that idolatrous hierarchical structuring is broken and replaced with what Power calls "the fundamental equality in baptismal dignity."[118]

The visible institution of the Church—its structures and activities—is only the surface of the primordial intersubjectivity of communal existence. As history demonstrates, these surface structures are the most susceptible to corruption. In other words, because redemptive existence is historical, it is also mixed with corruptions that can become institutionally sanctioned. Collins calls this element of redemptive existence the "self-protective schemes evident in human religiosity." When these schemes become dominant, she argues,

---

[116] Farley, *Ecclesial Man*, 146–9.

[117] Ibid., 152.

[118] Power, "Liturgical Praxis," 296, argues that Christian tradition seems to have lost touch with these roots. What is needed to restore our intersubjective consciousness is a renewed awareness of how humanity participates in rather than dominates cosmic history.

particularly when they are reflected in worship forms, the presence of God is obscured.[119]

A more precise outline of Farley's concept of christology and redemption will be necessary as this project continues. Important to the discussion to this point is his understanding that redemptive existence seeks the negation of corrupt social boundaries and of institutions that obscure the presence of God. What replaces these boundaries in authentic Christian community, says Farley, is "testimony to one whose death and resurrection was the occasion of this negation and the creation of ecclesia."[120]

Even without a fuller picture of the christological element of this argument, it is clear that redemptive ecclesial existence as Farley understands it centers on (1) how the sacred is known and interpreted within and in spite of the experience of human corruptions, and (2) how our mediations of the sacred break the hold of ideological dynamics both in the Church and in the world.[121]

In authentic ecclesial existence, primary metaphors for God's relation to human beings reflect how the sacred confronts the dynamics of evil.[122] Historically, monarchical metaphors for God have been predominant. Farley's argument suggests an interpretive shift to more interpersonal metaphors. Within the Christian paradigm, interpersonal metaphors find their clearest and most dynamic expression in the historical person and compassionate action of Christ.

As Farley argues, when sovereign rule and punishment are the controlling images for God, "God's relation to the world order is analogous to the maintenance of a social system through rule and punishment." Such judicial metaphors foster a distorted interpretation of evil.

Interpersonal metaphors for God, on the other hand, also grow out of biblical texts. These metaphors focus on God's creative power, on

[119] Mary Collins, "The Public Language of Ministry," *The Jurist* 41 (1981) 292.
[120] Farley, *Ecclesial Man*, 219.
[121] In Western methodologies centered in redemption history to the exclusion of other expressions of God's presence, what Schüssler Fiorenza calls "hegemonic christological discourses" have dominated. When this happens, even christology becomes a manipulative tool in the hands of the powerful, who will use it either explicitly or implicitly to maintain their dominant role. See Elisabeth Schüssler Fiorenza, *Jesus: Miriam's Child, Sophia's Prophet* (New York: Continuum, 1994) 5–8.
[122] Farley, *Good and Evil*, 143.

how God compassionately "lures the world process toward its best possibilities." When interpersonal or relational metaphors for God are central, persons within the faith community are empowered to live within the tragic structure of existence "without insisting on being secured by goods at hand."[123] God's interpersonal and creative relationship with creation is ultimately reflected in communal relationships as people learn to co-exist with one another and co-intend one another in their sense of obligation and in their actions.[124]

To articulate more clearly what he means by this interrelational aspect of redemptive ecclesial existence, Farley appropriates Emmanuel Levinas's concept of the "community of the face." As Farley explains, the presence of God, or the "universal face," is evident in the distinctive social and historical mediator which he calls the "community of the face." The purpose of a community of the face is more than to enable face-to-face relations. Other social institutions or groups can accomplish that. The primary impetus of a community of the face is the mediation of the universal face, a face which is what Farley calls "transregional." The universal face is expressed by relational language and through creation-oriented metaphors rather than judicial or monarchical ones. Because of this, it negates cultural and class boundaries and is present to all people, to all of creation.

When the Christian community is a community of the face, it is not primarily an institution of political change or moral change, although historically these emphases have drawn much methodological and theological focus. The Church's role is not to replace or compete with political institutions; nor does it exist as a resource for grace, morals, or forgiveness for individuals.

Rather, a community of the face exists primarily as a horizon of redemption, as a community of relation within which the spheres of human reality are drawn toward the ultimate reality of God's presence. To that end, a community of the face exists within history and directs its dialogue toward and with all human institutions; however, its most

[123] Ibid.

[124] Edward Farley, *Deep Symbols: Their Postmodern Effacement and Reclamation* (Valley Forge, Pa.: Trinity Press International, 1996) 49, suggests that in communal understandings wherein "obligation" remains as a word of power it includes "a refusal to reduce the other to an object for use and an acceptance of the irreducible mystery of the other." Obligation involves moving beyond self-oriented agendas and taking responsibility for that which is other than ourselves.

vital function is to disrupt the discourse of evil within these institutions and within the lives of human beings. It accomplishes this through the metaphorical language of the universal face—the Word of God—and through actions and responses that are shaped by that Word.[125]

To summarize, Farley argues that the universal face is mediated by communities of the face. This concept grows out of his rootedness in reflective ontology and its attendant criticism of monarchical metaphors for God that result in various forms of patriarchalism and hierarchy.

Craig Dykstra makes two claims that help to clarify Farley's understandings outlined above: (1) congregational life is engaged in socially acceptable patterns of mutual self-destruction, and (2) through congregational life these patterns are being redemptively transformed.[126]

The pattern of mutual self-destruction Dykstra refers to corresponds to Farley's assertion that within the spheres of human reality there is a tragic structure, a pattern of corruption that influences human language, thought processes, and actions. Similar to Farley, Dykstra explains that this destructive pattern is inherent in the achievement-oriented lifestyle of our society, a society in which one's self-image is dependent on claiming significance through what one does.

This pattern, says Dykstra, is reinforced at every level of the American cultural system. Human beings have a hungering need to be found worthy, but this need is not unconditionally met from childhood. Eventually, those who do not achieve success by society's standards are marginalized. The destructive nature of this pattern is reflected in people's lifestyles and actions. For instance, many people in our society are highly productive or "successful." However, their desire for success, or a sense of self-worth, is so strong they manipulate others in order to obtain it. The ultimate result is that corrupt behavior patterns become institutionalized, establishing oppressive or hegemonic institutional forms.

[125] Farley, "Toward a New Paradigm for Preaching," 165–75, does not offer a precise explanation of what he means by the "universal face." The sense is that as much as he resists forms of absolutism as idolatrous, so too he resists absolutizing God. In this, Farley exhibits a departure from Levinas and seems to propose an understanding of the transcendence of God that is more dependent on Tillich. See Peter Hodgson, "The Face and the Spirit," *Theology and the Interhuman,* ed. Robert R. Williams (Valley Forge, Pa.: Trinity Press International, 1995) 45.

[126] Craig Dykstra, "The Formative Power of the Congregation," *Religious Education* 82 (Fall 1987) 530–46.

According to Farley's argument, participants in the faith community are caught up in the entanglements of a tragic existence and bring these entanglements with them to the worship event. In other words, because the Church is made up of people, it is also characterized by socially approved patterns of mutual self-destruction. Because it exists within the tragic structure of human reality, the Church will always contain potential for corruption and potential for transformation.[127]

The greatest danger for the Church, then, arises when destructive patterns are institutionalized as doctrines, pedagogical forms, and liturgical forms, and passed on uncritically from generation to generation. When this happens, liturgical forms tend to foster a false sense of community. As Dykstra argues, however, liturgical forms can also mediate reconciliation, love, and communion, thus cultivating within the community a sense of common Christian identity.

Like Farley, Dykstra argues that

"since the patterns which destroy us lie at the pre-reflective level, and since the roots of these patterns lie in the desperate attempts at self-securing that characterize our historical existence, the redemptive power of the congregation must be a transformation of self-securing and must somehow be mediated at a pre-reflective level."[128]

Expanding on Farley at this point and echoing many voices within liturgical theology, Dykstra suggests that because it is through worship forms that our pre-reflective intuitions of God are mediated, it is also primarily through worship that patterns of mutual self-destruction can be redeemed.

Through the language of confession, the community acknowledges its participation in destructive patterns. Through repentance, we articulate the inadequacy of human efforts to achieve a sense of self-worth or unity with others. Finally, through proclamation and prayer, we recognize and celebrate the sustaining and liberating presence of God. It is in worship, says Dykstra, that the redemptive potential of the community finds its generative source and its most focused moment. Primary theology, as habitus, is rooted in worship, the center of the Church's transformative potential.

Farley's emphasis on the intersubjectivity of the community of faith accomplishes several things. First, it reminds liturgical scholars that

[127] Farley, *Good and Evil*, 291.
[128] Dykstra, "The Formative Power of the Congregation," 539.

truth, or knowledge, is more elusive and complex than many educational models imply. As noted at the outset of this chapter, knowledge, in addition to having an objective element, is also something that people do; meaning is participatory and cannot be reduced to isolated facts or principles. This understanding rekindles an awareness of the inherently reflexive or intersubjective nature of worship. As Ronald Grimes says, liturgy and the truth it mediates do not exist outside of concrete communities.[129] *but ...*

Second, Farley demonstrates how human inability to deal with the tragic condition of existence leads to distortions in communal identity and to oppressive institutional ideologies. This depiction challenges scholars to look more closely at liturgical forms that remain unreflective. It also urges the scholarly community to reexamine how liturgical renewal continues to be hierarchical and limiting.[130]

A transformed consciousness, such as that implied by Farley, will lead to inclusion of metaphors for God that are more relational, aesthetic and creation-centered. Power suggests that this means "retrieving what has been suppressed in human and religious experience." To accomplish this retrieval, Power calls for the recovery of Wisdom or Sophia as a metaphor for God. Wisdom, he explains, is acquired experientially as people learn to "cope" with reality.[131] As Farley might express it, wisdom, or habitus, is a disciplining of mind and emotions that happens as people learn to exist within the tragic structure of human existence in freedom and courage.

Finally, Farley's understanding of redemption challenges scholars to embrace an alternate vision of the Church, a vision determined not by the Church's political force or by its existence as an agent of moral

[129] Ronald Grimes, *Ritual Criticism* (Columbia: University of South Carolina Press, 1990) 35. See also Aune, "Worship in an Age of Subjectivism Revisited," 233–5.

[130] David Power, "Liturgical Praxis: New Consciousness at the Eye of Worship," *Worship* 61 (July 1987) 292–305.

[131] Ibid., 301. See also Elisabeth Schüssler Fiorenza, *In Memory of Her: A Feminist Theological Reconstruction of Christian Origins* (New York: Crossroad, 1992) 105–59; Ben Witherington, *Jesus the Sage: The Pilgrimage of Wisdom* (Minneapolis: Fortress Press, 1994); James White, *Christian Worship in North America—A Retrospective: 1955–1995* (Collegeville: The Liturgical Press, 1997) 201–7; J. Frank Henderson, "The Names and Images of God," *The Landscape of Praise: Readings in Liturgical Renewal*, ed. Blair Gilmer Meeks (Valley Forge, Pa.: Trinity Press International, 1996) 263–7.

change, but by its ability to exist within the tragic structure of human reality in a mode of reconciliation, love, and communion.

Kevin Seasoltz discusses how such a vision of the Church impacts eucharistic practice. Authentic community, he says, is made up of persons who gather around Christ's table to share their lives with one another; when people struggle to know and love themselves and one another, new life is made possible. This transformed "life" is similar to what Power refers to as the "ethical and agapic" foundation of liturgical praxis. True community happens, Seasoltz insists, as people "facilitate life for one another" on deeper and deeper levels.

The theme of the intersubjectivity of communal existence is also implicit to Lathrop's work. For example, reflective ontological concerns related to communal integrity emerge in his treatment of the "signs" of worship and how they mediate a mystery that only God can give. As he insists, congregations that push rigidly toward more dogmatic "signs" without attending to the agapic dimension of community lose the richness and meaning of the thing signified. Surface structures become primary. The task of the community in light of this is to push beyond institutional "wrappings" to grasp the ultimate realities that are at the center of tradition.

Always, Lathrop continues, the signs, actions, and objects of worship must draw the community into the mystery of Christ and urge it toward dialogue with the stranger in all of us and with the stranger in our midst. Lathrop challenges the community, much as Farley's reflective ontology does, to reflect constantly on how structures of power in liturgy succeed in reordering power structures in the world.[132]

The particular knowledge mediated by liturgical praxis is grounded in mutuality, love, and compassion.[133] This knowledge becomes transformative when communities intentionally invite all people to the eucharistic table. When this happens, Lathrop suggests, worship is no

[132] Lathrop, *Holy Things*, 164–9.

[133] Browning, *A Fundamental Practical Theology*, offers a definition of *agape* that corresponds to this understanding. In his reconstruction of Niebuhr's theological ethics, Browning defines *agape* as "mutuality and equal regard" and argues that valuing one's self as well as the other is an obligation implicit in the New Testament principle of neighbor love. For Browning, mutuality and equal regard are the core of practical reason; it is a principle that reminds people that any claim they make on another person in their decision-making, that person has the right to make on them.

longer a place where people clamor for "ownership" of the objects of worship but rather participate in an act in which God's mystery and self-gift are celebrated.

CONCLUSION

This chapter began with the depiction of a recent development in North American religious life, namely the increasing gap between what North Americans believe and how they incorporate these beliefs into their daily lives. Emerging along with this development is the question of how liturgy is to provide meaning for people's lives today. To address this question, this chapter sought to create a dialogue between Farley's philosophical theology and contemporary liturgical theology. As this journey into Farley's theology draws to an end, a conclusion can be drawn. At the heart of Farley's work and at the heart of liturgical theology stands a challenge for the Church to rethink what redemption or conversion means.

Traditional methodologies address the issue of conversion from the perspective of redemption history and how christology and christological discourse derive from that perspective. Farley and a number of contemporary biblical theologians have carefully scrutinized these positivistic historical approaches; the result has been to rethink the role of redemption history in theological method and in our construals of christology. Insights emerging from this work are transformative for our understandings of conversion and communal existence.

To summarize, this chapter points toward the need for a biblical matrix that (1) allows for a wider diversity of metaphors for God's relationship to humanity, (2) grounds a revised christological discourse, (3) provides foundational elements for the communal vision that grows out of such a metaphorical and christological shift, and (4) reappropriates ontological discourse for communicating the structure of creation and how it is related to the mystery of God. The following chapters will propose wisdom literature as providing such a biblical matrix.

Chapter 4

Wisdom and Liturgical Theology

At the heart of *The Elusive Presence*, Samuel Terrien's work in biblical theology, is a thought-provoking axiom of the Hebraic-Christian tradition: "The reality of the presence of God stands at the center of biblical faith. This presence, however, is always elusive."[1]

The dynamic interplay between the presence and elusiveness of God is also central to Christian liturgy. Through the juxtapositions inherent in worship, the gathered assembly catches a glimpse of God's presence and discovers a cohesiveness that shapes participants' thoughts, their actions, the totality of their lives. At the same time, however, divine mystery is only partially revealed in worship. Part of God's truth remains veiled, engaging the faith community in an ongoing dialectical journey of discovery. The mediation of God's truth, of God's presence, is the most dynamic purpose and action of worship.

As outlined in the previous chapter, the truth claims of the Church have been drawn into question by contemporary epistemological understandings. The faith community also faces complex challenges to its integrity as scholars from various disciplines expose the ideological underpinnings of many of the Church's institutions and activities. Farley has demonstrated, for example, that some of the "truths" mediated by traditional structures are in actuality selective versions of truth that serve to maintain prevailing power systems. In short, these are difficult times for the Church, times in which traditional formulations of the faith are at best in danger of collapsing and at worst already considered obsolete by contemporary skepticism.[2]

---

[1] Samuel Terrien, *The Elusive Presence: Toward a New Biblical Theology* (New York: Harper and Row, 1978) xxvii.

[2] Walter Brueggemann, *In Man We Trust: The Neglected Side of Biblical Faith* (Atlanta: John Knox Press, 1972) 7.

The previous two chapters of this project examined how both Farley and contemporary liturgical theologians are working to demonstrate that those things claimed "by faith" to have life-determining value meaningfully impact everyday existence. The theological proposals emerging from these perspectives struggle both to elucidate the distinctive reality of God's presence and to avoid formulating it into inflexible and limiting intellectual categories that diminish its mysterious quality.[3] This chapter invites wisdom literature scholars into this dialogue with Farley and liturgical theologians. Such a dialogue is important for several reasons.

The primary reason emerges from a closer examination of Brueggemann's and Terrien's work in biblical theology. While Israel's affirmation of faith is multifaceted, appropriations of that faith throughout the Church's history have focused on some facets to the exclusion of others. At least two aspects of Israelite faith have been neglected by a scholarly community and Church that have tended to understand all of Scripture and faith in terms of redemption history.

First, the predominant commitment of Western Christianity to a theology of sin and salvation has largely overlooked dimensions of Scripture which affirm creation, celebrate God's presence in culture, and emphasize human potential as created in God's image.[4] At this particular historical juncture, these neglected elements of Scripture seem to offer a possibility for building a bridge between a skeptical culture and biblical faith. As such, they invite more extensive examination.

A second overlooked aspect of Israelite faith is the motif of presence. According to Terrien, the "reality"of God is what stands at the center of faith and provides a unifying purpose for human existence. Thus, the Hebraic theology of presence, more than redemption history, provides an interpretive thread of continuity throughout the biblical corpus. This understanding resonates at several points with Farley's reflective ontology.

Chapter 2 outlined Farley's notion that there are elements or patterns of being that endure over time. These elements are not to be defined as

<hr />

[3] Terrien, *The Elusive Presence*, xxix.

[4] Brueggemann, *In Man We Trust*, 8, insists that Old Testament theology develops out of various kinds of dialectics rather than out of a central normative foundation. See Patrick D. Miller, "Introduction," *Old Testament Theology: Essays on Structure, Theme and Text*, ed. Patrick D. Miller (Minneapolis: Fortress Press, 1995) xv.

"universals" in the traditional objective or delimited sense. Rather, they represent modes of existence. A similar methodological grounding can be detected in Terrien's development of the "mode of presence" as foundational for biblical theology.

Terrien does not seek to impose on texts an objectifiable or universal theme that exists apart from contextual realities. He argues instead that the theme of "presence" is a mode of human relation to God that perdures throughout both Old and New Testaments, uniting "the vision of the ultimate with a passion for the service of man [*sic*]."[5] Terrien's theology of presence implies that there is a dynamic interplay of vision and ethics at the center of Scripture.

Allowing the motif of divine presence to provide a jumping off point for biblical theology restores the faith community as the primary locus for biblical faith and theology, a concern central to much contemporary liturgical theology.[6] A focus on "presence" also opens an avenue for rethinking the place and role of redemption history in theological method.

This chapter will discuss the above aspects of contemporary biblical theology in relation to wisdom literature. As consequent insights are connected with the work of Farley and liturgical scholars, the second axiom of the project's thesis will be supported:

[5] Terrien, *The Elusive Presence,* xxviii. The result of approaching biblical interpretation in this way is reflected in recent methods. These methods grow out of a hermeneutic awareness that theological interpretation is inherently constructive. In other words, they recognize that Scripture does not provide a universal program. See Leo Perdue, *The Collapse of History: Reconstructing Old Testament Theology* (Minneapolis: Fortress Press, 1994) ix.

[6] Terrien, *The Elusive Presence,* 22.

At various points in its history, biblical theology has attempted to discover a universal factor or theme within the diversity of the biblical corpus. As with these efforts, Terrien's theme of "presence" risks abstraction. Biblical texts, the history of biblical study has shown, resist imposed unifying schemes. See Steven J. Kraftchick, Charles D. Myers, and Ben Ollenburger, eds., *Biblical Theology: Problems and Perspectives—In Honor of J. Christiaan Beker* (Nashville: Abingdon Press, 1995) 7.

To his credit, Terrien's theology does not appear to impose a particular structure on texts. Rather, it points to an "interplay of theological fields of force at the center of scripture." A more detailed examination of what he means by this will be undertaken later in this chapter.

"A liturgical theological method grounded in the dialogical movement between the horizons of everyday reality and tradition evident in Old Testament wisdom theology contributes to the ongoing work of the liturgical movement by . . . (2) maintaining a rootedness in the Judeo-Christian biblical tradition that is methodologically centered on cosmology and anthropology rather than solely on redemption history."

The argument will consist of several interrelated parts.

First, one reason for changes in biblical theology is that traditional historically-oriented methods can no longer maintain dominance on the basis of authoritative claims of normativity. What is now required of these methodologies, says Steven Kraftchick, is "to hold themselves accountable—without recourse to assumptions held implicitly to be self-evident."[7]

Directly intersecting Farley's argument for a renewal of theology as habitus, in an era when the Church's authority is under siege, biblical theology needs to recognize the intersubjective or communal nature of truth. The first part of this chapter will address these authority issues by describing what Farley calls the "collapse of Christianity's house of authority"; implications of this for biblical theology and for liturgical theologies that operate within the "house of authority" as their methodological home will also be examined.

The second part of the chapter will look at recent developments in Old Testament theology that challenge the dominance of historical norms. Two aspects of these developments engage my project of correlating wisdom methodology and liturgical theology: (1) the critique of the dominance of historical norms in biblical study and interpretation, and (2) the emergence of alternative methodologies that rely on different philosophical underpinnings and that seek to establish how the questions of this era and culture are to be addressed to the text.[8]

[7] Kraftchick et al., eds., *Biblical Theology*, 11.
[8] Walter Brueggemann, *Theology of the Old Testament: Testimony, Dispute, Advocacy* (Minneapolis: Fortress Press, 1997) 42–60, examines how Old Testament theology has changed since the dominance of Eichrodt and von Rad. The primary reason for shifts in Old Testament study is that currently, within the parameters of contemporary epistemological and sociological understandings, there is increasingly evident a pluralism of interpretive contexts that points to the diversity of articulations of faith and God within the Old Testament corpus itself.

Finally, this chapter will propose that a wisdom perspective on liturgical practice, growing out of these changes in biblical theology, offers a methodological framework that dialogues with and expands upon the renewal initiated by the liturgical movement. A wisdom perspective accomplishes this by providing a broader epistemological base, by addressing Farley's critique of traditional theological method, and by suggesting a foundation for liturgical method that remains rooted in the Judeo-Christian tradition while addressing itself meaningfully to the rest of the world.

Not too long ago I journeyed with a friend down a narrow dirt road to a place in the woods hidden behind oaks and pines. Standing there were the skeletal remains of a building that used to be a church, now abandoned, with only the trees gathered around to hear its message. The steps leading to its entranceway were crumbling; even its eyes were empty and hollow, the glass broken out. In the eave where a vent used to be, two buzzards stared out at us. The church belongs to the forest now.

The image of that "church" serves as a metaphor for the difficult questions plaguing faith communities of our era. For many, the Church exists today primarily as a reminder of an outmoded historical time period, a time when faith and its institutions stood at the center of the community and provided a nucleus for people's actions. Emerging theological methods seek to restore the Church to its place as a vital dialogue partner at the center of personal, spiritual, communal, and societal concerns.

The three-way conversation created here between liturgical theology, Farley's philosophical theology, and biblical theology is a mutually critiquing and influencing dialogue that at the very least can (1) challenge the liturgical movement to expand the parameters of its biblical foundation, (2) suggest a corrective to Farley's reflective ontology, and (3) redefine biblical theology, from a revised reflective ontological perspective, as critical contextual activity that both resists a limiting universal scheme and uncovers enduring matrices of God's presence that can serve as a foundation for the Church's mediation of that presence today.

These three points of intersection form the general parameters of the discussion that follows. Implicit to the argument is the conviction that the crumbling walls of that abandoned church in the woods do not have to symbolize the future of the Church. The theological conversation developed here, one that integrates the discoveries and concerns of previously fragmented disciplines, has the potential to renew our worship forms and restore the Church's place as a bold participant at the discussion tables of the larger world without abandoning our rich history or our denominational and traditional distinctiveness.

BIBLICAL THEOLOGY IN TRANSITION

Kathleen O'Connor summarizes how the place and role of wisdom in biblical theology has changed in recent years:

"Aspects of Wisdom literature that in the past caused it to be ignored by biblical theologians are the very features of the literature that are provoking its rediscovery today. Wisdom's preference for daily concerns of human existence, for example, attention to creation, its depictions of God as mysterious and elusive—perspectives that once kept wisdom on the edges of historically oriented biblical theology—now seem to provide essential theological resources for a postcolonial, postmodern world."[9]

As she suggests, the focus on wisdom in biblical theology is rather recent, related to the faith community's struggle to appropriate its classic texts more adequately for changing existential realities and needs. Biblical theology is undergoing tremendous methodological change, change that has resulted in and been shaped by more intensive study of Old Testament wisdom.

In general, twentieth-century Old Testament theology has been dominated by the work of Walter Eichrodt and Gerhard von Rad. Models of biblical theology dependent on their work, rooted in the epistemological categories of the modern era and grounded in the historical-critical method, consistently push wisdom to the sidelines. By their standards, wisdom does not contain a clear reference to redemption history, an account of the revelation at Sinai, or a clearly developed concept of Israel as God's chosen people, all of which are normative for traditional methods cast primarily in historical categories. In short, traditionally dominant Old Testament theologies, presented in terms of the history, cult, and institutions of the Hebrew

---

[9] Kathleen O'Connor, "Wisdom Literature and Experience of the Divine," *Biblical Theology: Problems and Perspectives—In Honor of J. Christiaan Beker*, ed. Steven J. Kraftchick, Charles D. Myers, and Ben C. Ollenburger (Nashville: Abingdon Press, 1995) 183.

people, exclude wisdom and other parts of the Old Testament that are centered primarily on creation and providence.[10]

Wisdom has gained more attention recently because of increasing criticism of traditional paradigms of biblical theology. Several prominent theologies have emerged in the period from 1970 to 1990 that are in large measure critical responses to von Rad's thematic of "God's mighty acts in history."[11] The resulting emergence of wisdom as a viable partner in establishing new modes of doing theology intersects with the contemporary epistemological shifts outlined in the previous two chapters.

These developing approaches to biblical study share a hermeneutical awareness that theological interpretation is inherently constructive. Much as the goal of liturgical theology is not to abstract universal principles from the contextual framework of worship's ordo, the primary goal of much contemporary biblical theology is not to establish a dogmatic or absolute "message."[12] Rather, echoing Farley's focus on the "wisdom of the enduring," the predominant function of recent biblical theologies is to recover an enduring pattern or dialectic within the classic texts, a framework within which contemporary persons can discover ultimate truth.

Newer methods of biblical study depart from the epistemological and philosophical underpinnings of historical criticism in order to respond to an increasingly pluralistic sociopolitical ethos. Many of these methods have discovered in the wisdom corpus a neglected theological voice, one that reflects their concerns for a more constructive approach and avoids the positivistic and ideological tendencies common to classical tradition.[13]

As Perdue notes, scholarly voices now gaining a hearing in biblical circles are rooted in epistemologies other than Enlightenment models

[10] John F. Priest, "Where Is Wisdom to Be Placed?" *Studies in Ancient Israelite Wisdom*, ed. H. M. Orlinsky (New York: KTAV Publishing House, 1976) 281–8.

[11] Brueggemann, *Theology of the Old Testament*, 48, suggests the 1970s as marking the "break-point" in Old Testament theology. He argues that Gerhard von Rad's own work, *Wisdom in Israel* (Nashville: Abingdon Press, 1972), begins to "move beyond von Rad." Brevard Childs, in the same year, also issued his book *Biblical Theology in Crisis* (Philadelphia: Westminster Press, 1970), which explicitly called attention to the shifting landscape of Old Testament Theology.

[12] Perdue, *The Collapse of History*, x.

[13] Ibid., 5–7.

—social-scientific interpretations, liberation and narrative theologies, phenomenology and feminist theology. These methodologies, to phrase it in Farley's terms, "set the problem" of biblical study in a way much different from classical methods. This is reflected in the questions they bring to their study and to the text:

"Is the purpose of the biblical theologian to describe the theology or theologies of the biblical books and writers, that is, to set forth a historical theology; or is the purpose to construct a biblical theology that engages the present world, that is, to shape a contemporary hermeneutic? Should the purpose be to set forth the distinctive theologies of various books and corpora of literature in the Bible or to select a central theme and then compose a systematic rendering of biblical faith?"[14]

The current diversity of hermeneutical frameworks in biblical theology is paralleled by a similar plurality in liturgical circles where feminists, linguists, phenomenologists, and others have begun to propose liturgical methods from their particular perspectives and expertise.

Within biblical study in particular these new voices challenge traditional methodologies, arguing that wisdom and other neglected parts of Scripture show that Israel's intellectual life and understanding of God were much more expansive than a primary focus on the prophets and historical writings indicates.[15] This is a central reason why the renewed focus on wisdom is valuable for dealing with the current liturgical crisis.

Specifically, wisdom literature's framework for mediating God's presence intersects with and expands upon liturgical responses to the current crisis by implying in its structure the three kinds of discourse highlighted in Chapter 3 as central to authentic liturgy:[16] (1) discourse of memorial and blessing in which metaphorical language dominates, (2) revised ontological discourse that points to the enduring modes of revelation while maintaining an awareness of the mysterious quality of God's presence, and (3) secondary theological discourse that interprets and describes how persons within faith communities are related to one another and to tradition.

[14] Ibid., xi.

[15] James Crenshaw, "Prolegomenon," *Studies in Ancient Israelite Wisdom,* ed. H. M. Orlinsky (New York: KTAV Publishing House, 1976).

[16] David Power, *Eucharistic Mystery: Revitalizing the Tradition* (New York: Crossroad, 1995) 326.

Before examining in greater detail those biblical methods that more readily embrace Old Testament wisdom, it is important to have a clearer understanding of the precipitating factors of what Perdue has termed the "collapse of history" and what Farley calls the "collapse of Christianity's house of authority."

For archaic people, Farley explains, "tradition" provided an accumulation of wisdom that assisted them in making decisions in current situations. Having a distinctive "tradition" meant that they did not have to reinvent or rediscover "truth" in its entirety each time they faced a new situation; they could turn to the wisdom of their history to find the enduring elements of truth and construct on this foundation a solution to problems appropriate for current circumstances.[17]

The Judeo-Christian "tradition" initially developed, Farley continues, as Israel reflected on those times in its history when God provided the people with liberation or renewal. The wisdom or knowledge mediated by tradition and handed down from generation to generation was rooted primarily in the faith community's experience of God's presence in its particular context. When the Diaspora threatened the continuity of this rich tradition, Judaism created what Farley calls "vehicles of social duration," such as the Torah and the rabbinate, to insulate tradition from outside threat.

Later, when the religious plurality of the Mediterranean world jeopardized Christian identity, Christianity also created vehicles of duration for protecting its distinctiveness—namely frameworks such as the concept of an infallible text and a hierarchical institute of authority. These protective structures operated out of the presupposition that the content of Scripture and the doctrinal conclusions of the historical Church councils were God's revealed "truth" and could thus serve as the foundation for an authoritative cosmology, ethic, and Scripture principle. In Farley's terms, a "house of authority" was created.

A number of scholars from various perspectives have suggested recently that many of the principles and interpretations growing out of the "house of authority" are incompatible with the nature of earliest

---

[17] Don Browning, *A Fundamental Practical Theology* (Minneapolis: Fortress Press, 1991), outlines a similar understanding of how tradition is appropriated for particular historical contexts. He draws on the work of several contemporary intellectual traditions, including revisiting several practical philosophies. His work stands in the tradition of practical wisdom, or practical reason, that is associated with Aristotle, Augustine, Kant, and others.

Christian communities. Farley's own critique of the house of authority demonstrates how these principles have diminished the faith community's existence as a redemptive presence and thus undermined its ability to maintain a position of influence in contemporary culture.[18]

In an intriguing section in *Ecclesial Man* entitled "Ecclesia as the Abolishment of Salvation-History," Farley argues that the shaping of human existence toward redemption is inherently connected to divine presence. As noted in Chapter 3, Farley asserts that the chief motivating factor of human existence is the desire to fulfill the elemental passions. Redemption occurs within the community as both affective and cognitive dispositions are shaped toward reconciliation with God, reconciliation which results in non-idolatrous actions motivated by freedom, obligation, and communion.

Because redemption concerns how God's presence breaks through idolatrous human tendencies toward self-securing, the locus of divine presence is decisive for the formation of the faith community. This is one of the points at which Farley's critique of the house of authority dialogues with both biblical and liturgical theology.

In Israel, he argues, divine presence is tied to a covenantal framework. Within this covenantal framework, God's presence is mediated through particular forms of sociality. Initially, the social form was tribal, eventually developing into a nation that occupied a specific geographical territory. As the nation of Israel grew, "institutions" of God's presence developed. Ultimately, in ancient Judaism, the most definitive locus for God's presence was believed to be the city of Zion and in particular the institution of the temple. Even in the Diaspora, this focus on the temple as the authoritative locus of God's presence was not abandoned.[19]

What the advent of Christ meant for the faith community, Farley continues, was actually an abolishment of these institutional conditions of God's presence, a possibility always implied in the prophecies and worship of Israel:

---

[18] Edward Farley's critique of the foundations of "authority" is found primarily in *Ecclesial Reflection: An Anatomy of Theological Method* (Philadelphia: Fortress Press, 1982), but actually originated in *Ecclesial Man: A Social Phenomenology of Faith and Reality* (Philadelphia: Fortress Press, 1975), in which a slightly different thesis is advanced that leads to similar conclusions.

[19] Farley, *Ecclesial Man*, 165–7.

"The most striking thing about ecclesia is that the presence of God has absolutely no existing social or ethnic conditions. Ecclesia presupposes no land, no holy nation, holy city, no geographical center, no central temple, no particular language. In ecclesia Zion is abolished. The breaking of necessary connections between the divine presence and divinely established (or permitted) societal structures, always a possibility in Israel, is actualized in ecclesia."[20]

With divine presence located in the paschal mystery, the faith community, or ecclesia, is no longer bounded by the history, language, social institutions, or traditions of Israel.

To understand redemption in this way does not require adopting an unhistorical interpretation of faith. In Farley's perspective, Israel is vital as ecclesia's historical matrix. The tradition of Israel and its textual expressions remain formative for the faith community. However, in that "modification of disruptive existence toward redemption" that occurred through Christ's self-gift, "'salvation history' is broken and transcended."[21] In other words, through Christ, the particular mode of authority for God's presence called "salvation history" and its attendant ecclesiastical edifices are revealed as inadequate for mediating the elusive and mysterious presence of God.

The implications of this argument are important for those seeking to recover the connections between liturgy and justice. In particular, it draws attention yet again to the intersubjectivity of redemptive existence. Further explication of Farley's thought helps to clarify this.

The faith community is a historical reality connected to concrete historical events and circumstances. Because faith is historically continuous in this sense, it is characterized by a constant re-appropriation of historical wisdom or tradition. In other words, acts of faith in past faith communities cannot be separated or isolated from acts of faith of subsequent communities.

---

[20] Ibid., 168. As Farley is careful to note, whether in Judaism or Christianity, there are elements of God's presence that go beyond institutional frameworks. Farley explains: "God is not tied to his [sic] people and their institutions in the way that the presence of sacred power is tied to the cyclical rituals of animism or totemism." There is always the sense that God transcends established institutions of faith. It is this "elusive" aspect of God's presence that has been obscured by historical focus on the institutional structures.

[21] Ibid.

At the same time, however, the presence of God presupposes a reality that stands outside historical formulations; as noted earlier in Terrien, an aspect of God's truth remains veiled. This is why redemptive ecclesial existence is a mode of existence that both incorporates the historical conditions of faith and envisions realities beyond those conditions. Redemptive ecclesial existence is both historical and eschatological. When this understanding is central, "institutional" forms are seen for what they are—temporal and limited in their ability fully to comprehend or grasp ultimate truth.

Paradigmatically, in the mode of redemptive existence, as the faith community struggles to maintain this dynamic balance between divine presence and historical structures of mediation, the status of the stranger is redefined and ecumenism is given a foundation since the "only conditions for participation in ecclesia are the religious a priori and disrupted historical existence."[22] In authentic ecclesial presence, ecclesia is not tied to any particular institution. Therefore, the stranger does not need to be "ethnically translated" from his/her own life-world in order to be redeemed. Instead, the stranger is a potential participant in ecclesia simply because of her/his existence within the tragic structure of humanity.

To the extent that Christianity substitutes temporal frameworks for intersubjective modes that allow reciprocal face-to-face relationships with the stranger, it diminishes or obscures the redemptive power of God's presence as mediated through Christ. This hazard is inherent in communal life, Farley says, because provinciality and its institutions are common outcomes of the human desire or need for self-securing.

A number of liturgical theologians have examined how institutional Church life tends toward idolatrous forms that judge and exclude the stranger. Central to much liturgical discussion in this vein has been a focus on anamnesis, or memory, which Farley cites as an essential feature of ecclesia's sociality.[23] Power and Proctor-Smith, for

[22] Ibid., 169. Peter Hodgson, "The Face and the Spirit," *Theology and the Interhuman*, ed. Robert R. Williams (Valley Forge, Pa.: Trinity Press International, 1995) 44–5, fleshes out this understanding of how ecclesia incorporates "face-to-face relations." The universal face pulls interhuman experiences toward compassionate obligation for all of life. This experience of the universal face is in effect an experience of the sacred and is embodied or mediated through ritualizations of the sacred, thus through worship.

[23] Farley, *Ecclesial Man*, 177. When the role of salvation history is juxtaposed to the intersubjectivity of the faith community, our understanding of how memory functions in the faith community and thus in liturgy is reconfigured.

example, argue that operating too exclusively within a methodological "house of authority" leads to the suppression of the memories of the marginalized.

One suggested revision of eucharistic thought that grows out of Power's partial retrieval of ontology is related to this, in particular to how the memorial of Christ's paschal mystery centers around the communion table. Echoing Farley, Power argues that a primary feature of the faith community is memory. In his understanding, as in Farley's, the purpose of liturgically remembering Christ's self-gift is not to connect all historical happenings to one thematic or universal narrative that reflects God's purpose and action.

To remember Christ, says Farley, "is not to remember an event which established a bounded community but one which disestablished that community and broke all ethnic conditions of God's presence."[24] Power would agree. The purpose of the eucharistic narrative, of *anamnesis*, is not, Power says, to establish a delimited vision of God's presence and purpose. Instead, the eucharistic narrative uses metaphorical language that is more dynamic, constructive, and inclusive to connect the community with the past and the future.

Such a metaphorical framework for remembering points to the discontinuity of history and to God's intervention in the tragic structuring of historical existence. This makes it possible for the Church, in its eucharistic celebration, to embrace the world's suffering, past and present, and to engage the hope that through its actions the community can embody freedom and reconciliation.[25]

---

[24] Ibid.

[25] Power, *Eucharistic Mystery*, 334. The hope implicit to this understanding of Christian remembrance is that tradition will be more authentically and completely remembered. The faith community is challenged to "give recognition to the place that Jewish people still hold in testifying to God's presence in the world. . . ." It is also challenged to repent for those victims whose suffering has not been remembered within the house of authority and to embrace previously excluded images of God and Christ represented within Third World, feminist, and other experiences of God's presence. See also David Tracy, "Religious Values after the Holocaust: A Catholic View," *Jews and Christians after the Holocaust*, ed. Abraham Peck (Philadelphia: Fortress Press, 1982); James White, *Christian Worship in North America—A Retrospective: 1955–1995* (Collegeville: The Liturgical Press, 1997) 175–88; Mary Barbara Agnew, "Liturgy and Christian Social Action," *The Landscape of Praise: Readings in Liturgical Renewal*, ed. Blair Gilmer Meeks (Valley Forge, Pa.: Trinity Press International, 1996) 44–52.

When the faith community is defined within the above parameters, as a mode of redemptive existence, then face-to-face relations become one of its defining features. Not only does this establish a different position for the stranger, but a second danger of settling into a house of authority is overcome, the danger of becoming a sacred "cult" to which individuals can escape for help with individual religious needs.

As Kavanagh argues, echoing the discussion in Chapter 2, the Church's recent history reflects a tendency to restrict the sacred to cultic understandings. By contrast, ancient theologians viewed the "Church" as a "function" of the faith. For them, the Church was a "holistic enterprise whose faith crisscrossed and interacted with every human experience and institution."[26] Their discussions of Church, Kavanagh argues, centered on the fact that early Christian communities emerged within an urban frame, their worship spilling over into the city in a transformative way.[27]

In the Constantinian era, for example, even as the service of the Lord's Day settled into a more "institutional" structure, worship had a "space-scale" that permeated the whole city. By making various aspects of its liturgy public, Christianity spread throughout the city's diverse neighborhoods. This was a primary goal of stational liturgies that developed in the fourth and fifth centuries; people moved from worship station to worship station throughout the city, connecting the streets and plazas, as well as churches and shrines, to God's presence.[28]

The ethos for worship in a contemporary mindset is quite different from this. The Church's institutional structures have become more cultic and individualistic. Farley's critique suggests that this development parallels the collapse of the "house of authority." Restoring ecclesia's redemptive potential, he insists, involves rediscovering the dialectical balance between its existence as a historical entity and its ability to mediate the elusive presence of God, a presence that transcends and transforms historical boundaries. It also means recogniz-

[26] Farley makes a distinction between "church" and ecclesia. "Church," in his conception, is the "totality which combines intersubjectivity, ecclesia's sociality and institutional structures." The distinction is not a clear one, but Farley seeks to differentiate between community at the level of its determinate intersubjectivity and how it presents itself to the world institutionally. See *Ecclesial Man*, 107–8; 179.

[27] Kavanagh, *On Liturgical Theology*, 29–30.

[28] John Baldovin, *Worship: City, Church, and Renewal* (Washington, D.C.: Pastoral Press, 1991) 5–8.

ing that participants in ecclesia are not those to whom are added the capacity to act in a certain way. As noted in Chapter 2, worship does not exist primarily to mediate individual salvation or to fulfill particular individual needs. Such a concept of worship reduces salvation and grace to idolatrous objects of self-securing. Rather, in ecclesia, the tendency toward self-securing is broken and authentic love for the other is made possible.

The function of what Farley calls a "post-authority" theological method, similar to liturgical theology, should be to establish a process of critical reflection through which the deep structures of communal action can be discerned. The goal of this method is to discover how pre-reflective truths or realities can be mediated in such a way that the meaning of those truths for everyday life is transformatively revealed.

Primary dependence on a biblical matrix of redemption history is not adequate for such a method. To establish an adequate method requires a reconfigured biblical foundation; arguments in support of an alternative biblical matrix can be found in the arena of recent biblical theology.

DEVELOPMENTS IN OLD TESTAMENT THEOLOGY

Biblical historical criticism intersects with Enlightenment assumptions that value objectivity, positivism, and scientific precision in the study of texts, assumptions that have held epistemological dominance until this recent era. Finding its most definitive form in the late nineteenth century, historical criticism has attempted to reconstruct the history and thought of ancient Israel and early Christianity using the tools of source criticism, textual criticism, biblical archaeology, form criticism, and traditions history.

Within this model, perhaps most fully developed in the work of von Rad, the central aim of Scripture is to describe God's actions in the historical circumstances of people. As Robert Gnuse notes, the Exodus and Resurrection are perceived within the historical model not only as primary theological symbols but also as the hermeneutical framework for interpreting other events depicted in Scripture. Scripture is viewed as a witness to God's actions in the course of history. This theme of "salvation history," or Heilgeschichte, has dominated the content and method of Old Testament theology.[29]

[29] Robert Gnuse, *Heilgeschichte as a Model for Biblical Theology: The Debate Concerning the Uniqueness and Significance of Israel's Worldview* (New York: College Theology Society University Press of America, 1989) 1.

With the lessening of history's dominance in contemporary times, alternative methods of Old Testament study have emerged. These approaches focus on how the biblical text and tradition provide within themselves a framework for various interpretations in a plurality of contexts. This focus intersects with current liturgical concerns for ecumenism and for dialogue with an increasing societal plurality. Kraftchick's insights point to this important liturgical theology/biblical theology intersection.

As he explains, recent biblical methods are more attuned to the role of biblical theology in drawing into conversation a diversity of communities of discourse and their individual values and commitments. This focus emphasizes that each type of interpretation that presents itself, whether it be feminist, liberation, phenomenological, or literary, is challenged by the current intellectual ethos to justify its use of a particular method. Similar challenges are directed toward the underlying assumptions of contemporary liturgical methods.

As these biblical models struggle to respond to societal questions and to existential realities that challenge their underlying presuppositions, it is increasingly apparent that claiming a place of dialogue in the public arena is an intersubjective undertaking: "It [justification] goes on in—but also between—communities of discourse whose rhetorical practices not only depend on and shape shared values and commitments but also disclose them on their intersubjective grounds."[30] Recognizing the intersubjective nature of biblical interpretation means that issues emphasized by biblical theology now center on how the social and political commitments of interpretive communi-

---

[30] Kraftchick, "Introduction," 7–12, uses feminist interpretations as an example of his point. The objective of some feminist models is to address issues of subordination. This objective, "together with the values and commitments funding that objective, play a role in justifying feminist interpretive strategies, methods, and theories." These objectives are different from those of historical-critical approaches and result in goals and methodological forms that diverge from historical-critical ones. It is at this point of divergence that a horizon of mutually-critical dialogue is possible.

In terms of liturgical theology, Marjorie Proctor-Smith, *In Her Own Rite: Constructing Feminist Liturgical Tradition* (Nashville: Abingdon Press, 1990) 30–5, suggests that it is at the point of the authority of tradition—and thus also of Scripture—that the feminist movement and the liturgical movement diverge most significantly; therefore, it is also at this point that lies fruitful ground for dialogue.

ties, both contemporary and biblical, influence the "truth" that is uncovered by the methodological process.

Most of the newer biblical methods point to the potential of biblical theology to provide a framework within which the interpretive voices of diverse communities can enter into dialogue, thus uncovering both limiting hegemonies and shared values and commitments. As Brueggemann notes, an important goal of current Old Testament theology is to "make available the polyphonic character of the text."[31] The implications of such an approach for liturgical concerns are many, not the least of which is the extent to which such a framework can ground liturgical method and thus provide a similar avenue of intersubjective relation and dialogue both within and among faith communities.

Before examining some of these emerging methods in greater detail and drawing out the implications for liturgical method, it is helpful first to identify problematic areas in Old Testament interpretive categories that rely primarily on historical norms.[32] Perdue provides a summary of the criticisms of the historical method.

First, history provides a description of Israelite society and religion but offers no precise method for bridging the gap between the historical situation and the contemporary era. The historical-critical method commonly argues by analogy how the historical context parallels the contemporary situation. Engaging present culture is not the primary aim of the descriptive approach.

A related critique is that historical criticism describes the multiple theologies of Israel but provides no means of integrating them, of creating a synthesis. As Farley insists, such an approach results in the fragmentation of theology and leads to the current dichotomy between empirical study of texts and application. Similar to Farley, many biblical scholars now give greater attention to a reflective or constructive strategy of interpretation whereby the questions of contemporary society are invited to dialogue with the text. In other

---

[31] Brueggemann, *Theology of the Old Testament*, 89, focuses on the "processes, procedures, and interactionist potential of the community present to the text." In this way, he suggests, it is possible to respect the plurality of voices that constitute the substance of the Old Testament but also allow for the inherent conflict within the Old Testament as Israel negotiates and renegotiates its truth claims.

[32] Gnuse, *Heilgeschichte as a Model for Biblical Theology*, 23.

words, newer approaches are concerned with how biblical theology addresses itself, in Farley's terms, "toward the world."[33]

A third critique is that historical methods offer no clear process for critical evaluation of their historical description of tradition. This parallels the critique directed toward liturgical theologies that have not adequately examined their own presuppositions and that do not have an internal framework for self-critique. Recent biblical approaches attempt to be more intentional in examining how the social and political commitments of their particular contexts influence the "truth" that is uncovered by the methodological process.

In addition to these problems enumerated by Perdue, one other area of concern is raised by theologian George Lindbeck; this concern is related to the critiques of liturgical methods outlined in Chapter 2 and invites our attention. Lindbeck is in the company of several critics who argue that the historical-critical method is largely responsible for making Scripture less accessible to the average person; in short, he suggests that the historical-critical method has played a role in perpetuating the gap between clergy and laity, or as formulated in liturgical circles, between theory and practice.

Lindbeck argues that a particular way of reading Scripture was formative of the faith of the early Church. With the advent of Enlightenment categories of knowing and the subsequent removal of interpretation from the faith community to the "scholarly" arena, Scripture's function as a center or foundation for a core of communal beliefs was diminished. Walter Wink expresses a similar insight: "The historical critical method has reduced the Bible to a dead letter. Our obeisance to technique has left the Bible sterile and ourselves empty. . . . It was based on an inadequate method, married to a false objectivism, subjected to uncontrolled technologism, separated from a vital community."[34] As

---

[33] Edward Farley, "Thinking Toward the World: A Case for Philosophical Pluralism in Theology," *American Journal of Theology and Philosophy* 14 (January 1993) 51–63. A recent approach to biblical theology that engages the text and contemporary questions is Bernhard Anderson, *From Creation to New Creation: Old Testament Perspectives* (Minneapolis: Augsburg Press, 1994). His work grows out of the understanding that theology is both descriptive and constructive.

[34] Walter Wink, *Transformation: Toward a New Paradigm for Biblical Study* (Philadelphia: Fortress Press, 1973) 4–15, as quoted in J.J.M. Roberts, "Historical-Critical Method, Theology and Contemporary Exegesis," *Biblical Theology: Problems and Perspectives—In Honor of J. Christiaan Beker,* ed. Steven

discussed earlier, such a criticism also resonates with liturgical theology. For example, many "theologies from worship" have gone far toward reuniting the academic study of liturgy with the experiential matrix of communal worship. However, while liturgical scholars such as Wainwright make explicit that their work is an individual and contextually shaped presentation of one version of the Christian vision, their methods generally do not go far enough in examining how these contextual predispositions shape the doctrines that they deem as normative for doxological expression. What results is that the theologian and secondary theology continue to function as guardians over the "correct" expressions of truth generated in communal worship.

One reason for the continued gap between clergy and laity in liturgical practice is that the historical paradigm has shaped the parameters of liturgical theology's biblical matrix or foundation. While the bifurcation of theory and practice, of *lex orandi* and *lex credendi*, has been lessened by the liturgical movement, the predominant reliance on the historical-critical paradigm in liturgical study remains.

Perdue suggests that there is a fundamental question behind developments in biblical theology in the past two centuries: "Is Old Testament theology a discipline that originates within theology or is it more a history of Israelite religion that sets forth the ideas, values and beliefs of an ancient community?"[35] In attempting to answer this question, the contributions of the historical-critical paradigm cannot be dismissed nor can new approaches authentically address themselves "toward the world" if they fail to make explicit the historical particularity of texts.[36]

What is needed is a revised formulation of history that maintains the dynamic tension between historical positivism, as it reveals God's

---

Kraftchick, Charles Myers, and Ben Ollenburger (Nashville: Abingdon Press, 1995) 132.

[35] Perdue, *The Collapse of History*, 306.

[36] A number of scholars, while recognizing the weaknesses of the historical-critical paradigm in the face of the contemporary situation, have maintained a respect for the continuing contribution of this approach to the current task of interpretation. Roberts carefully answers Lindbeck's critiques in "Historical-Critical Method, Theology and Contemporary Exegesis," 131–41. See also Ben Ollenburger, "Biblical Theology: Situating the Discipline," *Understanding the Word: Essays in Honor of Bernhard W. Anderson*, ed. James Butler et al. (Sheffield: JSOT Press, 1985) 37–62; Perdue, *The Collapse of History*, 306.

presence in historical events, and creation theology or cosmology, as it critically defines our understanding of history and redemption.[37] Not a few scholars have argued that Old Testament faith must be interpreted in such a "bipolar" fashion. Brueggemann highlights examples of these approaches: Claus Westermann on blessing and deliverance, Samuel Terrien on the aesthetic and ethical, Paul Hanson on the cosmic and teleological.[38]

Common to these studies are several goals: (1) to urge a corrective balance to the overemphasis on historical tradition; (2) to uncover enduring patterns that are constitutive of the canonical material but that do not result in a universalistic credo; (3) to establish a biblical theology from an epistemological foundation that allows for ecumenical dialogue; and (4) to maintain a historical/covenantal focus that avoids the ideological limitations of proposing a universal theme within the diversity of the biblical material.[39]

As seen earlier, Farley's work also seeks to examine the enduring elements, the deep structures, of faith and its texts without adopting an "unhistorical" approach. Farley's theological portraiture may help to frame a mutually critical dialogue between historical-critical biblical methods and emerging alternative methods, a dialogue that can also provide fertile ground for establishing a revised biblical matrix for liturgical theology. Before examining how theological portraiture might accomplish this, it is important to describe three recent biblical

---

[37] Perdue, *The Collapse of History*, 115; Robin Lovin and Frank Reynolds, eds., *Cosmogony and Ethical Order* (Chicago: University of Chicago Press, 1985); David Tracy and Nicholas Lash, eds., *Cosmology and Theology* (New York: Seabury Press, 1983); Anderson, *From Creation to New Creation: Old Testament Perspectives.*

[38] Walter Brueggemann, "A Shape for Old Testament Theology, I: Structure Legitimation," *Old Testament Theology: Essays on Structure, Theme and Text*, ed. Patrick Miller (Minneapolis: Fortress Press, 1992) 1–2. The focus on the bipolar elements in the Old Testament is somewhat dated now and has faced a number of critiques. More evident now, according to Brueggemann, is that scholarship revolves around rhetorical and sociological disciplines. His current treatment, however, continues to use a bi-polar schematization as a "grid" to illuminate the ongoing "dispute" in Israel's faith regarding its truth claims. See Brueggemann, *Theology of the Old Testament*, 72–3.

[39] Brueggemann, "A Convergence in Recent Old Testament Theologies," *Old Testament Theology: Essays on Structure, Theme and Text*, ed. Patrick Miller (Minneapolis: Fortress Press, 1992) 95–110.

methodologies and examine their importance to the project of correlating wisdom theology and liturgical theology.

New Paradigms in Old Testament Theology

SOCIAL-SCIENTIFIC STUDY OF THE OLD TESTAMENT

One of the new models outlined by Perdue stands within the parameters of the historical paradigm but combines it with contemporary social-scientific study. This model utilizes tools from sociology and anthropology to delineate the changing social organization of ancient Israel throughout its history.

An important element in this method, related to uncovering contextual presuppositions in the interpretive process, is the recognition that biblical texts are social products, reflecting the interests of groups that interacted both with institutions and communal life. As social products, biblical texts reflect a given community's or group's particular view or understanding of reality; in other words, the truths mediated by these texts are not absolute but shaped by the categories of meaning prevalent at that time and in that place.

Such a methodological awareness is not uncommon to liturgical study. Irwin's emphasis within liturgical theology involves the recognition that "text shapes context" and "context shapes text." As Irwin suggests, much of the liturgical movement has emphasized the recovery of liturgical texts, both as found within the biblical corpus and as they have developed throughout the Church's history. While this effort has been productive for establishing the origins of Christian worship, Irwin seeks to balance this focus by examining how liturgy is primarily an enacted communal event that includes but is not restricted to texts. His method emphasizes scrutinizing liturgical texts without abstracting them from their historical setting, arguing that each text originally functioned to mediate God's presence for a particular historical circumstance.[40]

Social-scientific approaches to Old Testament study dialogue with liturgical study at this point, particularly as they seek to demonstrate how the theology of ancient Israel corresponded to the socioeconomic, political, and cultural interests of its time. A brief description of Brueggemann's social-scientific/anthropological treatment of wisdom both describes how this model works and begins to suggest the role of

---

[40] Kevin Irwin, *Context and Text: Method in Liturgical Theology* (Collegeville: The Liturgical Press, 1994) 31–2.

wisdom in establishing a different methodological foundation for biblical theology and thus for liturgical theology.

Brueggemann argues that the early "written" form of wisdom was intimately connected to the sociopolitical development of Israel during the pre-monarchical and early monarchical period.[41] Israel, in the pre-monarchical period, reflected a departure from conventional modes of state organization common in Canaan. This departure from the norm was a governing model that Brueggmann calls the "covenantal-egalitarian experiment." Part of this experiment focused on revelation in the form of the Torah as an alternate model for controlling the community's mode of acquiring knowledge. In addition, this model was based on an equal distribution of goods and wealth and until the Davidic monarchy and the later Solomonic "state," had no central authority.

This social and political organization, Brueggemann continues, paralleling Farley's summary of the development of the Judeo-Christian house of authority, required religious justification to tie it to the covenantal theology that was the primary framework of meaning for people's lives. The institution of the temple was thus constructed, and Israel's traditional and ritual practices became centralized in order to link the political organization and ethos to the perceived purposes of God. In other words, along with a centralized bureaucratic power, the Israelites developed a centralized religious authority. In this new theological articulation, God "took up residence" in the Temple at Jerusalem; as a result, God was no longer perceived as an agent of transformation but as the "guarantor of the dynasty."

Such efforts to "justify" institutional forms have continued throughout our religious history and are at the crux of feminist and Third World critiques of liturgy in particular. Recalling Farley's treatment of this subject in Chapter 3, similar developments have presented themselves in modern political and intellectual institutions. The risk is that these institutional forms will become substitutes for the reality content they mediate. In other words, when tradition fails to be self-critical and self-reflective, it risks merely protecting the status quo rather than mediating ultimate truth.

---

[41] Walter Brueggemann, "The Social Significance of Solomon as a Patron of Wisdom," *The Sage in Israel and the Ancient Near East,* ed. John G. Gammie and Leo Perdue (Winona Lake, Ind.: Eisenbrauns, 1990) 129–32.

This tendency, Farley argues, is common to institutions, particularly since institutional forms grow out of the human need and desire for self-securing. This is demonstrated in the development of the wisdom corpus. As Brueggemann points out, the early sages, as seen in Proverbs, had a role not unlike that of the court sages in Egypt and Mesopotamia, operating out of a pedagogical model that was inclined to be conserving of the established sociopolitical system.

What makes Proverbs a dynamic dialogue partner for the contemporary era is the fact that even as the sages attempt to preserve tradition amidst cultural changes that drew that tradition into serious question, they also demonstrate a willingness to enter into dialogue with the world and to create a community of faith that is a "world-in-process" within the created order.[42] As Brueggemann explains, the period of the United Monarchy (1000–921 B.C.E.) brought to Israel a visibility and affluence not experienced prior to that time. Faced with intellectual advances and cultural pluralism for which the Mosaic tradition had no adequate answers, the sages attempted "a radical reformulation of the old tradition with reference to the new situation."[43] In effect, the sages, not unlike many within the contemporary liturgical movement, sought both to maintain the distinctiveness of tradition and to dialogue meaningfully with the larger society.

Early wisdom, for example, maintains that there is a predictability within the created order; it also insists that human beings have the potential to discover within the created order the clues or "wisdom" necessary for virtuous living. This, along with the certitude that Israel was God's "chosen" community, gave the sages a peculiar optimism. They had a firm and continuing belief that virtuous living would lead to success or the "good" life, while vice would lead ultimately to destruction. Examples of this conviction can be found in Proverbs:

[42] To advance this argument does not mean that Wisdom escapes the cultural assumptions of the Near East; in other words, a direct parallel to contemporary concerns cannot be made. It does, however, offer an orientation different from that of the prophetic and historical books. See O'Connor, "Wisdom Literature and Experience of the Divine," 183.

[43] Brueggemann, *In Man We Trust*, 48, relies on scholarship that sees Proverbs as dated within the Solomonic period. Dated this early, Proverbs is viewed as a dynamic attempt at faith in a time when old traditions were considered inadequate. Proverbs 10:1 and 25:1 suggest an origin in the Solomonic period, and this corresponds to evidence that Wisdom was part of the Solomonic court (1 Kgs 4:29-34).

"The wicked covet the proceeds of wickedness,
  but the root of the righteous bears fruit" (12:12).

"Those who despise the word bring destruction on themselves,
  but those who respect the commandment will be rewarded" (13:13).

Eventually, historical events occurred that did not support the truth claims of tradition. Skepticism, already nibbling around the edges of traditional faith, intensified, and at least two responses to it emerged.[44] One response was the redemption theology of Deuteronomy, a theology whose development exemplifies how a community's perceptions of God's purposes can become concretized into dogma when historical circumstances draw tradition into question.[45]

In this response, the Yahwistic view prevailed. Belief in humanity's potential diminished while belief in God's sovereignty increased. Ultimately, in this perspective, knowledge of God or the world was denied to humans. The foundation for the epistemological crisis addressed by later wisdom was thus created.[46]

[44] James Crenshaw, *Old Testament Wisdom: An Introduction* (Atlanta: John Knox Press, 1981) 190–208.

[45] A similar response has emerged in the face of contemporary religious skepticism. As John Baker, "Epistemological and Historical Remarks on a Present Conflict," *Perspectives in Religious Studies* 15 (Summer 1989) 121–31, discusses, skepticism insists that the reasons offered as justification for particular truth claims are always subject to the same questions as the claim itself. Carried to its logical conclusion, this argument implies that it is not possible to know anything absolutely about the world; we can believe and act upon beliefs, but we cannot demonstrate absolutely that they are true. Dogmatists respond to this challenge by asserting that there are authoritative truth claims immune to skepticism and that these dogmatic claims are the foundation for all other knowledge claims. Fideists agree with the skeptics but insist that there are basic beliefs grounded "in faith" that nevertheless serve as the foundation for knowledge. For both fideists and skeptics, the prescribed set of beliefs is the foundation of knowledge.

This discussion is of particular interest to liturgical theology because one of liturgical theology's goals has been to discover a foundational pattern or deep structure that is common to a multiplicity of liturgies. See also Crenshaw, *Old Testament Wisdom*, 191–5.

[46] Crenshaw, *Old Testament Wisdom*, argues that skepticism plays an important role in theological development. See also Franklin Baumer, *Religion and the Rise of Skepticism* (New York: Harcourt, Brace and World, 1960).

An alternative response to skepticism, argues Crenshaw, was that of the sages, particularly as it is found in the canonical books of Job and Ecclesiastes. In the Joban narrative, wisdom confronts challenges to faith that emerge when the authoritative teachings of tradition do not respond adequately to the existential realities of a particular historical circumstance.

As we shall argue in greater detail later, a different aspect of Judaism's theological thinking emerges in Job; as Job struggles to defend his integrity in the face of undeserved suffering, a more eschatological view of faith is expressed. The Joban narrative voices the firm conviction that God will one day vindicate Job's innocence; it also insists that God's creation, in spite of all appearances to the contrary, is good and that meaning for life can still be found within it.

The response to skepticism in Ecclesiastes is even more radical than that of Job. Koheleth, facing the troubling situations of his era, is unable to overcome the sense that God is indifferent to human concerns. He concludes that all human searching for knowledge is absurdity.

Taken together, Job and Ecclesiastes represent a shift in world view in which the sages attempted to account for realities of life that made traditional theological constructs suspect. In this, they refused either to abandon tradition entirely or to support its principles uncritically. They offered instead a faith world view distinct from the Yahwistic one (in which God guides the events of history toward a particular goal or conclusion). In fact, the whole notion of God choosing a certain nation and fighting on its behalf became foreign to sapiential discourse as the sages increasingly understood truth to be revealed primarily in the creative act, in God's immanence.[47]

Again, Farley's understanding of salvation history intersects with this perspective; God's presence, in the sages' view and in Farley's theological model, is not limited to a particular institution or nation.[48] There is an unboundedness to God's presence, the sense that God's truth transcends established human institutions to permeate all of creation.

As the preceding summary of Brueggemann's social-scientific approach implies, biblical theology's dialogue with anthropology and

[47] Ibid., 190. See also R.B.Y. Scott, "Solomon and the Beginnings of Wisdom in Israel," *Supplements to Vetus Testamentum* 3 (1955) 262; and Terrien, *The Elusive Presence*, 351.

[48] Farley, *Ecclesial Man*, 168.

sociology has led to a reconfiguration of Old Testament theology. This configuration, Perdue notes, is linked in some ways to liberation theology, particularly as it illuminates how biblical writings are social products that reflect the interests and interactions of particular groups.

An example of the combination of liberation theology with Old Testament studies is the work of Norman Gottwald. Gottwald traces the structural development of Israel's social organization through three major movements: "the intertribal confederacy (Israel's revolutionary beginnings), the monarchy (Israel's counterrevolutionary establishment), and home rule under great empires (Israel's colonial recovery)."[49] His basic hermeneutical foundation, intersecting both with critical theory and current efforts at liturgical renewal, is that religion and its symbols reflect, criticize and legitimate social systems. Faith communities, in effect, are a matrix of institutional, personal and social forces that shape the ideologies and world views of participants. The theological enterprise cannot legitimately extract universal or dogmatic values and principles from the social matrix that shaped them.

Similar arguments have emerged within the liturgical movement on at least two levels. First, liturgical theologians within Fagerberg's methodological type of "liturgical theology" argue, similar to Gottwald, that theological knowing is generated through participation in the worship forms of a faith community that is in actuality a matrix of personal, social, and political factors. The knowledge mediated in worship forms, thus understood, cannot be extracted from participation in the ritual itself.

On a second level, liturgical scholars such as Power, Saliers, and Wainwright bring to their work an eschatological focus, particularly in reference to the Eucharist. A major aim of liturgical reform since the Second Vatican Council has been to recover the eschatological hope of early Christian worship. Saliers demonstrates how this eschatological focus is actually rooted in the act of liturgy.[50] For him, as for Wain-

---

[49] Perdue, *The Collapse of History*, 79–80, notes several works of Gottwald. See Norman Gottwald, *The Tribes of Yahweh* (Maryknoll, N.Y.: Orbis Books, 1979); and Norman Gottwald, *The Hebrew Bible—A Socio-Literary Introduction* (Philadelphia: Fortress Press, 1985). Gottwald's work is not specific to the Wisdom corpus but elements of it pertain to Wisdom's historical development.

[50] Don Saliers, *Worship as Theology: Foretaste of Glory Divine* (Nashville: Abingdon Press, 1994) 49–69, suggests that a primary impetus of Christian prayer and worship is "the cry for God's will and covenant promises in Jesus

wright and Power, the redemption of history occurs as the memory of the oppressed is recovered, as creation is seen as a unified whole, and as all of humanity is invited to gather around Christ's table as equal participants in the feast and in the dialogue.

A complementary eschatological focus grows out of the connection between Old Testament theology and liberation theology cited above. In sociological models of Old Testament theology, for example, the goal of salvation history is the realization of God's reign. God's reign is perceived as present in only a partial manifestation. The purpose of theology, in this eschatological framework, is to challenge faith communities to embody in their praxis a continually renewed vision of God's reign.

While a liberation approach to Old Testament theology is actually an adaptation of the history paradigm, its appropriation in liturgical theology involves at the very least an expansion of our understanding of redemption history. As noted earlier, Farley describes redemption as a mode of existence in which disruptive or tragic human existence is modified and salvation history is transcended. As he argues, in line with liberation theology and much of liturgical criticism, this eschatological goal is undermined by the fact that in every age the Church has been tempted to exchange ecclesia for other modes of sociality. The ancient form of such a substitution was institutionalism; a contemporary version is individualism.[51]

Perdue notes that social-scientific study is seen more as a partner to historical-critical method than as a replacement for it. More radical departures from the historical paradigm have also developed in contemporary scholarship.

CREATION IN CONTEMPORARY OLD TESTAMENT THEOLOGY

A second emerging model for Old Testament study that Perdue links specifically to the wisdom corpus is focused on creation. Several stimuli for this focus can be highlighted.

First, cosmology and anthropology have increasingly gained attention in theological circles.[52] These interests are because of the contemporary existential crises alluded to throughout this work.

Christ to be made real." See also Geoffrey Wainwright, *Eucharist and Eschatology* (London: Epworth Press, 1971).

[51] Farley, *Ecclesial Man*, 184.

[52] See Lovin and Reynolds, eds., *Cosmogony and Ethical Order*; and Tracy and Lash, eds., *Cosmology and Theology*.

A second stimulus is the recognition that our understandings of human nature, history, and redemption are intimately related to how we understand cosmology. Contemporary scholars are increasingly aware that the question of human salvation cannot be abstracted from our connectedness to and understanding of the rest of the created world.[53] Scholars in this arena give voice to the insight that humanity's eschatological hope and vision of redemption are inseparably connected to the destiny of the cosmos for which we are ethically responsible.

Such an understanding is not uncommon to liturgical theology. For example, Lathrop also emphasizes that liturgy's concept of creation is eschatological. The juxtapositions of worship constantly praise God for the goodness of creation; however, the dynamic framework of worship implies that "thanksgiving for creation does not need to be the same thing as affirmation of certain static orders of creation." The structure of the ordo itself, says Lathrop, reminds us that God continues to create. Reflected even in the act of gathering on the "eighth day" is the eschatological sense that creation is not complete.[54]

Similar to what the sages recognized in their daily discoveries of God's presence and purpose, the liturgy's gatherings and symbolic meanings insist that the world is still "in-process." Thus, while liturgy points to the fact that the cosmos is humanity's home, created by God, it also urges people of faith to challenge those structures within the cosmos that cause suffering or that impede the justice of God.[55]

One scholar whose focus is on creation is Claus Westermann. His work brings together two major theological poles in the Old Testa-

---

[53] John Collins, "New Testament Cosmology," *Cosmology and Theology*, ed. David Tracy and Nicholas Lash (New York: Seabury Press, 1983) 3–7.

[54] Gordon Lathrop, *Holy Things: A Liturgical Theology* (Minneapolis: Fortress Press, 1993) 210–1. Brian Gerrish has noted a similar eschatological vein in Calvin's eucharistic theology. Gerrish emphasizes that for Calvin, "authentic humanity is constituted by the act of thanksgiving to the Maker of heaven and earth whose goodness has prepared a table before us." For Calvin the Creator's love and the Redeemer's love are the same. Creation and redemption are both the work of God. See Brian Gerrish, *Grace and Gratitude: The Eucharistic Theology of John Calvin* (Minneapolis: Fortress Press, 1993) 128.

[55] Walter Brueggemann, foreword to *From Creation to New Creation: Old Testament Perspectives*, by Bernhard Anderson (Minneapolis: Fortress Press, 1994) vii.

ment—soteriology (history) and blessing (creation).[56] Westermann's soteriology is closely tied to von Rad's work. He focuses on the ancient historical credo that developed in Exodus and was expanded in the covenantal theology of the Deuteronomist. In this perspective salvation is the ultimate goal of history.

In discussing the second pole, Westermann focuses on creation texts, including wisdom, explicating the often ignored theme of blessing in the Old Testament in which God is viewed as enhancing and sustaining life. Westermann argues that creation is more than the first of God's historical acts; for him, creation is the foundation of a history that finds its specific redemptive focus in the people of Israel.[57]

Perdue rightly observes that for Westermann history and creation operate dialectically to embrace all of Old Testament theology. In this way, Westermann restores a balance between the historical paradigm and those elements of the Old Testament that have been overlooked or marginalized.

As Brueggemann notes regarding Westermann's dialectic, structuring biblical theology in this way draws the Old Testament out of its isolation in the historical-critical arena and focuses on its rootedness in a believing community. We have already seen how this move correlates with liturgical theology and with Farley's efforts to restore the notion of theology as a habitus.

A number of scholars argue that wisdom functions within a creation framework. Currently, however, no comprehensive studies explicitly set forth the creation theology of wisdom. Perdue suggests four major approaches to wisdom that point in this direction: anthropology, world order, theodicy, and the dialectic of anthropology and cosmology.[58]

First, Walther Zimmerli argues that wisdom represents the human quest to master life. He suggests that anthropology is actually at the center of sapiential reflection. The goal of the wise person is anthropological: to rule over creation as God's representative and to seek the "good" life through virtuous living.[59]

[56] Claus Westermann, *Creation* (Philadelphia: Fortress Press, 1974); Claus Westermann, *Blessing in the Bible and the Life of the Church* (Philadelphia: Fortress Press, 1978).

[57] Perdue, *The Collapse of History*, 124–5.

[58] Ibid., 129.

[59] Walther Zimmerli, "The Place and Limit of the Wisdom in the Framework of the Old Testament Theology," *Studies in Ancient Israelite Wisdom,* ed. H. M. Orlinsky (New York: KTAV Publishing House, 1976).

World order, or cosmology, is a second major approach to examining creation in wisdom theology. Several scholars, including Harmut Gese, Hans Heinrich Schmid, Hans-Jurgen Hermisson, and Bernhard Anderson, have produced studies that focus on world order. Schmid argues, for example, that prior to the end of the state of Judah, order or "justice" was not a static or dogmatic principle; order was believed to be historically or contextually conditioned. After the Exile, an ahistorical concept of order developed. In this it was determined that certain human actions led to particular consequences. This aspect of tradition is challenged in the Joban narrative.[60]

In his work "Creation, Righteousness, and Salvation: 'Creation Theology' as the Broad Horizon of Biblical Theology," Schmid makes a sweeping claim for creation, conceived within the parameters of world order, as the fundamental theme of biblical theology in its entirety.[61] Central to this understanding is a focus on how the faith community is formative of a person's character and moral world view.

James Crenshaw approaches wisdom from the perspective of theodicy. He argues that the central theme of wisdom is a questioning of the justice of God.[62] According to Crenshaw's argument, the sages challenged redemption history's picture of God. Faced with the skepticism and pluralism of their time, the sages turned from a predominant reliance on history to creation to defend both God's presence and God's justice.

Finally, Roland Murphy approaches creation theology in wisdom from the perspective of anthropology and cosmology. Framing his perspective as a convergence of anthropology and cosmology, Murphy argues that Israel made no real distinction between creation and redemption but understood both as constitutive of faith. The sages, he explains, believed that their observations and experience of creation provided a particular revelation of God; acquiring wisdom or knowl-

[60] This brief summary is paraphrased from Perdue's own summary. See *The Collapse of History*, 132–3.

[61] H. H. Schmidt, "Creation, Righteousness, and Salvation: 'Creation Theology' as the Broad Horizon of Biblical Theology," *Creation in the Old Testament*, ed. Bernhard Anderson (Philadelphia: Fortress Press, 1984). See also Hans-Jurgen Hermisson, "Observations on the Creation Theology in Wisdom," *Israelite Wisdom*, ed. J. G. Gammie, W. A. Brueggemann, J. M. Ward (Philadelphia: Fortress Press, 1984).

[62] James Crenshaw, "Popular Questioning of the Justice of God," *Zeitschrift für die alttestamentliche Wissenschaft* 82 (1970) 380–95.

edge of God is both a rational affair and an experiential one that involves a continuing dialogue with the created world.[63]

Having briefly outlined several emerging models of Old Testament theology that focus on wisdom in a creation framework, it is possible to suggest some implications for liturgical theology. In his work *From Creation to New Creation,* Bernhard Anderson makes a statement that establishes what is perhaps the most vital link between creation theology and liturgical concerns: "The affirmation that God is Creator arose originally out of the worship experience of Israel, not out of the reflections of a systematic theologian or philosopher."[64] To phrase it in terms similar to that of contemporary liturgical theologians, primary theology, or knowledge of God and of human beings as created in the image of God, is rooted in liturgical practices of the faith community. From this foundational link, several forays into liturgical theology can be made.

Much as contemporary existential crises have sparked a renewed focus within biblical theology on cosmology and anthropology, so, too, have issues such as the current ecological crisis and the threat of nuclear war influenced liturgical theology. Much of Power's work in liturgy, for example, arises from the cultural and sociological issues of this age.

One of Power's stated aims in *Unsearchable Riches: The Symbolic Nature of the Liturgy* is to examine how contemporary crises influence liturgy. Many of the crises of the contemporary era, Power emphasizes, are clearly cosmological ones—namely the "holocaust of the Jewish people under the Nazi regime, and . . . the imminent nuclear holocaust which threatens the entire world."[65]

As Power considers what it means to profess Christ in the midst of the despair created by these holocausts, he parallels the theological perspective inherent in wisdom that is described above. Power's method grows out of an awareness that human salvation is interconnected with the worshiping community's perception of and actions toward the rest of the created world.

[63] Roland Murphy, "Wisdom and Creation," *Journal of Biblical Literature* 104 (1985) 3–11.

[64] Anderson, *From Creation to New Creation,* 1. Arguing from the perspective of the creation stories in Genesis, Anderson points out that the Genesis story reaches its climax in the observance of the Sabbath, a fact that he says witnesses to the "existential foundation of the creation faith in the Israelite cultus."

[65] David Power, *Unsearchable Riches: The Symbolic Nature of Liturgy* (New York: Pueblo, 1984) 1–5.

As noted in the previous chapter, paralleling Farley's reflective ontology, Power approaches contemporary questions related to cosmology and anthropology by arguing for a renewed attention to ontology. In his revised ontological treatment of symbols, Power suggests that liturgy is both humanity's self-expression and a manifestation of God's mystery, of God's presence in creation.[66]

As Power explains, at one level the ontological question examines how the symbolic, how the juxtapositions in worship, are constitutive of persons and communities. At the same time, it points out that worship also mediates God's presence to humanity. Liturgy transforms human experience and expresses the inscrutable.[67]

Not unlike that adopted by the ancient sages, Power's model of theology draws upon tradition but also demonstrates the necessity of reappropriating that tradition in order to continue adequately to reflect God's presence. Because "truth" is elusive, Power argues, a process of critical reflection is needed that establishes an ongoing dialectic in which theology and culture are mutually influencing. Worship provides such a horizon:

"A kind of general principle is at work in the midst of such critical reflection which has to do with the nonidentity of the Word with any form in which it is spoken and of the Spirit with any voice in which it speaks. The absolute cannot be identified with any human culture, prayer or institution. . . . Worship in its very listening to God functions as a critique of life and culture. It is the fitting place to struggle for freedom to hear the Word and let the Spirit speak."[68]

An ongoing process of critical reflection can prevent the Church from rationalizing its symbols, from reducing them to their conceptual content.

Dominant epistemological models tend to reduce symbols to concepts. This means that in the Church's usage of symbols, concepts claim dominance, diminishing the authority of the truths mediated by the symbols. What happens, Power suggests, is that traditional and familiar concepts such as "original sin" or "institution" become substi-

[66] Ibid., 172–210.

[67] Ibid. As Power explains, symbols mediate between experience and reality, between the cognitive and the affective. They both penetrate the unconscious and provide the only language or expression of these deep structures available to humanity.

[68] Ibid., 174.

tutes for the more dynamic and metaphorical images found in the communal stories that generated the concepts—for example, the story of Adam and Eve in the garden or of Jesus' last meal with the disciples.

Related to this, as Farley explains, "words of power" or deep symbols empower religious communities. The current crises—epistemological, cosmological, and anthropological—have diminished the functionality of these symbols. One reason, Farley contends, is because the concepts or institutions through which these formative ideals found expression traditionally have been substituted for the ideals themselves.

In actuality, Farley continues, deep symbols have four essential features: "normativity, enchantment, fallibility (relativity and corruptibility), and location in a master narrative." What Farley illuminates in detailing these four features is that words of power point in several directions, "initially to the mysteries that attend our own personal being and also the world itself. . . . And beyond these things looms that far horizon that we only know as enfleshed in words of command, blessing, and warning, the divine mystery."[69]

There is a sense in which words of power are historical, expressing the determinancy of a community; as such they are relative to historical conditions and are fallible. They arise within a given community and mirror the ideological tendencies of that historical context. At the same time, however, words of power are "enchanted." They are connected to the mystery of creation and thus resist being limited by particular linguistic formulations.

When a community allows the "concepts," the expressive categories, of its deep symbols to become absolutized, both Power and Farley argue, then the historical and constructed character of them is lost; so, too, is the deeper meaning they originally sought to mediate.

In light of this, what is needed is a framework for critical reflection that restores to liturgy's symbols, to the Church's words of power,

[69] Edward Farley, *Deep Symbols: Their Postmodern Effacement and Reclamation* (Valley Forge, Pa.: Trinity Press International, 1996) 3. Farley cites Philip Rieff in this regard. Rieff is a social scientist who argues that in this contemporary "therapeutic" society, moral categories are replaced with management and psychological discourse. See Philip Rieff, *The Triumph of the Therapeutic: The Uses of Faith after Freud* (New York: Harper and Row, 1968). Such an argument parallels from a sociological perspective concerns voiced by Schmemann and others about how liturgy's symbols are affected when the Church becomes focused on the needs and desires of individual persons.

their ability both to establish historical moorings and also to point beyond themselves to the immanent and elusive presence of God. Cosmological language within the Old Testament in general and in wisdom in particular metaphorically connects creation and redemption. This widens the historical vision beyond the political and cultural horizons of Davidic and Solomonic Israel to embrace the rest of the created universe and to point to the cosmic design of salvation.[70]

As Anderson argues in his discussion of the Genesis creation narratives, and as we will see reflected in Proverbs and Job, creation is inseparably tied to the historical narratives of God's saving acts. Restoring the "creation" pole of the dialectic challenges us to see the meaning of human history as grounded in creation. As contemporary theologians Tracy and Lash have emphasized, this means that if the Christian tradition is fully to understand redemption, then it must recover a biblical understanding of creation. As they put it, "No Christian theology can claim adequacy to the Christian tradition by, in effect, retrieving only God and the self (including the social and historical self) while quietly dropping 'world' out of the picture."[71] An adequate understanding of Christian history is intricately tied to cosmological questions.

One key to revitalizing liturgy's symbolism lies in the restoration of its metaphorical framework and discourse, in moving beyond the facticity of "concepts" to the narrative and experiential world which generated them. This requires dialogue with creation, with the immense and interconnected data of the cosmos, rather than discourse only within the limited parameters of historical analysis and description.[72]

Wisdom reflects within its literary and theological framework the first two kinds of discourse that Power suggests are vital to authentic liturgy: (1) the metaphorical language of blessing and memorial, and (2) a level of ontological discourse that holds in tension the elusiveness of God's presence. As will be seen in the next chapter, a recognition of both the historicality and linguisticality of human existence is

[70] Anderson, *From Creation to New Creation*, 4–18, emphasizes that the understanding of God as Creator originates in the experiences of the worshiping community, Israel. The basic foundation of Israelite worship, he argues, is the confession of YHWH as Lord. Israel understands creation as affirming and expressing the same faithfulness that characterized the covenant relationship.

[71] Tracy and Lash, eds., "Editorial Reflections," 89.

[72] Power, *Unsearchable Riches*, 190–3; Brueggemann, *In Man We Trust*, 116–7.

central to sapiential discourse. The sages "constructed a world in which to live (historicality), and their tools for this world construction were metaphors that were embodied in both poetry and narrative (linguisticality)."[73]

Wisdom, using dynamic metaphorical language, discovers God in the midst of the struggles, doubts, and joys of daily existence. God's presence is consistently tied to creation because the presence of God is always found in ordinary life.[74] The same insight has been raised in contemporary liturgical discussions; the juxtaposition of the objects, actions, and questions of daily living with the Word of God allows for the disruption of the hold of evil and offers hope for change.

Discussions of metaphor in biblical texts have led to a field of study called the "theology of imagination."[75] Important to correlating wisdom and liturgical theology is David Tracy's use of a theology of imagination in treating classic texts, namely Scripture. A classic text, he explains, possesses a certain meaning at its origin. However, the same text also transcends that specific historical time to engage people in other generations. In other words, a classic contains meaning that both defines the values of a historical community and demands reinterpretation for contemporary communities.[76] Interpreting Scripture as a classic text involves historical, sociological, and literary-critical approaches that examine how the text speaks to the contemporary situation, a process that Tracy argues requires the use of imagination.

In *Analogical Imagination: Christian Theology and the Culture of Pluralism*, Tracy delineates the two classical types of theological language—

---

[73] Perdue, *Wisdom and Creation*, 57.

[74] O'Connor, "Wisdom Literature and Experience of the Divine," 188–9.

[75] Perdue, *The Collapse of History*, 264–5, explains that "imagination" in this sense is not to be equated with fantasy or non-truth. Instead, imagination refers to that which "is less bound by convention and orthodoxy as the psyche seeks to invent or reinvent new realities that suggest or open up the possibility of the reorientation of human life and devotion." What Perdue calls "religious imagination" is that constructive way of knowing that refuses to be limited to dogmatic constructs and that results in a "redescription of reality."

[76] David Tracy, *Analogical Imagination: Christian Theology and the Culture of Pluralism* (New York: Crossroad, 1981); and David Tracy, "The Analogical Imagination in Catholic Theology," *Talking about God: Doing Theology in the Context of Modern Pluralism*, ed. David Tracy and John B. Cobb Jr. (New York: Seabury Press, 1983). See also Sallie McFague, *Metaphorical Theology: Models of God in Religious Language* (Philadelphia: Fortress Press, 1982).

analogical and dialectical. He argues that primary theological language, generated within the faith community as it experiences God's presence in its own historical situation, is analogical or metaphorical language.[77]

As seen previously, Hilkert uses Tracy's categories to argue that the most significant differences between Protestant and Catholic theologies may occur at the level of "imagination." The dialectical imagination stresses the distance between God and humanity, the hiddenness of God, and the need for grace as redemption. The sacramental imagination, or what Tracy calls the analogical imagination, emphasizes the immanence of God, the creation of humans in the image of God, and the mystery of the incarnation. Some of the central tenets of sacramental imagination directly correlate elements of creation theology in the wisdom corpus explicated above—namely the goodness of creation, creation's redemptive power, the presence of the Holy Spirit (or wisdom) in the faith community, and the dialogical process of salvation.

Hilkert suggests that dialectical and sacramental imaginations diverge most prominently on questions of anthropology.[78] She maintains, however, that preachers "name grace" in human experience and history only when sacramental theology dialogues with the central categories of dialectical theology. The same could be said for how liturgical forms "name grace" or mediate redemption.

Tracy echoes her conclusion, arguing that "serious Christian theological speech about God will be ultimately analogical without abandoning the insights of negative dialectics." He suggests that an integration of these two modes of speech embrace both the disclosive and the elusive presence of God as revealed in Christ.[79] This notion will form the foundation for the specific treatment of sapiential language and liturgical language in the next chapter.

In terms of biblical theology, Brueggemann proposes a theology of imagination for appropriating Old Testament texts for the present. Brueggemann agrees with Terrien, Westermann, and other contemporary biblical theologians that the Old Testament develops within a

[77] David Tracy, "Analogy and Dialectic: God-Language," *Talking About God: Doing Theology in the Context of Modern Pluralism*, ed. David Tracy and John B. Cobb Jr. (New York: Seabury Press, 1983) 29–30.

[78] Mary Catherine Hilkert, *Naming Grace: Preaching and the Sacramental Imagination* (New York: Continuum, 1997) 30.

[79] Tracy, "Analogy and Dialectic," 38.

dialogical framework. Brueggemann's own framework for interpreting the Old Testament is found in two related essays: "A Shape for Old Testament Theology, I: Structure Legitimation" and "A Shape for Old Testament Theology, II: Embrace of Pain." In these foundational essays, Brueggemann argues that Scripture is a historical or classic text that also makes normative claims for faith communities of every era. Discovering what claims of tradition are transformative for the present involves seeing the structure of Old Testament theology in a particular way. Brueggemann describes this structure as an interplay of "structure legitimation" and "embrace of pain."[80]

The Old Testament, Brueggemann's sociopolitical model suggests, understands God from the perspective of the traditional theologies of a particular sociocultural world. However, it also pushes beyond tradition, imagining God as one who enters into existential realities. In the Old Testament, God is both immanent and transcendent.

In the "common" theology, or traditional theology, of the Old Testament sociocultural world, God rules over the cosmos by decisively acting in history. This common theology, argues Brueggemann, is contractual in nature; it is a crucial part of the structure of Old Testament faith and has been the primary conversation partner in most Old Testament theology until this time.[81]

This reliance on common theology, wherein there is an orderliness to life and actions that leads to certain consequences, is evident in the reality constructs of the wisdom corpus.[82] In fact, contractual theology, seen in the Mosaic traditions, the Deuteronomist, the prophets, and wisdom, can be said to be a foundation of Israel's faith.

However, as noted in relation to the development of the wisdom corpus, the danger of relying solely on common theology is that it

---

[80] Brueggemann, *Theology of the Old Testament*, xvi–xvii, has recently developed a new framework for interpreting the Old Testament, one that he believes is more appropriate to the epistemological and sociocultural realities of this contemporary age and that engages the plurality of Israel's own statements about its faith's truth claims. He calls this process "testimony-dispute-advocacy" and argues that it reflects the extent to which theological claims in the Old Testament are testimonies open to clarification, review, and counter-assertions. This process of clarification or "dispute" occurs within the Old Testament itself.

[81] Brueggemann, "Old Testament Theology, I: Structure Legitimation," 13–15.

[82] Von Rad, *Wisdom in Israel*, 122.

may become dogmatic to the point that God's institutional representatives are believed to transcend everyday life. If this happens, contractual theology becomes ideological hegemony that legitimates the power structures of the elite or controlling minority.

Proctor-Smith and other liturgical critics would agree with Brueggemann that this contractual theology, to the extent that it legitimates hierarchy and oppression, requires sharp critique. What Brueggemann suggests is the most transformative critique of common theology is the fact of pain in our world, or as Farley might state it, the fact of the tragic structuring of existence.

In the dialogue between Job and his friends, for example, the traditional contractual theology of coherence and empiricism reflected in the friends' speeches implies that where pain occurs there must be a human failure or sin that needs correction. The ultimate assumption? Those who face pain must have violated the "contract." The response of wisdom to this traditional theology, couched in the working out of Job's existential crisis, is to embrace pain.

Brueggemann explains what this means in his second essay. Contractual theology, as he describes it, focuses on God as creator and on God in relation to creation. This is only one pole of the Old Testament's structure. Old Testament theology often participates in structure legitimation; it tends to identify the "good" life and coherence in creation with the current dominant social structure. However, parts of Old Testament theology are also intent on acknowledging existential realities in which the assertions of contractual theology are not adequate or appropriate.[83]

When Israel's historical experiences fail to support the truth claims of this traditional theology, for example, a theological crisis results and an alternative theology develops, namely that represented in wisdom responses such as Job and Ecclesiastes. This alternative theology "embraces the pain" of living within the tragic structuring of human existence and challenges the oppressive structures of tradition.

One reason why Brueggemann's assessment of Old Testament theology is so important to liturgical concerns is that the current cultural perception of faith has been shaped by a kind of non-reflective contractual theology, one that too easily supports the status quo. As Brueggemann puts it, this contractual theology lacks a human face.

[83] Brueggemann, "Old Testament Theology, II: Embrace of Pain," *Old Testament Theology: Essays on Structure, Theme and Text*, ed. Patrick Miller (Minneapolis: Fortress Press, 1992) 22–44.

Farley's understanding of the "community of the face" necessarily emerges again at this point. When the Christian community functions as a "community of the face," it exists primarily as a horizon of redemption within which the spheres of human reality meet and are drawn toward the ultimate reality of God's creative presence. In this understanding, redemption is not solely nor even primarily contractual. Rather, redemption is intersubjective in nature; it occurs as the discourse of evil within human institutions is disrupted by God's Word and by the actions that are shaped by that Word.

Chapter 7 will examine how a non-contractual or non-transactional understanding of redemption liberates the traditional Christian symbol of the cross, freeing it from ideologies that use it to justify inequalities and to perpetuate injustice.

IMPLICATIONS OF CONTEMPORARY BIBLICAL THEOLOGY FOR LITURGICAL RENEWAL

This chapter began with the assertion that a three-way dialogue between liturgical theology, Farley's philosophical theology, and biblical theology is a mutually influencing conversation. As it reintegrates previously fragmented disciplines, this conversation can provide a foundation for renewal of worship forms that (1) maintain a rootedness in tradition, and (2) aid in restoring the Church as an authentic participant in public discourse. Several conclusions can be drawn that support this thesis.

First, as liturgical scholars and biblical scholars have separately demonstrated in recent years, Old Testament theology and liturgical theology can and should be both descriptive and constructive. The interpretation of historical texts is a conversation shaped by practical questions about how a particular text's traditional wisdom is to enter into dialogue with present concrete concerns.

Second, the fusion of horizons between tradition and contemporary culture finds its generative source in ecclesial presence, namely the faith community's liturgical expressions. The consequent question for liturgical renewal is how the critical-reflective interaction between present concerns and the wisdom of tradition is to be focused in the worship event. To address this issue requires an integrative approach cognizant of the horizons of meaning evident in both the historical and contemporary cultures; a solely descriptive and positivistic historical theology is not adequate. A dialogue between sacramental imagination and dialectical imagination, a dialogue inherent in the linguistic and developmental structure of Proverbs 1–9 and Job, offers a balance to an over-dependence on history.

Third, wisdom operates within a creation framework, thus providing a horizon of integration for dialectical and sacramental concerns. It is therefore an invaluable, if neglected, conversation partner in efforts to provide a corrective to liturgical theologies centered too exclusively on redemption history.

Finally, in this age of the "collapse of history" and the "collapse of the house of authority," the abandonment of Scripture is always a risk. A related concern is that all of our deep symbols will also be diminished, the ultimate consequence being that our distinctiveness as a tradition will be lost. Allowing wisdom to provide a methodological framework for liturgical theology enables a transformative dialogue with contemporary concerns without wholesale abandonment of classic texts and tradition.

Retrieving Old Testament voices that were marginalized by the dominance of contractual theology can recapture much of what has been suppressed or ignored in human faith experience. Power suggests that in this process, retrieving the name of Sophia for God is important; I argue that the renewal of the metaphorical language and hermeneutical framework of the wisdom corpus as a whole is vital to these retrieval efforts, efforts that lead to a more dynamic and authentic picture of who God is.

Chapter 5

Sapiential Imagination in
Wisdom Theology and Liturgy

A thematic question for liturgical renewal today is how to maintain the dynamic and transformative quality of worship in an era of increasing religious skepticism. How does worship paint a picture for people of who they are and where they "fit" in the world, especially when the Judeo-Christian tradition has become relativized? In a world that many have termed "post-Christian," how can the Church convincingly continue to offer itself as a place for shaping the "habits" of people's hearts and minds?

Liturgical theology's answer, noted earlier, is to search for meanings beneath the surface of the traditional words and actions of liturgical forms, to discover in the deep structures of the language and rituals a unifying pattern that meaningfully addresses the situation of our particular time and place. The liturgical movement seeks to accomplish this both by renewing traditional symbols and by creating new ones that are more reliable for uncovering those deep structures. This chapter will demonstrate that the discovery of deep structures requires a metaphorical process similar to the creative process that engaged the ancient sages.

The task of the wise person, the goal of sapiential imagination, was to discover the pattern of meaningfulness that permeates the spheres of the cosmos, society, and the realm of the divine.[1] In fact, a foundational

---

[1] Leo Perdue, *Wisdom and Cult* (Missoula, Mont.: Scholars Press, 1977) 11, suggests that from the perspective of ancient Wisdom, the wise person's task was to "discover his [*sic*] place, function and time within the structure of this order. . . . By successfully integrating himself within these spheres of reality

element of "knowing" in the wisdom corpus is a keen awareness of the integrative and thus intersubjective nature of knowledge and human understanding.

For the sages, obtaining knowledge was a journey with several primary goals: (1) to strengthen the sense of community; (2) to shape moral character; and (3) to establish a relationship with Woman Wisdom, a relationship they believed would provide insights into the mysteries of God's divine providence.[2]

The essence of this journey, the way the sages made metaphorical connections between creation and the Creator, is dynamically and pictorially captured in the wisdom corpus through the pedagogical form of the wisdom saying; it is a form that can provide a structural and biblical foundation for liturgical forms that correlates more directly with theology as habitus.

For example, liturgy, conceived as the experiential center to which all other theological investigation is connected, offers a pattern for making sense of the emotional, intellectual, and moral fragments that scatter the landscape of contemporary human living. As Lathrop argues, liturgy "creates a world." In liturgical juxtapositions, human understanding and knowledge of God are transformed; patterns of

---

or 'order,' the wise man thereby becomes aware of the meaning of existence for himself and may achieve self-understanding, knowing who he is and what he is about." By following the call of wisdom (see Proverbs 8), a person could acquire the blessings of a successful life. Later wisdom (Job, Ecclesiastes, Wisdom of Sirach) responds to the challenges of skepticism to the ancient community's foundational beliefs, making possible transformation of the traditional world view.

[2] Farley explains that since the Enlightenment, theological education has been seen as a journey that begins in the isolated towers of theoretical studies in Bible, history, ethics, and systematics. From there, clergy journey out into the world to "practice" what they've learned. When habitus is restored, theology is redefined as a "comprehensive mode of existence," as the way in which both individuals and the community as a whole respond to situations. Christian faith in particular, says Farley, is "existence in the mode of redemption," a way of being in the world that recognizes the fragility of life and of human corruption and seeks freedom from both. The interpretive and self-reflective pedagogical model implied by this perspective is similar to the pedagogical forms within the wisdom corpus. See Edward Farley, *The Fragility of Knowledge: Theological Education in the Church and University* (Philadelphia: Fortress Press, 1988) 89–92.

harmony emerge from within societal chaos; and worship becomes a mediating presence between humanity and the divine.[3]

The sages, like contemporary liturgical theologians, wondered how to articulate the wisdom of God in ways that would give their communities hope for making sense out of the absurdities and uncertainties of life. As noted in Chapter 1, they searched for a "prism" through which they could filter the sounds, sights, and actions of their world. For the sages this prism was wisdom; to follow the path of Sophia was to gain the means for shaping the experiences of life into a coherent pattern, a pattern through which one could gain insight into the deeper mysteries of God.

The sages did not construct their world view using the discursive and denotative language of most second-order theologies. Rather, they painted the picture of wisdom and of their faith world in the vivid metaphorical language of first-order theology, a language that begins, as liturgical theologians insist, in the common objects and actions of daily living. In wisdom, as the traditional narrative of the community is juxtaposed with the narratives of individuals and with existential realities, new meanings are broken open, and transformation of world views is made possible. This epistemological model requires seeing wisdom or knowledge as dialogical.[4]

For the sages such a model, called "sapiential imagination" by Perdue, operates on several levels. On one level, sapiential imagination "observes"; it examines the "stuff" of reality and seeks inherent relationships between objects and actions that on the surface do not appear to be related.

Examples of this can be found in Proverbs, where such everyday entities as the persistence of the ant are observed and commented on by the sages in the lively form of wisdom sayings. As Perdue explains,

"the sages observed such things . . . sought out their relationships with other objects . . . then used them as the substance of wisdom

[3] Gordon Lathrop, *Holy Things: A Liturgical Theology* (Minneapolis: Fortress Press, 1993) 87–9.

[4] Clifford Geertz, "Thick Description: Toward an Interpretive Theory of Culture," *The Interpretation of Culture: Selected Essays,* ed. Clifford Geertz (New York: Basic Books, 1973) 46, explains that "communal meaning is a configuration of signs and metaphors organized by systems of rules or codes." Communal meaning is not static.

teaching. Sayings of various kinds were used to incorporate into moral discourse what was learned from reflecting on the images of sense perception. Comparisons . . . were made that contributed to a body of knowledge that made sense of the world."[5]

In addition to observing, sapiential imagination operates on another level.

At this deeper level, beyond human sense perception, sapiential imagination "moves from more conventional portrayals of images to unconventional ones by associating with objects and segments of reality new features, or by putting them into unusual configurations or combinations."[6] The creative juxtaposition of images in wisdom sayings has the potential, says Perdue, to reorient existing meaning structures, allowing the mind to transcend the present world and perceive realities beyond the immediacy of human experience. In other words, sapiential imagination nudges back the boundaries of more orthodox renderings of God and the world to expose a new life-orienting reality, a reality that emerges from the unexpected realm of ordinary experience.

The study of metaphor, as emphasized in Chapter 4, is no stranger to theological circles.[7] In recent study, a number of liturgical scholars have become interested in how the liturgical event, not just its language but all of its constitutive elements, is intrinsically metaphorical.[8]

This is an important insight, particularly if Farley's assertions about the diminishment of society's words of power are true. As noted earlier, faith communities continue to function by way of traditional symbols and metaphors. Appeals to such symbols emerge in the public sphere as well. Public and religious discourse alike remain rooted to a degree in deep symbols such as "life," "obligation," "integrity," "truth," "freedom," and "rights."

[5] Leo Perdue, *Wisdom and Creation: The Theology of Wisdom Literature* (Nashville: Abingdon Press, 1994) 50.

[6] Ibid., 51.

[7] Janet Martin Soskice, *Metaphor and Religious Language* (Oxford: Clarendon Press, 1985) 1–23, traces the development of an understanding of metaphor from Aristotle through John Locke's rationalist critique of rhetoric and figurative speech.

[8] Mark Searle, "Liturgy as Metaphor," *Worship* 55 (March 1981) 98–9.

Even though they remain in use, however, deep symbols have been reduced to surface language that lacks clear connection to historical roots. In addition, because of the current epistemological focus on empirical data, the dynamic interchange between the concrete and abstract, between presence and elusiveness, a quality necessary to symbolic structures, has collapsed.

For this reason, even as the liturgical movement moves toward renewing or redefining its central metaphors, it must also revisit the ontological nature of its discourse, how liturgy engages persons in a relationship with something "real" which cannot be contained in empirical categories.[9] A look at the metaphorical nature of wisdom sayings can aid the liturgical movement at this stage of renewal.

In addition, as already argued, the continued progress of the liturgical movement depends on establishing a clear framework of self-critique. Farley's appropriation of Erazim Kohak illuminates how this framework of self-reflection is linked to the metaphorical process:

"Reflective thinking, he [Kohak] says, is not the daytime thinking that views its objects in the full luminosity and clarity of mathematics and laboratory research. It is not the nighttime thinking of the dim and shadowy mysteries of the poet's world. Combining the two, reflective thinking embraces both luminosity and darkness. In other words, its time is the time of dusk."[10]

Reflective thinking is a horizon that merges mystery and clarity. Sapiential imagination in the wisdom corpus creates such a horizon; its thinking is inherently reflective.

A primary tenet of twentieth-century liturgical renewal is that while attention to historical texts is necessary to liturgical renewal, so, too, is attention to the sense that the language of praise and prayer is more than words. It is the interplay between the contextual circumstance of

[9] Gordon D. Kaufmann, *God the Problem* (Cambridge, Mass.: Harvard University Press, 1979), makes a distinction between what he calls the "available" God and the "real" God. As he emphasizes, the ultimate reality of God is only known to us in a mediated and thus incomplete way. We know God only in relationship.

[10] Erazim Kohak, *The Embers and the Stars* (Chicago: University of Chicago Press, 1984), quoted in Edward Farley, *Deep Symbols: Their Postmodern Effacement and Reclamation* (Valley Forge, Pa.: Trinity Press International, 1996) 24–5.

the community and classic texts that breaks open new meanings, that establishes an avenue for persons to encounter the mysteries of God's presence.[11] The wisdom corpus is a biblical model for such an understanding. The creation of meaning in wisdom depends on both the verbal expressions of language and on the non-verbal framework of interaction. We turn now to examine the framework of interaction that constitutes the form of wisdom sayings.

THE FORM AND FUNCTION OF PROVERBIAL SAYINGS

Since the 1960s, literary criticism and the phenomenology of language have gained an important voice in biblical interpretation. Central to this developing area of biblical study is the understanding that religious language is essentially metaphorical and that the faith community communicates its beliefs about God primarily by means of metaphor or words of power.[12]

Similar emphases are emerging in liturgical study. One reason for this is the shift in Western ways of knowing. Another reason, noted by

[11] Don Saliers, *Worship as Theology: Foretaste of Glory Divine* (Nashville: Abingdon Press, 1994) 139–41, argues that to focus primarily on the surface language of liturgy is to neglect the deep meanings to which that language points: "The central issue is not 'what are the theological truths contained and stated in the texts?' but 'what is being said and done in the liturgical action and use of these words.'" In other words, the juxtaposition of the language with people's actions and with the community's existential realities suggests a metaphorical process in which both current and historical meanings are transformed. Such a treatment involves concentration not only on form-critical methods in dealing with texts but also on examination of the sociocultural situation out of which the text originates and to which it currently addresses itself. Echoes of Brueggemann's sociopolitical perspective on biblical texts, discussed in the previous chapter, can be heard here. See also Lawrence Hoffman, *Beyond the Text: A Holistic Approach to Liturgy* (Bloomington: Indiana University Press, 1989).

[12] Leo Perdue, *The Collapse of History: Reconstructing Old Testament Theology* (Minneapolis: Fortress Press, 1994) 199–201, notes the centrality of this focus to feminist scholars (whose criticism is also prominent in liturgical dialogue) and to social-scientific models such as liberation theology, which as we saw in the previous chapter provide important insights into our understanding of wisdom. Elisabeth Schüssler Fiorenza, *In Memory of Her: A Feminist Theological Reconstruction of Christian Origins* (New York: Crossroad, 1992), is an example of this effort by a feminist.

Searle, is that, through ecumenical dialogue, scholars and communities have encountered Oriental languages and non-Western ways of thinking, thinking more attuned to the importance of metaphor for human conception of reality.[13]

Renewed attention to metaphor in liturgy has heightened awareness that the language of the liturgy is symbolic language. Liturgy's language does not function primarily to describe God or to denote religious principles. Rather, it has a creative purpose in shaping and reshaping the community's view of reality by pointing toward those aspects of God's truth that elude linguistic expression. Catherine Vincie argues that "in liturgy we are called to speak what we already know, but we are also called to explore the mysteries of God and self that remain unknown."[14] Liturgy's juxtapositions, its metaphorical framework, nurture such a creative process of discovery and growth.

Related to this, noted in the previous chapter, is biblical theology's insight that Scripture consists of essential dialectical patterns that are constitutive of the whole. The work of Brueggemann and others to interpret the Old Testament in such a fashion points to the metaphorical structure of biblical language.

Wisdom contributes to this discussion through its use of sapiential language, language that metaphorically creates meaning by framing a dialogue between issues of order or justice and the realities of beauty, emotion, and delight in creation.[15] This framework in wisdom for mediating truth correlates with liturgical frameworks. Before making the connections between sapiential imagination and liturgy, however, it is necessary to outline the form and function of wisdom sayings. Central to the discussion that follows is the presupposition that linguistic forms and the content of those forms cannot be isolated from one another; meaning is constructed by and is the result of the interaction between both.[16]

---

[13] Searle, "Liturgy as Metaphor," 104.

[14] Catherine Vincie, "Tension and Transformation in Public Prayer," *The Landscape of Praise: Readings in Liturgical Renewal*, ed. Blair Gilmer Meeks (Valley Forge, Pa.: Trinity Press International, 1996) 101.

[15] Perdue, *Wisdom and Creation*, 48.

[16] Ibid., 49. Perdue establishes some methodological parameters that help to clarify this presupposition: (1) sapiential imagination creates or shapes a world view or understanding of reality; (2) the sages used metaphor to establish coherence to their perceptions about creation; (3) the language of wisdom

The Pedagogical Form of Proverbial Sayings

James Crenshaw describes the proverb as "a winged word, outliving the fleeting moment."[17] Proverbial sayings dot the landscape of contemporary American life; Americans enjoy popular wisdom found in everyday conversation, advertisements, signs, and songs.

Most proverbs grow out of a longer narrative or experience of persons within particular communities. To quote Crenshaw again, a proverb is "a short sentence, founded upon long experience, containing a truth."[18] While the longer narrative or experience may be forgotten, the proverb generated by the experience is passed from generation to generation.

Even though proverbs use only a few words to express a great deal more, they are not the isolated or individualistic views of one person. Proverbs embody truths that have the rich layers of tradition as a backdrop. It is this aspect of proverbs that gives them their "hermeneutical openness."[19] Patterns of truth endure from generation to generation in proverbial wisdom, but the use of a proverb and aspects of its meaning continue to depend on the wisdom of the theologizing community, a use that does not require either the adoption or abandonment of tradition in its entirety.[20]

This ability of proverbs to be both historically specific and general, their hermeneutical openness, is what makes it possible to reappropriate the truth they mediate in varying historical and cultural contexts. Central to the liturgical movement is a similar question of how historically specific texts and liturgical forms can mediate meaning in quite different and diverse current situations. A clearer understanding of how proverbs accomplish this may help to answer this liturgical question.[21]

---

is not merely "external trappings"; and (4) sapiential language is historically particular; the social location of the teachings is intrinsic to the teachings themselves.

[17] James Crenshaw, *Old Testament Wisdom: An Introduction* (Atlanta: John Knox Press, 1981) 67.

[18] Ibid.

[19] William McKane, *Proverbs: A New Approach* (Philadelphia: Westminster Press, 1970) 23.

[20] Alyce McKenzie, *Preaching Proverbs: Wisdom for the Pulpit* (Louisville: Westminster/John Knox Press, 1996) 32.

[21] Proverbs have often been relegated to a marginal place in theological study and have been virtually absent from the pulpit. Still, they are not mere

Carole Fontaine operates out of the perspective that an oral phase of transmission existed prior to the written and canonized form of wisdom sayings. Her work *Traditional Sayings in the Old Testament* investigates the application of sayings to daily life. In her examination of wisdom sayings in the historical books of the Old Testament, Fontaine concludes that at an early date proverbs were being handed down orally within communities.[22]

Fontaine's analysis of the form of proverbs, what she calls "proverb performance," grows out of a branch of folklore studies called paroemiology, which focuses on the "folk ideas" or cultural presuppositions underlying the meaning and use of particular sayings.[23] She is interested in the hermeneutical process by which a saying is selected from a given stock of proverbs and applied within a given context, particularly the rules or frameworks that determine how the saying is interpreted by hearers.

The way Fontaine develops her inquiry into proverb performance is related to what Schon calls the "epistemology of practice." As he argues, there is a "knowing-in-practice" that is central to the actions people take in everyday living.[24] As noted in Chapter 2, communities often encounter situations for which the foundational knowledge of the university does not provide a clear answer. In these situations, the

---

rhetorical flourishes that have outlived their original usefulness. As Gerhard von Rad suggests, proverbial wisdom was arguably more vital to daily decision-making than were the Ten Commandments, which were proclaimed in the cultic assembly only infrequently on festival occasions. See Gerhard von Rad, *Wisdom in Israel* (Nashville: Abingdon Press, 1972) 26.

The same can be said of liturgical forms. The deeper meaning of some worship forms and rites may have faded, but these forms are still more than mere decorative overlay. While liturgical forms have at varying times in history become disconnected from their moorings in God's truth, the essential elements of the ordo provide generative patterns, rooted in the early Church, that are vital to mediating the truth of the Gospel.

[22] Carole Fontaine, *Traditional Sayings in the Old Testament* (Sheffield: Almond Press, 1982).

[23] Ibid. With the growing recognition of the importance of context, paroemiologists struggle with how to evaluate proverbs that have been canonized at a later time, particularly when their original context and usage have been lost.

[24] Donald Schon, *The Reflective Practitioner: How Professionals Think in Action* (New York: Basic Books, 1983) x.

pragmatic wisdom mediated by the structural form of the proverb finds its most transformative usage.[25]

In the pedagogy of proverbs there is respect for and reliance on "tacit" knowledge. While this knowledge is generated in a particular situation, as noted above, an element of its truth can be made explicit and put in a form that can be generalized. Differing from empirical models of knowing, however, this generalization does not exist in dogmatic form but rather offers a particular lens for viewing situations.

In other words, the generalization of knowledge in proverbial forms "frames" or "sets" problems in a different way. Thus formulated, the knowledge implicit within a particular historical situation can join the common stock of knowledge and be appropriated for use in other situations.

Kurt Lewin, speaking from the perspective of the human and social sciences, calls this process "reflective transfer." As people utilize "knowledge in action" and reflect on that action, he argues, certain themes become evident that give rise to "actionable" theories. These theories are related to Farley's "wisdom of the enduring." They are verbally explicit and derive from particular situations; however, they can also be generalized methodologically and thematically to other situations, not as "law" but as theories to be put to work, tested, and reinvented.[26]

How one sets or frames the problem, as discussed in Chapter 3, determines in large measure the knowledge that will be used to resolve it.[27] Farley suggests that a rethinking or resetting of the entire problem of theological method is necessary for theology to dialogue meaningfully with contemporary concerns. A similar process of reframing lies at the heart of the form and function of wisdom sayings. Fontaine turns her attention to this ability of proverbs to reframe hearer's attitudes, behaviors, and perceptions in specific situations.[28]

Appropriating Peter Seitel's model of proverb performance, Fontaine examines how both the internal dynamics and the social dimensions of wisdom sayings in the Old Testament frame problems

[25] McKenzie, *Preaching Proverbs*, 11.

[26] Kurt Lewin, *Field in Social Science* (New York: Harper, 1951). See also Schon, *The Reflective Practitioner*, 319.

[27] Lewin, *Field in Social Science*, 40.

[28] See also McKenzie, *Preaching Proverbs*, 10. She suggests that proverbs use indirect language to shape hearers' attitudes and behaviors.

so that new meanings are revealed.[29] Fontaine uses Job 34:1-3 to exemplify this:

"Then Elihu continued and said:
'Hear my words, you wise men,
    and give ear to me, you who know;
for the ear tests words
    as the palate tastes food.'"[30]

Seitel's model has three important characteristics. First, in each proverb there is the "interaction situation," or the event in which the proverb was originally used. The interaction situation points to who the user and hearer/receiver of the saying are, what the occasion of the saying is, and the intent of the saying. In Job 34:2 the "user" is Elihu and the "receivers" are Job and his three friends. The implied intent or strategy of this saying is to affect the attitude of Elihu's hearers. Elihu wants them to respect what he has to say on the basis of its content rather on the basis of a preestablished cultural hierarchy of authority.

The second characteristic is the "proverb situation." The proverb situation refers to the actual "terms" used in the saying, the relationship between them, and the underlying message. The terms in Job 34:2 are (1) "the ear tests words" and (2) "the palate tastes food." The dialogical relationship between dissimilar terms or images, their juxtaposition to each other and to the particular context, allows the saying to be applied metaphorically to situations that do not pertain to the image literally.

The final characteristic is the "context situation," the underlying or hidden terms to which the elements of the proverb situation are being related. In the example here, Elihu uses the imagery of "ear" and "words," metaphorically linked to imagery of eating and food, to challenge his listeners to hear his argument on its own merit rather than

---

[29] There are various forms of proverbial sayings. Crenshaw, *Old Testament Wisdom*, 68–9, notes three types of parallelism in proverbial sayings: antithetic (Prov 11:1), synonymous (Prov 4:7), and progressive (Prov 25:18). Claus Westermann, *Roots of Wisdom: The Oldest Proverbs of Israel and Other Peoples* (Louisville: Westminster/John Knox Press, 1990), delineates proverbs of observation, of contrast, of antithesis, and of comparisons.

[30] Job 34:2.

on the basis of his age or social standing. He uses a wisdom saying to invite his listeners to reappropriate traditional understandings of authority in order to hear his voice.[31]

The primary function of the traditional wisdom saying, then, is to orient the hearer and user cognitively and affectively toward the existential realities of daily living and through the metaphorical process to urge them to a greater awareness of the web of relationships that exist in life. Proverbs function to stimulate recognition of the interconnections between the surface structures of existence and the deep structures wherein we discover the mysteries of God's presence.

In this process, Roland Murphy notes, daily human experiences are a field of operation for both communal insight and divine presence.[32] The sages sought not primarily to impose order on the world but to discover the harmony and justice that is implicit to creation. This insistence on directing their theological thinking "toward the world," as Farley would express it, provided the community with many rich insights that were too easily obscured by the rigid dogmatic norms of those who were "wise in their own eyes" (Prov 3:7).[33]

Perdue utilizes different terminology to describe "proverb performance," terminology that relates to Farley's discussion of Christianity's "vehicles of social duration." What Perdue calls an "interactional model" defines metaphor as the "interfacing of two distinct subjects within a sentence."[34] In this model, the "tenor" is the primary subject and is conveyed by a "vehicle" or secondary subject. In other words, the vehicle becomes the tool of mediation whereby the tenor is interpreted or given meaning.

In wisdom sayings, however, the interpretation of the tenor is not understood as dogmatic or absolute. As vehicle and tenor are juxtaposed to one another, they both become conveyers and receptors of meaning. Their interactional relationship is mutually influencing and partici-

---

[31] Fontaine, *Traditional Sayings in the Old Testament*, 170. McKenzie, *Preaching Proverbs*, 5–6, formulates the structure of proverb performance using different terminology. See also Perdue, *Wisdom and Creation*, 59–60; von Rad, *Wisdom in Israel*, 24–50.

[32] Roland Murphy, *The Tree of Life: An Exploration of Biblical Wisdom* (New York: Doubleday, 1990) 114–6.

[33] Alyce McKenzie, "Different Strokes for Different Folks: America's Quintessential Postmodern Proverb," *Theology Today* (July 1996) 209.

[34] Perdue, *Wisdom and Creation*, 60.

pates in the construction of meaning. Vital to the process is the fact that as vehicle and tenor define one another, neither one loses its own identity. Distinctiveness is retained even as new meaning is created.

This interactional relationship between terms or objects is an aspect of metaphor that makes it vital to liturgy. Searle notes the distinction between "steno-language" and "tensive language" in liturgy. Steno-language refers to those words and symbols that have a relatively clear reference, particularly for those who speak the same language. Such symbols lend themselves to clarification and definition by scientific discourse.

Tensive language, or metaphorical language, tends to be more ambiguous, pointing not to a particular referent but rather to patterns of associations. The "literal" meanings of the two objects or images in the metaphor are held in tension, allowing a new or reconfigured meaning to break through. Searle notes the importance of tensive language for liturgy. Sacraments, for example, are transformative to the degree that they are able to retain the literal meaning of their objects and at the same time point beyond that literal meaning or surface structure to deeper structures of meaning.[35]

Such an understanding is echoed by Lathrop, who discusses how the objects or the "holy things" of worship have both a literal and symbolic meaning prior to their usage in worship. In worship, these objects point to these prior meanings. Juxtaposed to God's Word in the ordo, they also point beyond themselves and beyond cultural limitations to God's presence:

"All the sacred connections of our central things, all of our conventions of holiness . . . finally represent simply ourselves and our culture. They suggest transcendence, but it is our hope for God they speak, not God's own presence. Then, however, the ordo puts these symbols in motion, juxtaposes them to each other. The juxtaposition is meant to speak and sing Jesus Christ in our midst, God's presence of mercy."[36]

---

[35] Searle, "Liturgy as Metaphor," 105–7, appropriates the work of Max Black and Philip Wheelwright on metaphor for liturgical concerns. See Max Black, *Models and Metaphors* (Ithaca, N.Y.: Cornell University Press, 1962); and Philip Wheelwright, *Metaphor and Reality* (Bloomington: Indiana University Press, 1962).

[36] Lathrop, *Holy Things*, 97.

The objects of worship are rich with meaning, but they mediate even more expansive meanings of God's presence as they become secondary to the interactions of the ordo. What is important in the ordo, as in wisdom sayings, is not solely the images' referents but also the patterns of associations and meanings that use in a particular context gives them.[37]

The process of integration and interaction in wisdom sayings, particularly the way in which the objects and actions of ordinary life become a field of God's revelation, provides a framework from within the biblical corpus for the construction of meaning invited by the ordo. In addition, the focus of sayings on observing creation, their use of metaphor to make connections between ordinary existence and God's presence, and their refusal to concretize knowledge into inflexible doctrinal norms or principles—these characteristics of wisdom dialogue with contemporary epistemological developments in ways that a primary focus on redemption history does not.[38] In fact, it can be

[37] Power, *Unsearchable Riches*, 186–7, notes that one of the ways symbols change human perspective is by challenging us to shift from perceiving persons and things as objects to perceiving the meaning with which they are constituted. For instance, the data of liturgy are the signs, words, and actions used. Metaphor and symbolism in liturgy urge us to move away from preoccupation with the data to encounter what the patterning of these objects in a given context "means."

[38] Related to this, Sallie McFague, *Metaphorical Theology: Models of God in Religious Language* (Philadelphia: Fortress Press, 1982) 14–29, makes a distinction between metaphorical thinking and sacramental thinking. As she states, one problem of religious language in this era is that people no longer perceive the world as inherently sacramental. Traditional sacramental language of analogy, whereby the "things" of this world are understood to be related analogously to the divine, is no longer considered a viable possibility in our era.

What is required, she argues, is a transformation of religious language to focus on its metaphorical character. I contend that adopting such a focus from within the parameters of a wisdom foundation pushes beyond traditional ontological categories of thought without entirely dissolving the ontological element of our understanding of God's presence. A wisdom foundation also aids in redefining the "sacramentality" of all life by using a metaphorical framework to enable the faith community to discover those threads of continuity or similarity between two dissimilar objects without establishing some sort of normative or dogmatic analogy that results in diminishing the intersubjective character of both.

argued that wisdom can help in bridging the gap between institutional models of theology and theology as habitus.

A recurring theme in Fontaine's discussion is the universal nature of wisdom sayings. As seen in Chapter 3, contemporary epistemology's insistence that there is no universal foundational knowledge has resulted in a skeptical attitude toward any form of ontological reasoning. It has also resulted in the fragmentation of human understanding.

Wisdom's epistemological framework joins hands with Farley's reflective ontology to challenge this. Almost without exception, the images found in traditional wisdom sayings reflect the daily life and attitudes of the community. This means that at their most basic level, these images are not specific to a particular religious belief, to a particular political standpoint, not even necessarily to a particular socioeconomic class. Rather, they are drawn from the everyday experiences of people, experiences that are familiar, common, even universal to a degree.[39]

Related to this, Nigel Barley, a folklorist cited by Fontaine, calls the message of the wisdom saying its "context-free core." He means that the image of the saying is contextually determined, but the message it mediates could be applied metaphorically to a number of other contexts because it is a message that speaks to some universal experience or need. The "context-free" core of the saying, or pre-reflective intuition as Farley would call it, is expressed cognitively through the matrix of the metaphor.[40]

Gilkey develops a similar understanding with reference to the faith community and liturgical ecumenism. In a world replete with skepticism toward traditional faith claims, Christian communities can only approach a true sense of liturgical unity when they retain their distinctiveness and then aim for a "self-transcending particularity." Within each tradition, Gilkey asserts, there is a "non-relative core of interpretation that becomes that tradition's hermeneutical principle for assessing all other faiths." This non-relative or "context-free" core enables a particular tradition to define and understand faith metaphors such as "salvation."

The object of ecumenism, says Gilkey, is not to relativize this distinctive core. Instead, unity is made possible when each community maintains some aspects of its core of non-relativity but at the same

---

[39] Westermann, *Roots of Wisdom*, 132–3
[40] Fontaine, *Traditional Sayings in the Old Testament*, 170.

time recognizes that its knowledge, even within this foundational set of beliefs, is intersubjective and incomplete. Within these parameters, dialogue with differing traditions is possible.

Important in relation to this is the way wisdom provides not a dogmatic universal principle but a framework for "mapping one field of experience onto another," thereby unifying people and communities at the point of their commonality and providing them with an arena for communicating and interacting with one another.[41] What is foundational to sapiential imagination (and to the metaphorical process inherent in the ordo) is that "meaning" is not discovered in a particular linguistic "container." Meaning occurs as the result of human interaction with the various fields or horizons of living, as they are "mapped onto one another" through the metaphorical process.[42]

To move in the direction of ontology in this way represents a rather radical departure from traditional ontologies that have been the subject of contemporary scrutiny. The importance of revisiting some elements of the ontological question were discussed at length in Chapter 3. Joining wisdom's understanding of metaphor with the question of symbol in liturgy enables us to retrieve, at least in part, an aspect of ontology not discussed there—the ontology of symbols. A brief discussion of this will make clearer the value of wisdom's dialogue with liturgical renewal.

As Power discusses in *Unsearchable Riches,* scholastic understandings of sacrament insisted that the "created partakes of the being of the Creator." An "ontology of participation" provided the basis for this understanding. In Aquinas's working out of the ontology of participation, sacraments "represent a world in which human persons participate in the life of God and a world in which God is immanent." At the same time, however, God is also distinctly transcendent or separate from humanity.[43]

[41] Langdon Gilkey, *Society and the Sacred* (New York: Crossroad, 1981).

[42] Michael B. Aune, "Worship in an Age of Subjectivism Revisited," *Worship* 65 (May 1991) 224.

[43] Power, *Unsearchable Riches,* 182, suggests that Aquinas sets up a three-fold task: (1) creation's participation in God must be spoken of in a way that avoids blurring the distinctions between Creator and created; a sense of transcendence must be maintained. (2) The relationship between God and creation must be expressed so that the distance between what is infinite and what is finite is maintained; and (3) this distance is also to be expressed in such a way that God's immanence in creation is also respected.

As noted earlier, Power suggests that aspects of this ontology of participation can be retrieved from Aquinas's hierarchical symbolic world and appropriated for this contemporary situation. Such a retrieval involves seeing metaphor similar to its formulation in the wisdom corpus. Several connections can be made.

For instance, liturgical metaphors mediate a knowledge that transcends their particular vehicles; this knowledge, Searle says, originates in the unfathomable and mysterious aspect of reality. In order for metaphors or symbols to be disclosive of God's mystery requires the engagement of the community in contemplation of creation and the Creator.[44] Metaphor invites hearers to let go of their assumptions about reality to experience new insights and meanings. However, the reality experienced through metaphor resists categorization in linguistic forms. This means that all linguistic attempts to describe the "real" are "open to correction by the experience itself as well as by other experiences."[45]

The ultimate goal is that perspectives of persons in the community will be changed. The above example, Job 34:2, reflects this desired outcome. Similarly, the juxtapositions of liturgy challenge the presuppositions of participants, inviting them to reconfigure the traditional meanings or perspectives that they brought with them to the worship event. When this restructuring occurs, the community can resist the idolatrous desire for self-securing and autonomy and become open to God's gift of grace and freedom through Christ.[46]

A major difference between this understanding of an ontology of symbols and that expressed by Aquinas can be underscored here. Aquinas, paralleling the sociocultural influences of his time, embraced

[44] Searle, "Liturgy as Metaphor," 110, suggests that participation of the hearer "requires an act of contemplation, rather than analysis, which takes it apart and destroys it, dissipating its power." Contemplation, he argues, involves an "entering into" or participation in that which is contemplated. What this means in terms of wisdom will become clearer as we examine Job.

[45] Ibid., 111. Paul Ricoeur, *Figuring the Sacred: Religion, Narrative, and the Imagination,* ed. Mark I. Wallace (Minneapolis: Fortress Press, 1995) 46–7, suggests, echoing Farley, that "faith" is the "attitude of one who accepts being interpreted at the same time that he or she interprets the world of the text." Such an understanding is inherent in the form of wisdom sayings, wherein hearer and speaker are mutually influenced.

[46] Edward Farley, *Good and Evil: Interpreting a Human Condition* (Minneapolis: Fortress Press, 1990) 133–5.

a hierarchical ordering of world and Church. In this sense, Aquinas aimed to conserve the status quo. At the same time, however, his thought broke with tradition in making clear that the vehicles used to mediate God's presence are not to be substituted for the actual reality of that presence.[47] It is this second aspect of Aquinas' understanding of symbol that Power proposes to retrieve and appropriate for this era.

The form of wisdom sayings accomplishes what Power seeks by implying something other than a hierarchical model of authority and by reflecting the sense in which knowledge of God is both attainable and elusive. In the historical development of wisdom, outlined in the previous chapter, the early sages tended to be conserving of tradition when cultural change seriously questioned that tradition. They sought what their tradition promised, an implicit order and harmony in life and in the cosmos.[48] At the same time, they respected the complexities of life that resist traditional formulation.

The second half of this dialectic is reflected in the interactional model of authority inherent in wisdom forms. As Fontaine notes, biblical wisdom has an implicit authority, derived from its proven effectiveness on the playing field of daily existence rather than from its use by the intellectual or theological elite.[49]

Wisdom's relational framework of authority is most apparent in the linguistic form of individual sayings. In most of the sayings, the strategy is to confront the hearer with seeming contradictions in order to encourage reflection, evaluation, and possible transformation. As the speaker speaks indirectly of universal truths, the hearer is challenged to become engaged in the metaphor as his/her mind works to "break the code," to discover the deeper message, and to make application to his/her own life.[50]

In this process, the speaker is not the authoritative dispenser of some isolated fragment of knowledge of which he/she has owner-

[47] David Power, *Eucharistic Mystery: Revitalizing the Tradition* (New York: Crossroad, 1995) 237–8.

[48] Dianne Bergant, *What Are They Saying About Wisdom Literature?* (New York: Paulist Press, 1984) 10–11.

[49] Fontaine, *Traditional Sayings in the Old Testament*, 170. The controlling authority of wisdom did not end within the parameters of the court of Jerusalem. It can be seen at work at various levels of society in resolving conflicts or orienting users to respond to life's problems in an integrative way.

[50] Ibid., 122.

ship.[51] Truth is rather mediated through what McFague calls the "grid" or "screen" of metaphor, making it possible for the metaphor to take on a life of its own as the hearer interacts with it and with its message.[52] The movement between hearer and speaker is no longer linear as both are shaped by the interaction.[53]

In wisdom, primary expression of faith takes the form of the metaphorical process, a process that dialogues with the liturgical movement's insistence that primary expressions of faith occur in the juxtaposed symbols, actions, and language of liturgy. Discussion now turns to how traditional metaphors in wisdom are redefined or appropriated for contexts other than the ones in which they were generated and how this process intersects with liturgical renewal.

THE METAPHORICAL PROCESS

"Hear, my child, and accept my words,
    that the years of your life may be many.
I have taught you the way of wisdom;
    I have led you in the paths of uprightness,
When you walk, your step will not be hampered;
    and if you run, you will not stumble.
Keep hold of instruction; do not let go;
    guard her, for she is your life.
Do not enter the path of the wicked,
    and do not walk in the way of evildoers.
Avoid it; do not go on it;
    turn away from it and pass on."[54]

These verses from Proverbs 4 highlight what Norman Habel says is a primary symbolic expression in Proverbs 1–9—the symbol of the

[51] Westermann, *Roots of Wisdom*, 133, argues that a distinctive quality of proverbs is that they allow those being addressed to maintain their own autonomy in observing, reflecting, and making decisions. There are proverbs which Westermann says are "pedagogic" in orientation. These sayings are more exhortational in nature and lack the relational or interactional quality. However, even these exhortations are not authoritarian in nature, primarily because of their "handed-down" quality. They are generally acknowledged as having a more social function.

[52] McFague, *Metaphorical Theology*.

[53] Fontaine, *Traditional Sayings in the Old Testament*, 9.

[54] Prov 4:10-15.

"way."[55] This symbol represents a central goal of "wise" persons in early wisdom, namely to choose those actions in daily living that will lead to well-being and to avoid those situations that bring failure or destruction. At a deeper level, to follow the path of wisdom was to discover the means for shaping the experiences of life into a coherent pattern through which one could gain insight into the mysteries of God. Such a process of decision-making involved both the appropriation and reformulation of traditional faith images and understandings.

The model out of which the sages operated to appropriate tradition constitutes what Perdue calls the metaphorical process. This section will briefly describe that process. Connections will be made between this process and how meaning is constructed in contemporary faith communities, particularly in worship.

As Browning explains in *A Fundamental Practical Theology*, religious communities are communities of memory and practical reason. As noted earlier, when a community's usual practices or tradition do not provide an adequate solution to a particular problem, the community begins to ask questions about those practices, practices which Browning says are "theory-laden." To say that practices are "theory-laden" means that they are rooted in and shaped by various underlying presuppositions—tradition, doctrine, the history of the community, environmental crises, and Scripture, to mention a few.[56]

When a crisis in practice develops, Browning argues, the community does several things. First, it reflects on the traditional practice and may attempt to describe it in order to gain a better understanding of it. Second, it reexamines the sacred texts and traditional norms that

---

[55] Norman Habel, "The Symbolism of Wisdom in Proverbs 1–9," *Interpretation* 26 (1972) 131–57. As he discusses, the symbolism of the "way" is elaborated, clarified, and intensified in terms of its polar opposite. The symbolism of the two ways in Prov 4:10-19 is related to several other bipolar choices—the two hearts in 4:20-27 and 6:12-15, the two companions in 5:5-8 and 6:20-24, and the two houses in 7:6-27.

[56] Don Browning, *A Fundamental Practical Theology* (Minneapolis: Fortress Press, 1991) 2–3. Brueggemann develops a foundation from biblical theology for this understanding of how classic texts are appropriated for contemporary times. The concept "theology of traditions," in his *Theology of the Old Testament: Testimony, Dispute, Advocacy* (Minneapolis: Fortress Press, 1997), expresses the understanding that what is said in classic texts about God and humanity, particularly in narrative traditions, involves a reconfiguring of isolated or individual narratives into a coherent and meaningful sequence.

have guided the practice in question; in this, the community invites its current questions into dialogue with these texts.

What happens next, Browning continues, depends on how willing the community is to continue the process of self-critique. The most transformative outcome of the conversation between contemporary questions and classic texts occurs when traditional meanings are reconstructed or new religious understandings are created.

Browning suggests that "religious communities go from moments of consolidated practice to moments of deconstruction to new, tentative reconstructions and consolidations." When yet another crisis presents itself, the community begins the process once more.[57]

To put it more succinctly, Browning, like liturgical theologians who argue that liturgy is primary theology, suggests that theology is inherently "practical." It moves from present theory-laden practice to a retrieval of more normative or traditional theory-laden practices to the creation of more critically held theory-laden practices.[58] In this process, as exemplified in Farley's retrieval of a Judeo-Christian paradigm of good and evil, certain deep structures or enduring elements of truth emerge over time if the community maintains a consistent process of self-critique.

This mode of appropriating tradition finds one biblical counterpart in wisdom's metaphorical process. First, as already seen, sapiential imagination uses language to construct a world view. Geertz's work on symbol parallels the insights raised earlier in this regard. As he explains, communal meaning or wisdom is a "configuration of signs and metaphors." In effect, it is a web of reciprocal relationships that work together to shape a moral world view. What is important for communities to recognize, Geertz continues, is that meanings do not settle rigidly into certain world views. Rather, as the community's narrative

---

[57] Browning, *A Fundamental Practical Theology*, 6–7.

[58] McFague, *Metaphorical Theology*, 6–7, reminds us of the rather conservative nature of this whole process. As she suggests, and as Farley would likely agree, people depend on their constructions of reality to fulfill their elemental desires. Because of this, communities tend to be more conserving of traditional constructions when they face threats or crises. Often, as Farley enumerates in *Ecclesial Reflection: An Anatomy of Theological Method* (Philadelphia: Fortress Press, 1982), the result is actually a more literalistic or absolutist approach to our construals of reality. McFague argues for a metaphorical way of embracing reality as an alternative.

is juxtaposed to the narratives of individuals in that community, to the Judeo-Christian narrative, and to the sociohistorical narrative, the metaphorical process functions to make continual transformation of world views possible.[59]

For the sages, the world view shaped by sapiential imagination provided a context in which they could choose the "way of wisdom." Through root metaphors derived from sapiential imagination, a community communicates the constitutive features of its world view or religious understanding. These metaphors, however, are not static; they exist in relationship with other words and images.

What makes metaphors work, Perdue continues, is that they take hearers through a process in which traditional meanings are deconstructed so that more appropriate and transformative visions can be formed. As Ricoeur argues in relation to reading biblical texts, the process is "a creative operation unceasingly employed in decontextualizing its meaning and recontextualizing it in today's *Sitz-im-Leben*."[60] Perdue outlines the stages of the metaphorical process in *Wisdom and Creation* as well as in *The Collapse of History*.[61]

The first stage in the metaphorical process is "destabilization." Metaphors combine images from conventional life and challenge common understandings by posing a meaningful contradiction; they "pose a meaning that, if taken literally, is nonsense."[62] An example from Proverbs illuminates this:

"Wisdom has built her house,
  she has hewn her seven pillars. . . .
She has sent out her servant-girls, she calls from the highest places in
    town,

---

[59] See Clifford Geertz, *The Interpretation of Cultures: Selected Essays* (New York: Basic Books, 1973); *Local Knowledge: Further Essays in Interpretive Anthropology* (New York: Basic Books, 1983); and *Myth, Symbol and Culture* (New York: Norton, 1971).

[60] Paul Ricoeur, "The Bible and Imagination," *Figuring the Sacred: Religion, Narrative and Imagination,* ed. Mark I. Wallace (Minneapolis: Fortress Press, 1995) 145. See also Paul Ricoeur, *The Rule of Metaphor: Multi-disciplinary Studies of the Creation of Meaning in Language,* trans. Robert Czerny (Toronto: University of Toronto Press, 1977) 216–56.

[61] Perdue, *Wisdom and Creation,* 61–3; Perdue, *The Collapse of History,* 202–5.

[62] Perdue, *Wisdom and Creation,* 61.

'You that are simple, turn in here!'
  To those without sense she says,
'Come, eat of my bread
  and drink of the wine I have mixed.
Lay aside immaturity, and live,
  and walk in the way of insight.'"[63]

To picture "reality" as a palatial house into which the wise are invited by a woman of wealth and intelligence is not logical in terms of rational discourse. In addition, to personify Wisdom as a woman challenged understandings common to that cultural context and tradition and posed a picture that could not be taken as literally true.

The purpose of the metaphor is to draw hearers out of a rational framework and into a more imaginative one where it is possible to consider new meanings. When common perspectives are challenged in this way, the hearer experiences what Perdue describes as a disorienting shock.[64]

The second stage in the metaphorical process is called "mimesis." The seemingly contradictory associations created by the juxtaposition of the vehicle and the tenor of the metaphor invites the hearer to an awareness that there is something in this interaction that is "truth."

The third stage of the metaphorical process is transformation. As Perdue argues, if a metaphor is particularly engaging, it has the potential to "re-create the meaning system of the audience, redescribing reality by shaping a new cosmology that provides instruction in the way to live within the world."[65]

The final stage is "restabilization." When a metaphor is recognized as mediating truth, it can become an accepted part of tradition. As noted earlier, however, even these moments of restabilization are temporary; when the community encounters another crisis or problem the process is initiated again.

The essence of the metaphorical process's transformative potential is this ability to stimulate a continual process of reflection and reconstruction. Metaphors defy concretization and cannot be contained in one-dimensional definitions. It is this tensive quality of metaphor that gives it its dynamic energy and vitality. Perdue suggests that the

---

[63] Prov 9:1-9.
[64] Perdue, *Wisdom and Creation*, 62.
[65] Perdue, *The Collapse of History*, 203.

tension occurs on two levels: between the tenor and vehicle of the metaphor and in the transitional stage between traditional meaning systems and new or altered ones.[66]

In other words, as Searle argues from the perspective of liturgical theology, metaphors cannot be given "steno-meanings," or literal definitions, that remove the tension. When this happens, when the tensive quality of metaphor is lost, the transformative process becomes stymied by uncritical assertions or inflexible dogma.[67] Several connections between wisdom's metaphorical process and liturgy can be made at this point.

First, as noted above, Browning's approach to interpretation and appropriation of classic texts is based on the insight that religious communities make decisions in particular situations by moving from practice to theory to practice. While not explicit, a kind of praxis-theory-praxis framework can be discovered within Lathrop's liturgical method.

As Lathrop explains, liturgical theology accepts traditional patterns and symbols as having some level of authority among us. At the same time, liturgical theology also engages in a contemporary critique of tradition. Liturgy, in this sense, is primary theology; it is that event in which tradition and its resources intersect with and are challenged by the lives of people in the community. The organization of *Holy Things* into three interrelated sections highlights this metaphorical, praxis-theory-praxis quality of worship.

The first section of Lathrop's book addresses the "primary patterns in which meaning occurs in the Christian assembly."[68] This section, says Lathrop, is "secondary liturgical theology." It is written discourse that attempts to explain the experience of liturgy and to discover its structures. Secondary liturgical theology is both reflective and descriptive and operates to clarify the structures of meaning in worship for a contemporary society. As such, it involves historical theology as the community examines normative traditional texts and rituals and seeks

---

[66] McFague, *Metaphorical Theology*, 29, argues that when theology is conceived as primarily metaphorical it does not result in a mere "baptizing" of the existing tradition. Instead it seeks to nurture the tension between the contemporary and traditional horizons, arguing that this metaphorical tension houses the potential to reform and transform.

[67] Searle, "Liturgy as Metaphor," 105–6.

[68] Lathrop, *Holy Things*, 6.

to appropriate them in light of contemporary needs and concerns. As will be seen in greater detail later, the structure of Job reflects this form of secondary reflective discourse.

In his second section, Lathrop deals with the actual event of worship's primary patterns; Lathrop calls this section "primary theology."[69] As he explains, the meaning of liturgy is known to us first of all as we participate in the worship event. The symbols and actions of worship create a unique world of meaning through their interactions, a world that cannot be experienced through secondary discourse.

In the final section, Lathrop attempts to make application of primary patterns to current questions of liturgical renewal. As he explains, similar to Browning, the juxtaposition of the contemporary vision with the vision implicit to normative Christian texts, or in this case the primary patterns of the liturgy, makes transformation of worship and of world views possible. This section suggests that the purpose of liturgical theology is not only to articulate the patterns of worship as they have existed historically or as they exist currently; liturgical theology's task is not solely descriptive. Rather, it is also concerned with renewing traditional patterns so that they are more adequate for the needs of this age. Lathrop calls this movement "pastoral liturgical theology."[70]

While Lathrop does not develop an explicit praxis-theory-praxis model, the constant dialectical movement between praxis and theory is evident in his methodology. In fact, although Lathrop begins *Holy Things* with secondary theology, he makes clear that readers might begin with any of the three sections. For Lathrop, praxis and theory, or primary, secondary, and pastoral theology, are interrelated and interdependent. For him, then, a metaphorical process similar to that within the wisdom corpus is evident in the interactive pattern of ordinary actions and objects in liturgical rites.

A second connection between the metaphorical process and liturgy is related to the metaphorical nature of liturgy's discourse of memorial and blessing. A number of scholars have worked to overcome differences and controversies between varying traditions' eucharistic celebrations. Important to this has been a retrieval of a biblical understanding of memorial, particularly of the ritual structure of narrative and blessing in classic Judeo-Christian texts.

[69] Ibid., 87–160.
[70] Ibid., 161–226.

To develop a "theory," or secondary theology, of memorial out of this recovery of biblical foundations for eucharistic practice, says Power, involves examining the relation between the remembered event of the paschal mystery and present circumstances. Taking a methodological route similar to that of Browning, Power insists that this requires a better understanding of language's role in making past events or texts living realities in a community. It is through language that past events are appropriated in such a way that they transform world views.[71]

Echoing the earlier discussion, Power suggests that communities have "foundational narratives." These narratives are formative of communal identity and are passed from generation to generation. In time, however, events transpire that challenge traditional or foundational narratives, causing them to be reflected on and often retold in a new way.

What is important here is that a literal or dogmatic recital of an original narrative is not adequate for keeping a past event's meaning vital for current circumstances. Power implies that the power of narrative lies in its metaphorical dynamic. Because liturgy appropriates the narrative of the paschal mystery through complementary metaphorical forms such as poetry, lament, and proclamation, it both immerses itself in the constitutive meaning of Christ's death and resurrection and at the same time expresses how that reality cannot be confined within historical parameters.

When metaphorical forms of discourse become central to liturgical rite, says Power, "remembered event, ethical horizon, and community reality thus converge in the ritual act of appropriation that prompts an ongoing discursive and ethical appropriation."[72] Of vital importance to this process, he adds, is that the tension be maintained between a descriptive narrative of history that attempts to order events into a meaningful whole and a constructive form of history that leaves room for the elusiveness or inexplicability of the Christ-event. As noted earlier, it is this tensive dimension of metaphor that makes it transformative.

Mark Searle expresses an understanding similar to that of Power. Liturgy, he argues,

"is an enactment of the root metaphor of the paschal mystery of the death and resurrection of Jesus as the disclosure of God, yet it cele-

---

[71] Power, *Eucharistic Mystery*, 304–5.
[72] Ibid., 306.

brates that mystery in a whole series of rites and ceremonies. . . . All these serve to disclose, under the circumstances of particular times and places and occasions, the single, indivisible mystery, disclosed in the person of Jesus, which we intuitively know and encounter without either being able to understand it exhaustively or to articulate at all except in the metaphorical language of disclosure. The one unnameable mystery of reality is refracted through the variegated lenses of historical tradition and contemporary liturgical practices."[73]

Hints of the importance of ontological discourse recur at this juncture and provide a third connection between metaphorical discourse and liturgy.

The question addressed by both Power and Farley resurfaces when the issue of ontological discourse is raised, namely how a salvific event of the past is to become redemptive in the present tragic structure of the world. Power makes an important connection between liturgy, creation, and cosmology in this regard.

When the memorial language of eucharistic prayers incorporates the work of creation, he argues, both the created world and the need for human reconciliation with the created world are included in Christ's redemptive work. By juxtaposing the creation story and the story of Christ's death and resurrection in eucharistic celebration, by engaging these two stories in the metaphorical process, the community is reminded that even as salvation is tied to a constitutive historical event, it is also expressed by a creation story of mythic proportions that stands outside the parameters of any historical moment.[74]

To understand fully what Power means by this perspective on redemption requires establishing its biblical foundation from other than a primarily descriptive and positivistic historical perspective. One reason is that even as creation is adopted into the language of memorial in the Eucharistic Prayer, it is important that it not be interpreted

[73] Searle, "Liturgy as Metaphor," 112, argues that metaphor in liturgy represents the "intersection of the timeless with time."

[74] Power, *Eucharistic Mystery*, 312–5, explains that the proclamation of the cross stands at the heart of the narrative and of our remembrance. Citing Paul, Power argues that the wisdom of the cross is counter to the wisdom of the world. The mystery of God disclosed in the cross cannot be represented in either metaphysical or mythic thinking or language. The goal of liturgical discourse is to use language that respects this aspect of faith knowledge.

merely as belonging to a sequential continuum of historical developments. The mythic story of creation and the narrative of salvation do
not belong, says Power, on the same historical level. The creation
story, he argues, echoing Farley, is expressive of a condition or structure of human existence that is not tied to any particular historical
contingency. Christ's redemptive action, a historical event, disrupts
the tragic structuring of human existence and makes possible transformation of hearts and minds. Terrien's development of an "ecumenical theology of the Bible" emerges again here.

Terrien argues that the motif motivating the entirety of Judeo-
Christian faith—ancient Hebrews, prophets, and first-generation
Christians—is that of divine presence. In current Old Testament theology, he continues, two modes of divine presence have dominated. The
first interpretation of divine presence is rooted in the Torah. This
mode of presence emerges from the historical conditions of the Mosaic
covenant and raises the election of Israel to a universal responsibility.

The second mode of presence depends on temple ideology and ritual and relates primarily to the proclamations of the prophets. Terrien
argues that an Old Testament theology confined to the Torah and
prophets is faced with an unresolvable tension between these two
understandings of divine presence, unless the theology of presence
through wisdom is taken into account.[75] Just how the mode of presence
in wisdom operates as a pivotal center for Old Testament theology
will be raised in the next chapter. Primary to that discussion will be an
examination of how the inclusivity of *sophia* or Woman Wisdom in
Proverbs 1–9 metaphorically challenges and expands anthropocentric
interpretations of christology.[76]

A final connection between the metaphorical process and liturgical
theology is related to how communities retrieve and appropriate tradition and classic texts and how that process is formative of communal integrity. In liturgy, the Church seeks to image Christ, but Christ is
not fully present in any of our symbols, rites, or actions. What we are

[75] Samuel Terrien, "The Play of Wisdom: Turning Point in Biblical Theology,"
Horizons in Biblical Theology 3 (1981) 125–53.

[76] McFague, *Metaphorical Theology*, viii, has concluded within her feminist
perspective that it is not possible to continue to support an incarnational
christology or a canonical Scripture. She has adopted instead a "parabolic" or
metaphorical christological perspective and an understanding of Scripture as
the Christian "classic."

actually doing, then, in our liturgical representations, says Power, is "exploring the traces of God in history."[77]

Part of the process of retrieving the traces of God in our faith's history, highlighted by contemporary liturgical theologians in particular, is the effort to recover those things that have been suppressed in our religious experience. The kind of language that most authentically engages us in this journey of discovery of God's presence is the language of metaphor, particularly as we find it developed in the wisdom corpus. In dialogue with wisdom, liturgy becomes more intentionally focused on the metaphorical process and the destabilization inherent in that process that challenges tendencies toward patriarchalism and hierarchy, tendencies that deafen us to the voice of God in the marginalized or forgotten places of our tradition.

Religious communities are communities of memory and of practical reason. They carry with them an inherited tradition but also a predilection toward what is learned from lived experience. This is also reflected in the wisdom corpus where the focus is on a divine presence that wills the wholeness and harmony of all creation, that ties together *ethos* and *cosmos*.[78]

What this means, in effect, is that as *ethos* and *cosmos* are recognized as dialogically or metaphorically interconnected, the visional dimension, and subsequently the moral dimension, of faith is renewed. Farley's explanation is helpful here. As he argues, communal understandings in which "obligation" is restored as a word of power or as a root metaphor include a "refusal to reduce the other to an object for use and an acceptance of the irreducible mystery of the other." Obligation, or the ethical dimension of our faith world view, he says, involves moving beyond self-oriented agendas toward taking responsibility for that which is other than ourselves.[79]

This theme is central to Lathrop's liturgical theology as well. As he explains, it is not possible to create faith. However, local communities can recover the "wholeness and integrity" of the signs of the faith. A reflective process intent on determining the extent to which liturgical signs have remained authentic to the vision they were created to mediate can help to accomplish this. When the rich metaphorical

---

[77] David Power, "Liturgical Praxis: New Consciousness at the Eye of Worship," *Worship* 61 (July 1987) 298.

[78] Ibid., 301.

[79] Farley, *Deep Symbols*, 49.

dynamic of the signs is lost, says Lathrop, the meaning of the signs is in danger. Thus, a connection emerges between the "vision" of God that is shaped and mediated by the patterns of the ordo and the ethical dimension of communal life.

When a community pushes rigidly and dogmatically toward more objective delineations of liturgy's "signs" without concern for the "other," without what Power calls "agapic praxis," then the meaning of the thing signified is diminished. Always, Lathrop insists, the signs, actions, objects, and language of liturgy must draw the entire community into Christ and urge us toward openness and dialogue with the stranger in all of us and with the stranger in our midst.[80]

CONCLUSION

Scholars in various fields have noted a change in society's paradigm of reality construction.[81] Perdue concludes in response to this change that Old Testament theology should be both descriptive and constructive; in other words, it should examine texts within their own historical contexts but then take the hermeneutical steps necessary to appropriate those texts for contemporary questions and concerns. Such a move toward constructive theology is inseparably connected to the metaphorical process and metaphorical language.[82]

This chapter has demonstrated from the standpoint of the metaphorical process several ways in which a constructive rendering of Old Testament theology dialogues purposefully with the questions that currently face liturgical renewal. Central to the discussion of metaphor in this chapter is the recognition that a constructive treatment of classic texts requires a critical-reflective interaction. Such a

---

[80] Lathrop, *Holy Things*, 164–9, asks to what extent structures of power in the assembly reorder the structures of power in the world, to what degree love and service are present, to what extent situations of injustice are juxtaposed to the grace of Christ through liturgical forms.

[81] This "paradigm change" was the subject of an international, ecumenical, and interdisciplinary symposium at the University of Tubingen in the late 1980s. Gathered at this symposium were seventy men and women from all over the world, theologians from Catholic and Protestant traditions representing disciplines including sociology of religion, philosophy, and practical theology. See Hans Kung and David Tracy, eds., *Paradigm Change in Theology: Symposium for the Future* (New York: Crossroad, 1991).

[82] Perdue, *The Collapse of History*, 305.

process of critical reflection is inherent in both the content and framework of wisdom theology, particularly as it is developed in Proverbs 1–9 and Job. As such, it offers a biblical matrix for liturgical theology that houses within its parameters an established mode of self-critique.

The next two chapters will examine the development of this structure of critical reflection in Proverbs 1–9 and Job and will outline in greater detail how this particular biblical matrix can function as a foundation for liturgical theology.

Chapter 6

Creating a World: Proverbs 1–9

"Wisdom cries out in the street;
   in the squares she raises her voice.
At the busiest corner she cries out;
   at the entrance to the city gates she speaks . . ."[1]

"Does not Wisdom call,
   and does not understanding raise her voice?
On the heights, beside the way,
   at the crossroads she takes her stand;
beside the gates in front of the town,
   at the entrance to the portals she cries out:
'To you, O People, I call,
   and my cry is to all that live.
O simple ones, learn prudence;
   acquire intelligence, you who lack it.
Hear, for I will speak noble things,
   and from my lips will come what is right;
for my mouth will utter truth;
   wickedness is an abomination to my lips.
All the words of my mouth are righteous;
   there is nothing twisted or crooked in them.
They are all straight to the one who understands
   and right to those who find knowledge.'"[2]

[1] Prov 1:20-21.
[2] Prov 8:1-9.

In a contemporary situation where people are faced with tough ethical decisions everyday, particular questions continue to challenge the faith community. How are we to speak about the mysteries of God? How do our communal gatherings affect the hopes, dreams, ideas, and actions of daily lives? How does the mediation of God's presence in liturgy shape participants' moral and ethical character?

A word that emerged in relation to these questions in the last chapter was "imagination." Barbara Taylor offers a "picture" of imagination:

"A friend of mine clearly remembers the summer he lost his imagination. He was eleven years old, a distracted fifth grader who yearned for the last day of school so he could return full time to the fields of play. Memories of the previous summer spurred him on, long days spent lying on his belly in the back yard, racing miniature cars and trucks with his friends. When the last bell of the school year rang, he ran home to get everything ready, and next morning he hauled it all outside. With the sun heating up behind his back, he sat down in his special place surrounded by special toys and waited for the delicious feeling to creep over him, but nothing happened. He picked up his favorite truck and ran its wheels over the ground. "Rrrrr!" he roared, as he had done so many times before, but it was not the sound of an engine this time. It was the sound of a boy's voice pretending to be an engine. . . . The bridge to his old world was gone. He no longer had access to it, and the loss opened up a hollow place inside of him."[3]

Imagination, as this picture-definition captures it, has two characteristics: (1) it is the mind's ability to recall objects and actions of past experience through memory and (2) it is envisioning the future by projecting the continued existence of an object perceived in the present. Leo Perdue suggests that imagination "gives coherence to experiences, combines perceptions into integrated wholes, and places into relationships and categories things that are sensed and perceived."[4]

[3] Barbara Brown Taylor, *The Preaching Life* (Boston: Cowley Publications, 1993) 38.

[4] Leo Perdue, *Wisdom and Creation: The Theology of Wisdom Literature* (Nashville: Abingdon Press, 1994) 50. David Buttrick, "Speaking between the Times," *Theology and the Interhuman*, ed. Robert Williams (Valley Forge, Pa.: Trinity Press International, 1995) 151–2, notes that contemporary confidence in objective reason is gone. Now, particularly as revealed in the art world, depic-

A number of contemporary theologians have revisited the imaginative or metaphorical dimension of faith in an effort to restore to the faith community its ability to speak about, envision, and embody the mysteries of God's presence. By "imagination," they do not mean that faith is a fictional world of magic or make-believe; rather, as Newsom suggests, the imaginative dimension of faith refers to the process whereby the human capacity to form mental pictures of self, neighbors, the world, and the future is engaged and transformed.[5] David Power expresses it this way: "The imagination of faith seeks to name God between the cracks."[6]

The purpose of "sapiential imagination" in the wisdom corpus is similar to this; its goal, in a sense, is to name God between the cracks. As noted in the previous chapter, for example, the sages used sapiential imagination to encourage communal participation with God in building an earthly dwelling of harmony, order, and virtue. Perdue argues that the book of Proverbs hinges on this constructive purpose: "the purpose of the collection [Proverbs 1–9] and the larger book is instruction in wisdom or *musar*—that is, knowledge about God, the world, and human life; the embodiment of sapiential piety and virtue; and the construction of a world for human dwelling." The genre of proverbial wisdom, he suggests, was designed to teach and to persuade and through that process shape an "esthesis—a poetic world of beauty, harmony, order and balance that is to be actualized in the life of one seeking wisdom . . ."[7]

Using verbs that create images as mythic and cosmic as "dividing the primeval deep" (Prov 3:19-20; 8:24, 27-28) and "splitting open the chaos monster," while at the same time speaking of things as everyday

---

tions of "reality" are less boundaried because reality "is no longer defined by its objective thereness." Buttrick posits that the contemporary era may perceive the world as "phenomenally structured in consciousness." When this happens, the sense of mystery and awe that attends God's presence, the imaginative dimension of faith, can be restored. He calls this way of analyzing reality a "mode of metaphorical logic."

[5] Carol Newsom, "Wisdom and the Discourse of Patriarchal Wisdom: A Study of Proverbs 1–9," *Gender and Difference in Ancient Israel,* ed. Peggy L. Day (Minneapolis: Augsburg Fortress, 1989) 142–60.

[6] David Power, "Liturgical Praxis: New Consciousness at the Eye of Worship," *Worship* 61 (July 1987) 300.

[7] Perdue, *Wisdom and Creation,* 78.

as crops, the marketplace, and the streets of the city, the sages invite the community to engage in an imaginative *and* intellectual task of shaping a world where people can encounter God.[8] In this process, ethos and cosmos are metaphorically connected.

Similar to this aim of sapiential imagination, an important goal of liturgy is to enable communal encounter with God and call forth ethical decision and action through the narrative remembering of Christ's death and resurrection.[9] Imagination has a role in this encounter as it provides connections to past experiences and then projects the continued existence of these experiences into the future.

Through liturgical remembering a new vision of reality and a new way of interpreting life is made possible. In effect, this imaginative shift in vision, or fusion of past, present, and future horizons, is inherent in the process of conversion, wherein past values and contemporary concerns are reoriented. As Mark Searle suggests, "conversion" is a kind of transition through which a person's character, values, and relationships are reconfigured.[10]

What this means ultimately is that restoring to the faith community its imaginative ability to discover traces of God's presence in the surrounding world impacts both the visional and ethical dimensions of communal life. The "vision" of God shaped at the metaphorical level and mediated by ordo is interconnected with the community's moral praxis.

This chapter will examine Proverbs 1–9 in an effort to illuminate how the wisdom corpus models from a biblical perspective this necessary metaphorical connection between cosmos and ethos.

The first part of the chapter will suggest a working definition of the relationship between virtue (or the moral dimension of faith) and knowledge of God. Three implications of the fact that Proverbs is rooted in a particular moral context will be discussed: (1) that ethical

---

[8] Ibid., 84. Perdue notes that these themes in Proverbs 3 permeate other parts of the Old Testament (Gen 1:2; 7:11; Job 38:16; Psalm 74; Hab 3:8-10) and are found also in Near Eastern/Mesopotamian creation epics.

[9] Mary Catherine Hilkert, *Naming Grace: Preaching and the Sacramental Imagination* (New York: Continuum, 1997) 97, discusses how narrative language, or in this case metaphorical language, has the potential to reshape reality constructs. Through this, transformation is made possible not only of individual or personal identity but also of social and political structures.

[10] Mark Searle, "Journey of Conversion," *Worship* 54 (January 1980) 35-6.

praxis is inseparable from wisdom or knowledge of God, (2) that moral concerns are as much a part of shaping character, of shaping elemental features of human being, as they are of influencing conduct, and (3) that the notion of character so developed connects past and future and provides a bridge between the faith community and society.[11]

The second part of the chapter will address how conversion is tied to communal shaping of character and how liturgy functions in this process. Insights regarding the role of language in shaping moral understanding will also be examined in this section.[12]

For the sages, creation or conversion is a process through which "God shapes chaos into an enduring cosmos and sustains a world that is intelligible, orderly and good."[13] The frame of reference for this journey of conversion is the faith community (Prov 1:1-7); the mediating presence between Creator and the created is Woman Wisdom. As will become evident in the discussion, this framework suggests a critical pedagogical approach to character formation and communal integrity that maintains tradition's constitutive identity while entering into a mutually influencing dialogue with other societal voices.

As William Brown emphasizes, wisdom's theology creates a *paideia* or habitus that sees faith not as the mastering of information but rather as a hermeneutical journey of discovery.[14] It is a journey of practical wisdom—praxis to theory to praxis—that begins and ends with the primary theology of the faith community; by analogy, it is also a liturgical journey.

[11] Richard Bondi, "The Elements of Character," *The Journal of Religious Ethics* 12 (1984) 204.

[12] William Brown, *Character in Crisis: A Fresh Approach to the Wisdom Literature of the Old Testament* (Grand Rapids, Mich.: Eerdmans, 1996) 2–3, notes that while Perdue emphasizes that wisdom exists as a dialectic of anthropology and cosmology, he tends to favor cosmology. As Brown insists, the anthropological nature of wisdom is equal, if not primary, to the cosmological. This is evident in the emphasis in Proverbs on the importance of human language and observation in framing our knowledge of God.

[13] Perdue, *Wisdom and Creation*, 80.

[14] Brown, *Character in Crisis*. The entirety of this work focuses on the theme of "journey" as it can be uncovered in Proverbs, Job, and Ecclesiastes. He notes that "all three chart the self starting from a central, familiar locale that provides expected security and identity. But the moral subject does not remain in this position for long; it moves into certain realms of liminality, to the frontiers of the community, creation and knowledge."

Power suggests that an important element in the renewal of liturgy is a retrieval of the "transformational" elements of tradition, some of which have at times been suppressed in religious experience and by institutional formulas. A recovery of the name Sophia, or Wisdom, as an image for God and Jesus can play a central role in this goal of retrieval.

There are several reasons why a retrieval of "wisdom" is significant: (1) wisdom has a practical focus; (2) wisdom is acquired through everyday experiences and choices, as persons cope with the existential realities that come their way; (3) wisdom reflects an attitude of faith that wills the wholeness of all humanity; and (4) to be "wise" in the sense meant by the sages is to have a flexibility of heart and mind that enables one to discern appropriate choices for varying contexts.[15]

In effect, a recovery of wisdom in general and of the metaphor "Sophia" in particular focuses communal consciousness on questions of character, on questions of how the faith community's *lex orandi* and *lex credendi* issue in *lex agendi*.[16] Such a liturgical praxis, Power says, is founded on an integration of an ethical, agapic, and theoretical praxis, a notion that will be addressed later in this section.[17]

In the contemporary era, when "virtue" has become a household word, the discussion of the role of worship and the Christian community in character formation is no stranger to practical theology and social ethics.[18] Many scholars in these disciplines have asserted that the

[15] Power, "Liturgical Praxis," 301.

[16] Don Saliers, *Worship as Theology: Foretaste of Glory Divine* (Nashville: Abingdon Press, 1994) 3.

[17] Power, "Liturgical Praxis," 302, argues that Christ "and his transformation in the Spirit are testimony to that wisdom whereby the God who dwells in the cosmos, dwells in a people who through the pathos of suffering and compassion become a community in which there is neither Jew nor Greek, neither slave nor free, no male and female. This persuasion shapes the world in which, in the name of Christ, Christians are invited to live, and to which they can, in the same name, invite all humanity to enter."

[18] It is important to revisit Farley's contention here, namely that deep symbols such as "virtue" have diminished in function. In this case, where there has been a resurgence of attention to a discourse of virtue, it is vital to examine what "deeper normativity" is at work in society's appealing to the symbol. See Edward Farley, *Deep Symbols: Their Postmodern Effacement and Reclamation* (Valley Forge, Pa.: Trinity Press International, 1996) 23–4.

social significance of the Church, what gives it a distinctive integrity, is the way in which it is a "community capable of hearing the story of God we find in scripture and living in a manner that is faithful to that story."[19] In other words, one of the distinctive features of the Church is its role in shaping a moral world view.

A primary insight to be distilled from these discussions is that the Church does not exist solely nor even primarily to create moral rules or principles or to provide "religious" answers to "secular" questions. As Alexander Schmemann notes, operating out of such a dichotomy between the faith community and the world marginalizes the Church and impairs its ability to be a redemptive presence in the midst of the world. The most important task of the Church and its worship is to shape a "community of character" in which "habits" of the heart and mind are strong enough and pliable enough to witness to God's truth in a tragic and broken world.

As the faith community struggles to reconnect theory and praxis and overcome cultic categories, it is important that a more integrative understanding of the moral dimension of faith be established. Bruce Birch, from a biblical standpoint, argues that in general Protestants have tended to think of ethics in isolated categories, in terms of certain actions. Such a limited perspective perpetuates the bifurcation of theory and praxis.

What needs greater attention is the role of ethics in shaping character.[20] A more important question than "What should we do in a given situation?" is "How can the faith community nurture people in such a way that they have a disposition of heart and mind for making decisions grounded in the essence of the gospel?"

As seen in the previous chapter, this second question is critical to the structure of wisdom sayings. Alyce McKenzie expresses this when she demonstrates that the use of proverbial sayings requires a certain wisdom; appropriate connection of sayings with circumstances other than those in which they originated depends upon the decision-making ability of the interpretive community.[21]

---

[19] Stanley Hauerwas, *A Community of Character* (Notre Dame, Ind.: University of Notre Dame Press, 1981) 1.

[20] Bruce Birch, "Biblical Preaching as Moral Reflection," *Journal for Preachers* 5 (1982) 13.

[21] Alyce McKenzie, "Different Strokes for Different Folks: America's Quintessential Postmodern Proverb," *Theology Today* (July 1996) 207.

Edward Farley expresses a similar concern. Tradition, he explains, "is not the bare metaphysical fact that the past endures in the present." Interpretation of past wisdom and its appropriateness for the current praxis is shaped by a multiplicity of concerns—cultural location, economic situation, personal and communal crises, psychological needs, and political issues, just to mention a few.[22]

What this means for the question of how character is formed in a community and by that community's liturgy is that ethical norms that arise out of tradition cannot be interpreted as absolute. What is actually created in community is a metaphorical framework within which a critically reflective moral conversation can occur, a conversation that is constantly aware of the potential of its norms, interpretations, and principles to be both liberating and oppressive, both transformative and idolatrous.

"Virtue," Brown explains, is an attitude of the heart and mind; it is patterned within a particular tradition and a particular context and disposes one to certain actions.[23] Understood in this way, virtue cannot be seen as rigid conformity with certain rules. It is instead a sequence of moral impulses that guide persons as they choose what rules to follow.

For Aristotle, the highest virtue is practical wisdom, which brings heart and mind, reason and inclination, into dialogue, allowing persons to make sound decisions in particular situations. From an Aristotelian perspective, then, the exercise of virtue requires a unity of the soul, of its perception, intelligence, and desire. As Brown puts it, "there is an integrity to the person of character, a wholeness or completeness regarding the exercise of virtue."[24]

---

[22] Farley, *Deep Symbols,* 30. Even a so-called "traditionless" society "lives from the past in the sense that it preserves and institutionalizes its language, customs, policies and social organization. Thus, a specific past inevitably accumulates in and shapes the present of fire departments, committees, congregations, and music groups."

[23] Brown, *Character in Crisis,* 9.

[24] Ibid., 10–12. Brown provides a synthesis of a large body of work on the question of virtue. These include Aristotle, *Nichomachean Ethics,* trans. Martin Oswald (Indianapolis: Bobbs-Merrill, 1962); Alasdair MacIntyre, *After Virtue: A Study in Moral Theory* (Notre Dame, Ind.: University of Notre Dame Press, 1981); Stanley Hauerwas, *Character and the Christian Life: A Study in Theological Ethics* (San Antonio, Tex.: Trinity University Press, 1975); Bruce Birch and

Farley expands on this understanding. He suggests that human personhood is constituted by an intrinsic intersubjectivity. In spite of the fragmentation perpetuated by dominant epistemological models, a wholeness and interconnectedness is constitutive of human sociality.[25]

A biblical pedagogical framework for such character formation can be found in Proverbs. As Brown suggests, "through complex networks of rhetorical images and strategies . . . the book of Proverbs presents a powerfully compelling profile of normative character."[26] We turn now to look at how Don Saliers understands character formation to be a liturgical concern and how this is connected to the way wisdom in Proverbs functions to shape a life of integrity.

Proverbs and Liturgical Theology in Dialogue

An emphasis in Saliers' *Worship as Theology* is that questions concerning Christian ethics cannot be understood apart from the way the faith community worships God. Communal worship, he argues, constitutes the matrix through which the intentions and actions of persons are formed. Several themes in his work parallel the discussion above.

For example, Saliers argues that liturgy shapes a community's affective life through a patterning of emotions. This liturgical patterning occurs as people respond to the symbols and metaphors within their faith traditions. As he explains, however, even as liturgy's symbols and actions shape the community and guide persons in making moral decisions, the interpretive layering of cultural, personal, and geographical contexts is always present.[27] That is why worship must be understood as an ongoing dialectical process. Answers to the deeper questions of existence—who God is and who we are in relation to God—emerge only as worship shapes us over time, or as Farley would express it, as habitus is formed.

Larry Rasmussen, *Bible and Ethics in the Christian Life* (Minneapolis: Augsburg Press, 1989).

[25] Edward Farley, *The Fragility of Knowledge: Theological Education in the Church and University* (Philadelphia: Fortress Press, 1988). See also David Kelsey, *Between Athens and Berlin: The Theological Education Debate* (Grand Rapids, Mich.: Eerdmans, 1993) 45–6.

[26] Brown, *Character in Crisis*, 20.

[27] Saliers, *Worship as Theology*, 147–50.

One task of the faith community in light of this is to search for ways in which liturgical practice shapes our affections toward the things of God.[28] Much worship today has become an enactment of existing class values and goals; however, when liturgy is focused on shaping lives in the direction of God's purposes, it will seek to reveal the inadequacies of cultural practices and constructs of meaning.[29]

Liturgy, when it accomplishes this, is intrinsically eschatological; it invites participation in God's grace now but also contains an openness to the future, to a cosmic vision of a transformed creation. Saliers contends that the eschatological dimension of worship is central. It is an aspect of worship that has important implications for the issue of character formation.

First, as discussed above, virtue is a habitus of the heart and mind that disposes one to certain actions. As such, character cannot be dogmatically connected to any particular set of duties or obligations. Rather, developing the qualities of habitus is an ongoing process of "maturing into the mystery" of Christ's redemptive love:

"The Christian moral life is the concrete embodiment of a pattern of affections and virtues revealed in the pattern of God's self-giving in Jesus Christ. While many in our present social climate long for the certainty of conformity to a closed set of rules for behavior, Christian liturgy authentically celebrated compels us beyond the first-level certainty. . . . What is required is an actual reorientation of life, a

[28] In North American Protestantism, much of this emphasis on religious affections grows out of the Great Awakening. Such an emphasis is the focus of Jonathan Edwards, "Treatise Concerning Religious Affections," *The Works of Jonathan Edwards,* vol. 1, ed. Edward Hickman (Edinburgh: The Banner of Truth Trust, 1974). In his treatment of religious affections, Edwards wrestles with the question of character formation, making a distinction that hearkens back to the distinction between the two ways in Proverbs. He distinguishes between what he calls "gracious affections" and "false affections" and between "evangelical humiliation" (whereby a person gains a sense of transcendent holiness and begins to allow the beauty of divine presence to shape his/her heart and life) and "legal humiliation" (whereby a person acquires information about God but does not have an "answerable frame of heart"). For Edwards, a goal of the faith journey is a constant reflecting on life in an effort to plunge the depths of truth and change the disposition of the heart, the place where truly "gracious affections" shape virtuous living.

[29] Saliers, *Worship as Theology,* 161–70.

process of conversion of the heart and social imagination to the rule and reign of God that Jesus proclaims and embodies."[30]

Saliers contends that liturgical action and moral praxis are interdependent even though neither our lives nor our liturgies may reflect that fact.

As he explains, there is a "double work" of authentic liturgy. There is that aspect of liturgy that functions as *leitourgia*. This is the community's participation in the focused worship event as a gathered assembly. Interconnected with *leitourgia* is the people's liturgy in the world, the *diakonia*. What this means is that the Church's patterning of service as it gathers around the table and proclaims the Word shapes and permeates its service in daily life to those outside the community.[31]

To summarize, Saliers suggests that humans are formed in a multiplicity of ways by a combination of images, concerns, and communal and societal influences. For the Christian, however, the paschal mystery is the generative source of character formation. Because of this, the process of maturing in our participation in this mystery, the shaping of our dispositions toward God, can never be seen merely as a matter of adopting certain behaviors. The process of character formation is dialectical and always in process. It involves a continual "practicing" of the "good" through the patterns of liturgy. With that process in mind, we now turn to Proverbs.

Proverbs 10–31

An initial reading of this collection of short sayings is like reading a list of moral rules or principles. Each saying appears to be contained within its own individual frame with no apparent over-arching rhyme or reason. However, these sayings are more than isolated rules.[32] This becomes apparent when they are juxtaposed to the hermeneutical inclusio of Proverbs 1–9 and 31.

As Claudia Camp suggests, Proverbs 1–9 and 31 were created as an interpretive frame to restore to the collection of sayings in 10–30 their fullness of meaning. The proverbs in 10–30 have been cut loose from their contextual mooring. Considered individually, therefore, they

[30] Ibid., 175.

[31] Ibid., 180–2.

[32] J. J. Collins, "Proverbial Wisdom and the Yahwist Vision," *Gnomic Wisdom*, ed. J. D. Crossan (Chico, Calif.: Scholars Press, 1980) 1–18.

reflect a de-contextualization that can result in the diminishment of their meaning. The inclusio of 1–9 and 31, argues Camp, provides a theological "performance context" that recontextualizes the sayings.

The guiding metaphor for this framework is Sophia and Sophia's house. Proverbs 8 and 9, for example, allude to house imagery twice, and in 9:1, Sophia "builds her house" and invites all her hearers to come and feast at her table. The repetition of this imagery in poetic form in 1–9 and again in 31 establishes a literary framework for the collection that makes it a unified whole.[33]

While caution must be taken in drawing a liturgical parallel, several initial hermeneutical connections with Saliers' treatment of liturgy can be made. In particular, it can be suggested that, like the structure of Proverbs, when the Church provides a liturgical framework for the multiple rules, categories, and principles present to us in daily living, a focused moment of recontextualization guided by the redemptive presence of God becomes possible. Much as Sophia and Sophia's house in Proverbs 1–9 and 31 provide thematic and structural coherence for the moral actions prescribed in 10–30, so does the faith community, through its liturgy, invite persons to discover a unifying framework for their lives. A closer examination of how this process operates in Proverbs 1–9 will make this connection clearer.

In Prov 7:6, a narrative is begun:

"For at the window of my house
    I looked out through my lattice
and I saw among the simple ones,
    I observed among the youths,
    a young man without sense,
passing along the street near her corner,
    taking the road to her house
in the twilight, in the evening,
    at the time of night and darkness."

Painted here is a grim picture of a young man slipping away into the darkness, following the wrong path, the path of "foolishness."

The image of someone watching this scene through the "window" serves as a hinge or focal point for reading the rest of what Brown

[33] Claudia Camp, *Wisdom and the Feminine in the Book of Proverbs* (Sheffield: Almond Press, 1985) 179–208.

calls the "metanarrative" of Proverbs from a liturgical perspective. "Watching through the window of home" both directs our attention away from the community toward the world and reflects back to the context of the community. Two emphases emerge that parallel the "double work" of the liturgy outlined above: (1) the centrality of the community and tradition in shaping character and (2) the process of journeying out into the world where the testing of virtue inevitably occurs.[34]

The centrality of "home" and the communal values taught there are evident from the beginning of Proverbs. Brown's translation and interpretation of Prov 1:1-7 are helpful here:

"1:1 The Proverbs of Solomon, Son of David, King of Israel

1:2 To appropriate wisdom and instruction; to understand insightful sayings;

1:3 To acquire effective instruction, righteousness, justice and equity.

1:4 To teach the immature prudence and the young knowledge in discretion.

1:5 Let the wise (also) attend and gain erudition, and the discerning acquire skill (in counseling).

1:6 To understand a proverb, a figure, words of the wise, and their enigmas.

1:7 The fear of Yahweh is the beginning of knowledge; fools despise wisdom and instruction."[35]

As Brown notes, these opening verses of Proverbs cover virtue types ranging from concrete practical skills to more abstract qualities such as righteousness.

Brown also contends that these introductory verses are structured with communal and moral virtues at the center:

"This litany of values opens and concludes with reference to the intellectual values of wisdom and instruction (vss. 2 and 7) as well as to their literary conventions. . . . Sandwiched between this literary envelope are particular distinctions in virtue. Effective instruction,

---

[34] Brown, *Character in Crisis*, 152.
[35] Ibid., 23–4.

skill, prudence, and discretion constitute eminently practical or instrumental virtues that enable the person to pursue successfully certain goals and objectives. . . . At the center of this constellation of virtues are found the comprehensive moral traits of 'righteousness, justice and equity' which constitute normative communal relations and conduct."[36]

As Proverbs unfolds, these virtues reappear throughout the sayings in 10–30 to echo communal concerns and to reemphasize the importance of justice and righteousness as the community makes moral decisions.

The communal dimension of Proverbs, says Brown, is grounded in the "fear of the Lord" as both the beginning and ending of the journey toward wisdom (1:7).[37] "Fear" in this context means reverence for or awareness of the presence of the divine. In other words, as Brown puts it, virtues mark the external shape of ethical character, but the center of character is the person's relationship to God.

Gaining wisdom, then, is not a mere gathering of facts or the adoption of certain prescribed or normative behaviors. It consists in a shaping of the heart and mind toward God. Character in Proverbial Wisdom has a dialogical dimension in which several concerns are interconnected: (1) individual choice and relationship with God; (2) tradition and the community's interpretation of tradition; and (3) the way tradition is shaped and reconstructed as persons journey away from the community into the marketplace and encounter dissonant images and interpretations.

The Role of Wisdom Personified

Proverbs begins in a communal pedagogical setting where a father instructs his son in the way of wisdom.[38] Within the framework of community, root metaphors are established and taught. In 7:6, noted above, the son undertakes the journey into the marketplace. There, in the streets of the world, he encounters images that are vastly different from those he has learned in the setting of his community.[39]

---

[36] Ibid.

[37] See also Gerhard von Rad, *Wisdom in Israel* (Nashville: Abingdon Press, 1972) 65–73.

[38] K. A. Farmer, *Proverbs and Ecclesiastes: Who Knows What Is Good?* (Grand Rapids, Mich.: Eerdmans, 1991) 41–2.

[39] As Claudia Camp, "Woman Wisdom as Root Metaphor: A Theological Consideration," *The Listening Heart: Essays in Wisdom and the Psalms in Honor of*

At first these new categories of reality are disorienting. This disorientation, however, is inherent in the metaphorical process, and as these dissonant images are juxtaposed to traditional understandings, the possibility arises for reshaping traditional symbols and metaphors. What ensues is an on-going process of reformulation of moral principles and consequent shaping or reformulation of character.

Throughout this process, Sophia is present. In Proverbs 8, she

"takes her stand;
beside the gates in front of the town,
at the entrance of the portals she cries out."[40]

The virtues on which she focuses are related to what Brown calls "sagacious discourse": "They [Sophia's words] are straight to one who understands / and right to those who find knowledge."[41] As Brown outlines, in 8:6-9, Sophia first emphasizes values that constitute a just order. Values of truth and righteousness follow. All of these values are an integral part of her "straight talk," demonstrating that truth cannot be abstracted from its linguistic form.[42]

In 8:12-21, Brown continues, wisdom is depicted as rooted in the communal virtues of righteousness, justice, and prudence that were introduced in 1:1-7. In conjunction with this anthropological element, it then becomes apparent in verses 22-31 that Sophia also exists in the cosmic realm.[43]

Samuel Terrien argues that it is this cosmic/anthropocentric dialectic that makes wisdom a central biblical matrix for divine presence. On the one hand, as above, Sophia describes normative character. Then

---

R. E. Murphy, ed. K. G. Hoglud et al., JSOTSS (Sheffield: JSOT Press, 1987) puts it, as the discourse in Proverbs 1–9 continues, it becomes clear that there is another level of authority beyond that of the hierarchical one between father and son. The rhetorical structure urges the student to find underlying the voice of the father a second more revelatory voice. That voice, says Camp, is Woman Wisdom, who is the mediator between heaven and earth; and at an even deeper level of meaning is the voice of God, who speaks through both the teacher and Sophia.

[40] Prov 8:1.
[41] Prov 8:9.
[42] Brown, *Character in Crisis*, 36.
[43] Ibid., 37–8.

she departs from that anthropological level, illustrating through the metaphorical language of Prov 8:22-31 that wisdom also transcends time:

"God created me at the beginning of God's work,
    the first of God's acts of long ago.
Ages ago I was set up,
    at the first, before the beginning of the earth."[44]

Sophia is seen with God in creation, joyfully experiencing the work of God's hands:[45]

"When God marked out the foundations of the earth,
    then I was beside God, like a master worker;
and I was daily God's delight,
    rejoicing before God always,
rejoicing in God's inhabited world
    and delighting in the human race."[46]

Some scholars have even translated "master worker" in 8:30 as "child," suggesting that Sophia delights in creation as a child might, rejoicing in the wonders and mystery of the created universe. As Brown notes, the language of worship permeates this litany of creation as in it Sophia "embodies the irrepressible joy of witnessing creation unfold and receiving God's 'affections.'"[47]

---

[44] Prov 8:22-23. The NRSV has been altered here to reflect inclusive language for God.

[45] Samuel Terrien, "The Play of Wisdom: Turning Point in Biblical Theology," *Horizons in Biblical Theology* 3 (1981) 134.

[46] Prov 8:29b-31. The NRSV has been altered here to reflect inclusive language for God.

[47] Brown, *Character in Crisis*, 38. See also Bernhard Lang, *Wisdom and the Book of Proverbs: An Israelite Goddess Redefined* (New York: Pilgrim Press, 1986); and R.B.Y. Scott, "Wisdom in Creation: The AMON of Proverbs 8:30," *Vetus Testamentum* 10 (1960) 213–23.

Roland Murphy, *The Forms of The Old Testament Literature*, volume 13: *Wisdom Literature: Job, Proverbs, Ruth, Canticles, Ecclesiastes, Esther* (Grand Rapids, Mich.: Eerdmans, 1981) 61, suggests that this sense of Sophia's preexistence, or her being "begotten not made," reflects some Canaanite influence. See also von Rad, *Wisdom in Israel*, 151–7.

It is at this juncture that Sophia provides a "pedagogical link" of
sorts between humanity and the divine:[48]

"And now, my children, listen to me:
  happy are those who keep my ways.
Hear instruction and be wise,
  and do not neglect it.
Happy is the one who listens to me,
  watching daily at my gates,
  waiting beside my doors.
For whoever finds me finds life
  and obtains favor from the LORD."[49]

To join hands with Sophia, in the biblical tradition, is, in a sense, to
enter into relationship with God. Sophia's encounter with divine
presence and consequent rejoicing, expressed in Proverbs 8 in the language of worship, is something that human persons can participate in
as they accept the invitation to enter Sophia's house and strive to live
lives of virtue.[50]

Terrien argues that the belief implied in Proverbs 1–9, that there is a
bridge or mediating presence between Creator and creation, is the rich
soil in which the entirety of the biblical corpus is rooted. He also contends that the primary image for this mediating presence is Woman
Wisdom; she calls out at the city gates, participates with God in creation, and invites all in the city to enter her house.[51]

Of course, in this regard it is equally important to note that in Israelite religion, monotheistic beliefs did not allow for personifications to become real
deities. In this, Hebrew understanding of Sophia departs from these Near
Eastern myths.

Claudia Camp suggests that Woman Wisdom be treated as a root metaphor
that justifies embracing God as Goddess. Her treatment echoes David Power's
suggestion for broadening our imagery for God to include the female imagery
of Sophia. See Camp, "Woman Wisdom as Root Metaphor," 45–76.

[48] Brown, *Character in Crisis,* 40.

[49] Prov 8:32-35.

[50] Brown, *Character in Crisis,* 37–8.

[51] Terrien, "The Play of Wisdom," 136–7, says that "wisdom playing in the
presence of God is also wisdom delighting in the midst of the children of men
[*sic*]. She throws a bridge from cult to culture. She introduces the *oikoumene* to
an aesthetic, scientific and philosophical contemplation of the world."

As will be seen even more clearly in Job, wisdom seeks in its own era of skepticism and cultural change what the liturgical movement seeks for this era: to offer an imaginative and intellectual structure of contemplation that embraces all of creation. It accomplishes this, says Terrien, by opening an avenue of dialogue with culture that maintains a rootedness in tradition.

Some liturgical theologians conceive of liturgy in a way similar to this, understanding the role of liturgy as a sort of mediating presence between divine initiative and human response. For example, Kevin Irwin defines "theology" in terms that are not unlike the definition of "wisdom" that emerges in the wisdom corpus. In discussing liturgical theology, Irwin refers to Augustine's understanding of theology as speech *from* and *to* God as well as speech *about* God. Rather than maintaining the historical separation of nature and grace, faith and reason, scholarship and piety, theology and doxology, Irwin understands *theologia* to integrate not only the efforts of the intellect to speak scientifically about God but also the actions of the faith community through its liturgy to speak to God.[52]

Because it sacramentalizes creation and thus reminds humanity of the intrinsic mystery of the created world, liturgy restrains theology from becoming an "a-theological religious science." Liturgy is an event in which the ultimate realities with which theology is primarily concerned (such as God, sin, Christ, and redemption) are experienced within a framework of "thanks and praise," a framework that acknowledges the depth of the mysteries of God and the limits of even the best theological language.[53]

For the sages, the created world provided the matrix through which humanity gained a deeper understanding of the mysteries of God, mysteries which Irwin says liturgy also functions to reveal. As this brief explication of character formation in Proverbs 1–9 suggests, the sages believed that a person gained wisdom when he/she could observe creation and the chaos of the human world in juxtaposition and make the metaphorical connection between those observations and God's presence and purpose. In other words, a "wise" person looks beyond the tragic structuring of creation to the power and love of the Creator that disrupts evil and brings redemp-

[52] Kevin Irwin, *Context and Text: Method in Liturgical Theology* (Collegeville: The Liturgical Press, 1994) 266.
[53] Ibid., 268.

tion.[54] The movement toward redemption, in this sense, is not an isolated historical event; it is a journey.

PROVERBS AND THE "JOURNEY OF CONVERSION"[55]

Alexander Schmemann describes the eucharistic "journey" in *For the Life of the World:*

"The journey begins when Christians leave their homes and beds. They leave, indeed, their life in this present concrete world, and whether they have to drive fifteen miles or walk a few blocks, a sacramental act is already taking place, an act which is the very condition of everything else that is to happen. For now they are on their way to constitute the Church, or to be more exact, to be transformed into the Church of God. . . . The purpose of this 'coming together' is not to add a religious dimension to the natural community. . . . The purpose is to fulfill the church, and that means to make present the One in whom all things are at their end and all things are at their beginning."[56]

The connections must be made somewhat cautiously, but the sense of journey implied as Woman Wisdom calls at the gates of the city and by her invitation in Proverbs 9 has some intriguing parallels with liturgical concerns, particularly with how participation in liturgy is participation in what Searle calls a "journey of conversion." A brief look at what might be termed the "sacramental" aspects of Proverbs can further our discussion at this point.

As Kathleen O'Connor discusses, the marketplace, in addition to the faith community, is depicted as a primary place where persons meet

---

[54] Saliers, *Worship as Theology,* 183–8, discusses this in relation to character formation as he describes how prayer contains both glorification of God and sanctification of all that is created. For the faith community, there is the joy of contemplating the transcendent Creator and the challenge of active ministry to and in the created world. Both contemplative piety and compassion for creation are rooted in and flow out of habitus. To worship God involves not only ritual action and language in the liturgical event but also embodiment of the Word and sacrament in the world as participants are given wisdom to perceive God's presence everywhere in creation.

[55] Searle, "Journey of Conversion," 35. Brown, *Character in Crisis,* 152, prefers to call the journey inherent in wisdom a "journey of character."

[56] Alexander Schmemann, *For the Life of the World: Sacraments and Orthodoxy* (New York: St. Vladimir's Seminary Press, 1973) 160.

Sophia (1:20; 8:2; and 9:3). In ancient times, the city square was the center of social interaction. It is in this urban setting, in the "daily-ness" of things, that Sophia is to be found. Her voice is heard there in the "thick of things," in the mundaneness and brokenness of human social, economic, and political interaction.[57]

In Proverbs, there is no clear distinction between the sacred and the profane because all of life is understood as permeated by divine pres-ence. Several "sacramental" qualities of Proverbs can be highlighted in relation to this.

First, these passages have a "public" cast to them. This serves as a re-minder that the divine/human relationship cannot be categorized into one theological framework or world view. Sophia stands in the market-place, encouraging her students to recognize the sacredness of all life.

Second, Sophia, standing in the doorway to her house, calling out into the city, becomes a metaphorical intersection of meaning for persons who are part of both the faith community and the world. In a related sense, liturgy also stands as a kind of intersection of communal and societal horizons. As Gordon Lathrop argues, people who gather for worship bring with them their experiences of the world. As those experiences are juxtaposed to language about God, meanings are re-shaped and character is formed.

Finally, Sophia's location in the city square "signifies the breadth and prodigality of Wisdom's invitation."[58] Sophia's call is to all people, and particularly to those who are not yet wise (1:22, 32; 8:5; 9:4). The people to whom she appeals are "not a narrowly defined group, not the pious, nor the sinless, nor even the elect nation of Israel, but the 'simple' anyone in the squares of the city or at the cross-roads of the world."[59]

In other words, as the above quote from Schmemann demonstrates, the eucharistic journey begins for believers when they leave their

[57] Kathleen O'Connor, "The City Square and the Home: Wisdom's World," *Journal for Preachers* (1996) 10-11.

[58] O'Connor, "The City Square and the Home," 11.

[59] Ibid. As O'Connor notes, this "ecumenical" tendency inherent in wisdom does not mean that we are to read the text uncritically. In reinterpreting the metaphors and symbols of personified wisdom for our time, it is necessary to appropriate the dialogical structure of the text without embracing its stereo-typical and patriarchal leanings. See also Newsom, "Women and the Dis-course of Patriarchal Wisdom."

homes and make their way to the place of worship. This movement itself, says Schmemann, is a sacramental act. How the faith world is a world-in-process or a journey that occurs both within the church building and outside its doors is discussed at length by John Baldovin. As he explains, in its earliest stages, Christianity was an urban phenomenon. One of the significant means by which the Church made its faith a social as well as religious phenomenon was to make various aspects of its liturgy public.[60]

This sense of journey beyond communal parameters is reflected in Proverbs through the metaphor of "the way." Habel suggests that the symbol of the "way," or the "road," delineated primarily in Prov 4:10-19, functions to mediate some particular meanings.

As seen in Chapter 4, for example, in Proverbs 4 two "ways" are offered to the seeker after wisdom. To travel the way of wisdom and discipline is to choose life; the alternate way results in disruptions of life and chaos (4:16-19). The way of righteousness or truth is honest and public. In biblical understanding, explains Habel, a *derek* or way is an "open road whose direction is clear and whose end is known"; also implied by a *derek* is a special relationship between the road and the traveler, a mutual knowing of their respective directions.[61]

What does Habel mean by this? Because the *derek* has been traveled before, he says, it contains a certain wisdom or tradition. In other words, Habel continues, the tested wisdom of past experience has some power to "lead" new generations in a particular direction. Of course, the way of wisdom in Proverbs 1–9 is the way of YHWH; it is also apparent, as Habel notes, that the way *of* wisdom is at the same time the way *to* wisdom.

Searle contends that this metaphor of journey is an appropriate one for conversion. He suggests that the journey of conversion has three parts or movements; these parts parallel the several aspects of the metaphorical process outlined in the previous chapter. First, there is the beginning of the journey, initiated by some form of crisis. Sometimes the crisis presents itself in the form of a problem or question for which there is no adequate answer; crises also emerge as a result of

[60] John Baldovin, *Worship: City, Church, and Renewal* (Washington, D.C.: Pastoral Press, 1991) 5.

[61] Brown, *Character in Crisis,* 34, states that the *derek* is a communal metaphor as it can only be formed by the passage of many feet. See also Newsom, "Woman and the Discourse of Patriarchal Wisdom," 147.

more gradual life changes, as people become restless or dissatisfied with the direction their lives are going. Thus, the journey away from the safe confines of traditional or customary ways of being and doing begins. Within the metaphorical process, this marks the stage of disorientation or destabilization.

The journey itself sparks several stages of growth and reflection that include a "kind of dying to one's previous life and world" and a "recognition that long-held assumptions and beliefs about self and world are not true."[62] Accepting that one's assumptions are not ultimate, says Searle, is the turning point of the journey, the moment of growth and transformation. This incorporates the second and third stages of the metaphorical process—mimesis and transformation.

The "return" journey, as Searle terms it, begins when the perception of the situation is altered, when the ability to cope and to have hope in the midst of the tragic structures of existence is renewed. This enables persons to exist within the community and the world with a new vision. This is represented in the metaphorical process by the final stage of "restabilization."

This aspect of journey is inherent in the structure of Proverbs.[63] To revisit the earlier discussion, the son begins his journey into the marketplace, encountering the disorienting voices of a pluralistic world community, voices that are much different from those of his tradition. Engaging those voices, however, enables critical reflection and reconfiguration of traditional understanding. The result is a deepening maturity of character, a shaping of his affective and cognitive dispositions such that he is enabled to make ethical decisions that correlate more nearly to God's vision.

Finally, at the end of Proverbs is the "return."[64] The image in Proverbs 31, looking once again through the "window" to see the son settled into his own home with Woman Wisdom as his partner, hearkens back to the picture in 7:6. Implied here is the sense that the son has made his choice. He journeyed beyond the parameters of tradition, experi-

[62] Searle, "Journey of Conversion," 41–2.

[63] Brown, *Character in Crisis*, 49, states that "the book of Proverbs is eminently more than a catalogue of virtues. It is essentially about the journey from home to community and back again, a *rite de passage* that requires letting go of the parental ties of security to seek one's own security and identity through service to the community."

[64] Ibid., 154–5.

enced the challenges and vastness of the world outside the framework of his communal window, and then returned to establish his own faith identity. Important to this journey, as Brown highlights, is that the "return" destination of this journey in Proverbs is

"back home but never to the original domicile. All the practical and intellectual virtues with which one was raised, from discipline to piety . . . find their ultimate significance within the larger network of the community and the values that sustain it. The balanced and comprehensive repertoire of virtues serves to open up new vistas of maturity that, in turn, provide new levels of engagement within the community, including the opportunity for authentic intimacy."[65]

As noted above, Searle suggests that this "journey" metaphor for conversion is inherent in liturgy as well.

Synthesizing the work of Daniel Levinson and Arnold van Gennep, Searle argues that there are three moments in liturgical process. First, traditional understandings or ways of being are disrupted. Then, during a transitional stage, there are encounters with views of reality that challenge old ones and initiate a process of critical reflection. The transformations that occur as a result of these encounters finally reach a point of restabilization. Reentry into the community, with deeper levels of maturity, is then possible.[66]

Searle connects this understanding of ritual to Christian ritual in particular by discussing how the journey of Christ was a journey from the Creator into this world and back to the Creator through the cross. The climax of the journey is the paschal mystery. To participate in the paschal mystery through liturgy is to enter into Christ's journey, a journey that is an ongoing metaphorical process of crisis, reflection, and growth.[67]

---

[65] Ibid., 49.

[66] Searle, "Journey of Conversion," 45, suggests that this pattern aids in understanding numerous rituals such as marriages, funerals, initiation rites, and new year celebrations. See Arnold van Gennep, *The Rites of Passage* (Chicago: University of Chicago Press, 1960), and Daniel Levinson et al., *The Seasons of a Man's Life* (New York: A. A. Knopf, 1977).

[67] Searle, "Journey of Conversion," 48–9, states that every sacrament is a rite of passage or "an opportunity to live through the transition occurring within our own lives in explicit identification with the passage of Jesus through death

To conclude, Habel argues that in Proverbs 1–9 the symbol of journey, the "way," functions in several different symbolic zones or fields of human experience. It functions on a personal or individual level in Proverbs 4–6 where personal acquisition and appropriation of wisdom are urged. The symbol also operates within a communal zone; seekers after wisdom are rooted in the Israelite covenant community and its Yahwistic religion. While none of the major symbols of *heilgeschichte* are introduced in Proverbs 1–9 (for example, ark, exodus, or theophany), says Habel, Yahwistic religion still provides a broad frame of reference for the community's appropriation of wisdom's metaphors.

In addition to the personal and communal levels of meaning present in the symbol of the "way," a third field of meaning is designated by Habel as the realm of cosmological reflection. This field of meaning overlaps the others and mutually influences them. It is primarily concerned with "cosmic and primordial relationships to life."[68]

As this discussion of the "way" demonstrates, wisdom in Proverbs both encompasses redemption history and expands its parameters to the cosmic realm. This is a primary reason why wisdom is an appropriate and even necessary conversation partner for those liturgical theologies that seek to maintain traditional distinctiveness as well as direct their thinking toward the larger world.

CONCLUSION

"Wisdom has built her house,
    she has hewn her seven pillars.
She has slaughtered her animals, she has mixed her wine,
    she has also set her table.
She has sent out her servant-girls, she calls
    from the highest places in town,
'You that are simple, turn in here!'
    To those without sense she says,
'Come, eat of my bread
    and drink the wine I have mixed.
Lay aside immaturity, and live,
    and walk in the way of insight.'"[69]

---

from this world to the Father." He points to the fact that inauthentic celebration of liturgy can fail to enable such a journey of encounter and conversion.

[68] Norman Habel, "The Symbolism of Wisdom in Proverbs 1–9," *Interpretation* 26 (1972) 150.

[69] Prov 9:1-6.

O'Connor argues that Prov 9:1-6 presents a challenge to contemporary faith communities and their cultural assumptions. In this passage, Sophia invites all to come in and sit at her table. In her house, a banquet table is spread for all peoples; to feast at her table, Sophia proclaims, is to "discover meaning for the journey of life."[70]

Again, parallels to Schmemann's sacramental theology emerge. Schmemann argues that a central mystery of the eucharistic meal is the mystery of the Church existing for the sake of the world. In the Eucharist, we offer all things through Christ to God who created them. Returning these gifts to the world through our ethical praxis is also part of the Eucharist.

In the contemporary era, Schmemann continues, feasts of the liturgical year have diminished in meaning; for many people, they represent little more than breaks from the mundaneness of daily living.[71] This has happened in part because public life has been taken over by a market-driven mentality.[72] As Schmemann insists, however, there is a "non-transactional" quality to the Eucharist as we are given God's free gift of grace and then respond in gratitude through *leitourgia* and *diakonia*.

This understanding reflects the extent to which Schmemann's work is permeated by an emphasis on both the anthropological and cosmological dimensions of sacramentality.[73] We have already discovered how this dual focus is central to Proverbial Wisdom. To summarize, much as the sages insisted that knowledge of God permeates the cosmos and that humans have the potential to discover God's presence in the ordinariness of daily living, so Schmemann insists that the purpose of liturgy is to transform human awareness so that persons can perceive the sacramentality of the whole world.[74] It is this emphasis that links us, finally, to Farley's understanding of habitus.

One of Schmemann's focal points is that in worship, the faith community regularly "interrupts" common patterns of social interaction

---

[70] O'Connor, "The City Square and the Home," 13.

[71] Alexander Schmemann, *Introduction to Liturgical Theology* (New York: St. Vladimir's Seminary Press, 1986) 59–75.

[72] Aidan Kavanagh, *On Liturgical Theology* (New York: Pueblo, 1984) 29–30.

[73] Ibid., 54. Kavanagh suggests that the city and the Church within the city are necessary to a redeemed world. The Church is a holistic exigency "whose faith crisscrossed and interacted with every human experience and institution rather than a jumble of separate analytical categories."

[74] Schmemann, *For the Life of the World*, 120.

to participate in a radically different pattern. In doing this, as discussed in Chapter 2, the Church is not a cultic structure seeking isolation from a "profane" world.[75] Rather, the Church becomes what Lathrop calls a "sanctuary of meaning," a matrix within which all of our experiences and understandings of life are reoriented.[76]

Because Schmemann's work is rooted in the modern era with its own understandings of the categories of "sacred" and "profane," Farley's later work in philosophical theology contributes important insights if we are to make the most productive application of Schmemann's work to current liturgical concerns.

A brief recounting of material outlined earlier will help to clarify the discussion at this point. Farley argues that a crisis of contemporary theology is that faith is no longer recognized as the primary pattern or habitus within which knowledge of the world develops. One of his primary concerns is for a renewal of the understanding of theology as integrative of theory and practice. Contrary to dominant epistemological categories, he insists that the reflective life of the believer is a hermeneutical orientation that strives to make sense out of "all those things in life that present themselves to us for response and understanding."[77]

Within this perspective, the Church is a horizon of redemption through which this integration of personal, moral, communal, and social can occur. Farley, like Schmemann, asks how this redemptive horizon is to exist in relation to the surrounding culture. In answering this question, Farley insists that the Church is to provide an integrative intersection between the faith community and the world.[78]

Wisdom provides a biblical foundation for such an understanding. As seen in the above passage from Proverbs 9, for example, Sophia

[75] Mircea Eliade, *The Sacred and the Profane: The Nature of Religion—The Significance of Religious Myth, Symbolism and Ritual within Life and Culture* (New York: Harper and Row, 1957) 50–7.

[76] Walter Huffman, "The Concept of Sacred Space," *The Landscape of Praise: Readings in Liturgical Renewal*, ed. Blair Gilmer Meeks (Valley Forge, Pa.: Trinity Press International, 1996) 127–30.

[77] Edward Farley, *Theologia: The Fragmentation and Unity of Theological Education* (Philadelphia: Fortress Press, 1983) 31, 35–6.

[78] Thomas Ogletree, "Christian Social Ethics as a Theological Discipline," *Shifting Boundaries: Contextual Approaches to the Structure of Theological Education*, ed. Barbara Wheeler and Edward Farley (Louisville: Westminster/John Knox Press, 1991) 204.

stands at the intersection of the various dimensions of life that Farley describes and invites the world into that "sanctuary of meaning" where integration can occur.

Of course, standing in contrast to the "sanctuary of meaning," represented by the house of Woman Wisdom, is the house of the Woman Folly in 9:13-18:

"The foolish woman is loud;
 she is ignorant and knows nothing.
She sits at the door of her house,
 on a seat at the high places of the town,
calling to those who pass by,
 who are going straight on their way,
'You who are simple, turn in here!'
 And to those without sense she says,
'Stolen water is sweet,
 and bread eaten in secret is pleasant.'
But they do not know that the dead are there,
 that her guests are in the depths of Shē'ōl."

Throughout Proverbs, as Habel demonstrates, the contrasting metaphors are present, representing the two possible outcomes of one's journey—life and death.[79]

To pursue the way of "life" is to journey through the city and choose the house of Woman Wisdom, bringing our experiences of the faith community, our experiences in the marketplace, and our own personal struggles and questions. When wisdom becomes the goal of our journey, then the world and its objects are no longer ends in themselves; the tendency toward self-securing idolatry is disrupted.[80]

---

[79] Habel, "The Symbolism of Wisdom in Proverbs 1–9," 152–6. See also Perdue, *Wisdom and Creation*, 94–101.

[80] Edward Farley, *Ecclesial Man: A Social Phenomenology of Faith and Reality* (Philadelphia: Fortress Press, 1975) 142–4, argues that "alienated historical existence is marked by idolatrous relations with everything in the surrounding world. Alienated man [*sic*] intends the whole content of his surrounding world in the hope that any or all has the capacity to replace chaos. Idolatry, therefore, modifies one's transcendental consciousness and becomes a way of being temporal, a way of living in one's personal space, and an ingredient in all motivations and decisions."

Schmemann offers a similar insight that dialogues well with this passage from Proverbs 9:

"When we see the world as an end in itself, everything becomes itself a value and consequently loses all value, because only in God is found the meaning of everything, and the world is meaningful only when it is the 'sacrament' of God's presence. Things treated merely as things in themselves destroy themselves because only in God have they any life. The world of nature, cut off from the source of life, is a dying world. For one who thinks food in itself is the source of life, eating is communion with a dying world; it is communion with death."[81]

Sin, says Schmemann, is what happens when people fail to see all of life as a "sacrament of communion with God."

This happens, as Farley suggests in his discussion of the collapse of the house of authority, when people allow God to be defined solely in terms of religious structures. It also occurs when the Church is perceived primarily in cultic terms, wherein its purpose is to fulfill the elemental desires of individual persons. Redemption or reconciliation disrupts this way of being in relation to God and the world, empowering the faith community to affirm the sacramentality of all creation and to allow that conviction to shape its moral praxis.

Sophia invites the entirety of earth's family to her banquet. Some scholars contend that her house represents the "home of a rich woman who opens the doors to invite in poor and foolish to share in her plenty." Others see the house as an image for Israel's Temple. Some even argue that because Sophia's house is depicted as resting on seven pillars, it is representative of the entire earth.[82] In any case, Sophia's banquet, like the Church's eucharistic meal, has the multivalent quality of being rooted in a particular historical tradition while also embracing the world: "Wisdom's home is the earth imagined as a temple, as the dwelling place of the Creator, and as place of joyous feasting for all who come."[83]

---

[81] Schmemann, *For the Life of the World.*
[82] O'Connor, "The City Square and the Home," 13.
[83] Ibid.

Chapter 7

Job: The Journey of Conversion as Critical Reflection

A central goal of this project, outlined in the thesis statement, has been to address three urgent issues that confront the Church in the contemporary era: (1) how to provide a theological foundation for liturgical renewal that engages the question of the validity of the truth claims mediated by liturgical forms; (2) how to maintain a rootedness in the Judeo-Christian biblical tradition that is methodologically centered on cosmology and anthropology rather than solely on redemption history; and (3) how to establish within liturgy's hermeneutical framework an ongoing process of critical reflection.

Previous chapters have demonstrated that the societal circumstances precipitating these issues are multiple, ranging from shifts in world economic and political centers of power to monumental historical tragedies to the diminishment of culture's foundational symbols. In the midst of this tumult of change, the Church is experiencing a loss of credibility as its dominance as the "one true" religion is undermined by increasing religious pluralism, diversity, and relativity.[1]

What the faith community needs to do in these times of unprecedented change, says Gordon Kaufman, is to "enter into the most radical kind of deconstruction and reconstruction of the traditions we have inherited, including especially their most central and precious symbols, God and Jesus Christ and Torah."[2] As seen in Chapter 5, such

---

[1] Hans Kung, "A New Basic Model for Theology: Divergencies and Convergencies," *Paradigm Change in Theology,* trans. Margaret Kohl, ed. Hans Kung and David Tracy (New York: Crossroad, 1991) 445.

[2] Gordon Kaufman, "Nuclear Eschatology and the Study of Religion," *Journal of the American Academy of Religion* 51 (1983) 13.

a critical examination and reappropriation of historically rooted and foundational models for understanding religion is one of the most complex and exciting tasks the Church faces today.

The task is exciting because it offers the faith community several opportunities: (1) to embrace a greater appreciation for the created world, (2) to restore the dynamism and formative character of religious language, (3) to begin a dialogue of mutual growth and learning with other religious understandings, and (4) to reach a new awareness of the interdependence of all of creation, particularly of all humanity.[3]

However, the difficulty of this undertaking, of seeking to renew traditional models without diminishing the essential truths they contain, cannot be underestimated. Rediscovering and reconstructing society's deep symbols involves letting go of some "old" metaphors that have become entrenched in economical, social, and political distortions of privilege and power. Renewal ultimately means to propose a different vision of existence, one in which "delight in the other, not domination of the other, is central."[4]

Earlier chapters have demonstrated how liturgical theologians in recent years have struggled to reconstruct traditional liturgical forms in response to the Enlightenment's impact on the Church; enormous progress has been made toward establishing liturgical methods and practices that are more ecumenical and unifying rather than denominational and divisive. The liturgical movement has also increased awareness of the faith community's existence within and responsibility toward a larger cosmological context.

This project has proposed that a necessary element to the continuation of liturgical renewal emerges in liturgical theology's dialogue with contemporary biblical methodologies, in particular with biblical methods that are more attuned to the theological foundations of the wisdom corpus—anthropology and cosmology. The following analy-

[3] Sallie McFague, *Metaphorical Theology: Models of God in Religious Language* (Philadelphia: Fortress Press, 1982) x.

[4] Ibid., xi. See also Wendy Farley, "Eros and the Truth: Feminist Theory and the Claims of Reality," *Theology and the Interhuman,* ed. Robert R. Williams (Valley Forge, Pa.: Trinity Press International, 1995) 30–3; Peter Hodgson, "The Face and the Spirit," *Theology and the Interhuman,* ed. Robert R. Williams (Valley Forge, Pa.: Trinity Press International, 1995) 44–9; Marjorie Proctor-Smith, *In Her Own Rite: Constructing Feminist Liturgical Tradition* (Nashville: Abingdon Press, 1990) 56–8.

sis of the structural form and theological content of Job will address the third primary issue raised by this project's thesis, namely that

"A liturgical theological method grounded in the dialogical movement between the horizons of everyday reality and tradition in Old Testament wisdom theology as it is developed in the structural forms of Proverbs 1–9 and 31 and Job contributes to the ongoing work of the liturgical movement by . . . implying within its hermeneutical framework an ongoing process of self-critique."

To support this argument, the first part of the chapter will examine how the world view and norms of Job's tradition are challenged by his circumstance of inexplicable suffering. The structure of the narrative and the "journey of conversion" that Job undertakes addresses the question of how liturgy engages issues of oppression and suffering.

Job's faith journey brings him face to face with the reality of the tragic structure of existence and what "virtue" and redemption mean within that structure. The ultimate outcome for him is a redemptive encounter with God that transforms his world view.[5] The second part of this chapter will detail how that redemptive process suggests a biblical framework for critical reflection that can function foundationally for liturgical renewal.

The liturgical movement has helped the Church rethink the quality and nature of its worship for the contemporary era. However, by uncovering the extent to which many of the Church's institutional structures and worship forms continue to perpetuate marginalization and oppression, liturgical theologians have reminded us that much work in the area of critical analysis is yet to be done. This growing edge in liturgical renewal raises a host of satellite discussions touching on issues ranging from *anamnesis* to moral praxis to eschatology.

Although Rebecca Chopp's quote from *Alice in Wonderland* and her accompanying comments are directed primarily at theological education, they nevertheless support the contention that critically analyzing liturgical structures to make them more liberating and inclusive is at heart a eucharistic concern:

[5] Langdon Gilkey, "Power, Order, Justice and Redemption: Theological Comments on Job," *The Voice from the Whirlwind: Interpreting the Book of Job*, ed. Leo Perdue and W. Clark Gilpin (Nashville: Abingdon Press, 1992) 159–71, describes how power, order, moral justice, and redemption are juxtaposed throughout the book of Job.

"The table was a large one, but the three were all crowded together at one corner of it. 'No room, no room!' they cried out when they saw Alice coming. 'There's plenty of room!' said Alice indignantly, and she sat down in a large arm-chair at one end of the table.

'Have some wine,' the March Hare said, in an encouraging tone. Alice looked all around the table but there was nothing on it but tea.

'I don't see any wine,' she remarked.

'There isn't any,' said the March Hare.

'Then it wasn't very civil of you to offer it,' said Alice, angrily.

'It wasn't very civil of you to sit down without being invited,' said the March Hare.

'I didn't know it was your table,' said Alice; 'it's laid for a great many more than three.'"[6]

Chopp explains that women come to the theological table (and, by analogy, to the eucharistic table) ready "to contribute, to feast, to talk and to participate. Though the table, laden with rich foods, concepts, categories, symbols, practices, and relationships seems to invite women, they are often told that they haven't really been invited."[7]

Several questions arise. Is it possible for a tradition such as Job's, one permeated by hierarchical and patriarchal structures of authority, to be reconfigured so that marginalized voices enjoy equal participation at its table? Many traditional structures have historically been ideological and manipulative. Are there liberating elements within tradition, elements that can disrupt the structures of power in the world? Or, as some feminist theologians have concluded, is real ecumenism and community possible only when traditional structures are abandoned and new ones are created that are more inviting of the stranger?[8] These questions are not unlike the ones raised in Job: What,

[6] Rebecca Chopp, *Saving Work: Feminist Practices of Theological Education* (Louisville: Westminster/John Knox Press, 1989) 114, describes some feminist practices of theological education and the vision of education that these practices create. While great strides have been made toward hearing the voices of women, in many cases, women continue to be "strangers" struggling to participate equally in the discourse of theological education. The same is true in liturgical discourse, as feminist ritual critics such as Marjorie Proctor-Smith continue to emphasize in their work.

[7] Ibid., 115.

[8] Ibid. See also Kathleen Weiler, *Women Teaching for Change: Gender, Class and Power* (New York: Bergin and Garvey Publishers, 1988) 57–66.

if anything, about inherited traditional ways of knowing and being are adequate for his circumstance of tragic vulnerability and suffering?

Gordon Lathrop, as noted earlier, celebrates the rich juxtapositions that constitute the Judeo-Christian tradition. He argues that the answer to the above questions, to liturgical ecumenism and renewal, is not in the wholesale eradication or replacement of the historical symbols of our faith.[9] His argument parallels that of Edward Farley, namely that "words of power" never completely disappear from societal structures but rather fade into this contemporary era's vast sea of symbols, images, and categories.

Taken together, the insights of Chopp and Lathrop suggest that there are two complementary and continuing tasks vital to liturgical renewal. First, the Church's task is to rethink tradition rather than to reinvent it.[10] This task of rethinking cannot take place without a rediscovery of the deep structures of the faith, the primary and enduring patterns of the ordo.

Retrieval of the ordo, or deep structures, of worship is but a first step, however. If liturgical renewal is to be adequate to and meaningful for today's cultural situation, a second task is vital, one that establishes within the renewal process a continuing dialectic of critical reflection. This second task reflects Chopp's insights and reminds us that the discovery of faith's deep structures involves more than historical analysis and description; the faith community must also continually push beyond the tradition's "vehicles of duration" in order to grasp the ultimate reality at the center of that tradition. Such a critical process constantly aims at uncovering those ideological aspects of

---

[9] Gordon Lathrop, *Holy Things: A Liturgical Theology* (Minneapolis: Fortress Press, 1993) 4, explains that contemporary historical scholarship has illumined the ancient outlines of worship as it exists in a variety of cultural and theological settings. What has been revealed is that the earliest traditions or patterns provide for a diversity of faith communities a common inheritance. See also Paul Bradshaw, *The Search for the Origins of Christian Worship: Sources and Methods for the Study of Early Liturgy* (New York: Oxford University Press, 1992).

[10] Edward Farley, "Re-thinking the God-Terms—Tradition: The God-Term of Social Remembering," *Toronto Journal of Theology* 9 (Spring 1993) 68, argues that it is not possible to abandon tradition entirely. All beings inherit the past and retain some trace of it as they make choices in their existential situation. Even a "traditionless society lives from the past in the sense that it needs and institutionalizes its language, customs, policies, and social organization."

tradition and its institutions that conceal faith's essence and thus limit its transformative potential.[11]

When both of these tasks of liturgical renewal are engaged, when the recovery of ancient signs and symbols also involves a recovery of the essential meanings they mediate, then, as Lathrop suggests, worship resists being a place where people clamor for "ownership" of the elements; liturgy becomes instead a sanctuary of meaning where all people are invited to participate in the eucharistic banquet and encounter God's redemptive presence.[12]

The epistemological advances and global expansion of this era have not eradicated oppression, injustice, and marginalization. Ideological structures that create these conditions are a reality at God's table too. Although the table is laden with the gifts of God's grace and appears inviting to all, some still want to crowd together at a corner of the table and cry "no room, no room" when a stranger comes near.

When liturgical theology operates to break down these barriers to table fellowship, to initiate reconciliation with God, and to establish mutual dialogue with all the people of the community, then authentic renewal of worship is possible. Job's journey through suffering to redemption provides a framework for critical reflection that in dialogue with current liturgical methods can further this process.[13]

JOB 1–10: TRADITION IN CRISIS

As noted earlier, numerous efforts have been made recently to establish more integrative models of theological knowing. The contemporary epistemological shift related to this effort has made

---

[11] Ibid., 70.

[12] Lathrop, *Holy Things*, 121.

[13] The book of Job is a classic of Western culture. To assimilate the wealth of exegetical scholarship alone far exceeds the capacity of this project; thus, this discussion does not propose to provide a commentary on Job nor imply a theological resolution to the complex questions raised by the narrative. The insights in this chapter will be limited to those themes from contemporary theological interpretation that dialogue with the dual focus of this chapter and further the aim of establishing a wisdom liturgical method. The biblical aspects of the discussion will be guided principally though not exclusively by the work of Newsom and Brown. To enable the process of making connections between Job and liturgical renewal, elements from Farley's reflective ontology will be revisited and voices from critical pedagogy will be invited into the dialogue.

an impact on theological education, liturgical theology, and biblical theology.[14]

Critical education theory, with its goal of transforming ideological institutional structures, emerges as an important conversation partner for these disciplines.[15] A brief survey of the tenets undergirding this focus paves the way toward linking the structure of Job to contemporary liturgical method.

Observations and analyses of institutions by critical theorists have important implications for contemporary theological education. Some of the shared axioms of these theories dialogue meaningfully with contemporary interpretations of Job, particularly with those interpretations that focus on issues of justice, politics, and power.

Critical theorists, represented in this discussion by Paulo Freire, Patti Lather, and Peter McLaren, examine how a dominant minority maintains dominance or ideological hegemony through the structural forms of institutional systems. Their arguments focus on how what has been termed the "technology of power" shapes institutions:

"Critical theorists begin with the premise that men and women are essentially unfree and inhabit a world rife with contradictions and asymmetries of power and privilege. The critical educator endorses theories that are, first and foremost, dialectical; that is, theories which recognize the problems of society as more than just isolated events of individuals. . . . Rather, these problems form part of the interactive context between individual and society. The individual both . . . creates and is created by the social universe of which he/she is a part."[16]

These theorists recognize that institutions are a matrix of institutional, personal, and social forces.

[14] Barbara Wheeler and Edward Farley, eds., *Shifting Boundaries: Contextual Approaches to the Structure of Theological Education* (Louisville: Westminster/John Knox Press, 1991) 9.

[15] See also Mark K. Taylor, "Celebrating Difference, Resisting Domination: The Need for Synchronic Strategies in Theological Education," *Shifting Boundaries: Contextual Approaches to the Structure of Theological Education,* ed. Barbara Wheeler and Edward Farley (Louisville: Westminster/John Knox Press, 1991) 259–94.

[16] Peter McLaren, *Life in Schools: An Introduction to Critical Pedagogy in the Foundations of Education* (Miami: Longman, Inc., 1989) 167.

These forces exist together in deeply contradictory tensions that are neither exclusively dominating nor liberating. The dialectic between individual consciousness and structural determinants is a key to shaping ideologies and world views. These insights echo Farley's defense of reflective ontology.

For Farley, conceiving theology from the standpoint of reflective ontology combats the production of one-dimensional quantifications of knowledge by dominant epistemological and educational models. Such one-dimensional knowledge, he argues, fails to respect the interrelatedness of human beings and results in oppressive social systems that profit from ignoring the complexity of humanity.

Farley's expression of this parallels that of critical theorist McLaren above: "Individual agents are irreducible, complex, and multi-dimensional. Interpretations of human agency that ignore this multi-dimensionality not only invite over-simplification but lend themselves to violating and subjugating agendas. . . . The spheres of agency, the interhuman, and the social are mixes of causalities (influences), perduring structures and transcendings."[17] Farley argues that what McLaren calls the "interactive context" of human social life has a tragic character.

What this means is that conditions of human liberation are interdependent with conditions of suffering and limitation; these forces together establish the enduring dialectical structure of human existence.[18] Farley develops "an ontology of tragic finitude as the background for the retrieved Hebraic-Christian paradigm of good and evil," a paradigm that finds a focused and challenging expression in the biblical narrative of Job.[19]

Job's encounter with tragic finitude poses not a few questions for traditional theological constructs. How do persons experience God's presence in and through historic and natural events, particularly tragic events? When there is dissonance between traditional beliefs about God and human experience, are the traditional beliefs to be affirmed in spite of conflicting evidence? These questions can and

[17] Edward Farley, *Good and Evil: Interpreting a Human Condition* (Minneapolis: Fortress Press, 1990) 29.

[18] Ibid.

[19] Robert R. Williams, "Tragedy, Totality, and the Face," *Theology and the Interhuman*, ed. Robert R. Williams (Valley Forge, Pa.: Trinity Press International, 1995) 80.

have been directed at the faith tradition's liturgical forms. Job, in dialogue with Farley and critical theorists, aids in establishing a framework of response.[20]

Critical theorists have pointed to the fact that as people struggle with the circumstances of daily living, institutional structures often become arenas in which groups vie for power, in which groups and individuals strive to establish those "secure" conditions in which their elemental passions can be fulfilled.[21] A not uncommon result is that the structure itself reinforces the dominance of an exclusive and oppressive minority.

According to Farley, ecclesia is a form of corporate existence; its determinate intersubjectivity exists in conjunction with a specific historical and concrete corporate identity. Because of this, ecclesia tends toward institutionalization. A distinction needs to be made, however, between those enduring features that are "inherent to the sociality of ecclesia and the ever-changing forms of institutionalization which ecclesia undergoes." Faith structures historically have tended to blur this distinction, defining ecclesia's enduring features within the limiting parameters of institutional forms.[22]

A result of this tendency toward institutionalization is that some communities develop world views and practices that "by their idolatry of inherited contents and customs" suppress elements of the community that transcend institutional forms.[23] In its most distorted form, says Farley, ecclesia is exchanged for a "closed and provincial

[20] James Gustafson, "A Response to the Book of Job," *The Voice from the Whirlwind: Interpreting the Book of Job*, ed. Leo Perdue and W. Clark Gilpin (Nashville: Abingdon Press, 1992) 176.

[21] Farley, *Good and Evil*, 133.

[22] Edward Farley, *Ecclesial Man: A Social Phenomenology of Faith and Reality* (Philadelphia: Fortress Press, 1975) 174–7, interprets institutionalization as "the process by which an inclusive social grouping integrates into itself certain human enterprises and their distinctive intersubjectivities." Corporate groups tend to develop forms of order to assure their survival or to implement the aims of the group.

[23] Farley, *Good and Evil*, 162, uses a term from moral religious philosophy to describe this—"corrupted autonomy." Reference to the affections is implicit. When persons are unable to tolerate their "tragic vulnerability," they often press the "goods at hand," sometimes even other people, into service for fulfilling their elemental desire for security. When some aspect of creation is "objectified" in this way, then autonomy has been corrupted.

religious community"; in so doing, the seeds for ideological hegemony are planted.

A concern for liturgical renewal is how to overcome hegemony and
restore to ecclesia its ability to welcome the "stranger." Contemporary
interpretations of Job point to a model within the Judeo-Christian
canon for how dominant hegemonies can be challenged and even
transformed by the redemptive justice and love of God.

The Joban Narrative

"There was once a man in the land of Uz whose name was Job. That man
was blameless and upright, one who feared God and turned away from
evil. There were born to him seven sons and three daughters. He had
seven thousand sheep, three thousand camels, five hundred yoke of
oxen, five hundred donkeys, and very many servants; so that this man
was the greatest of all the people of the east. His sons used to go up and
hold feasts in one another's houses in turn; and they would send and
invite their three sisters to eat and drink with them. And when the feast
days had run their course, Job would send and sanctify them, and he
would rise early in the morning and offer burnt offerings according to
the number of them all; for Job said, 'It may be that my children have
sinned, and cursed God in their hearts.' This is what Job always did."[24]

The image in Job 1:1-5 is not unlike what we might see if we looked
through the window of the house of wisdom in Proverbs 31. Job is a
successful, virtuous man. He has chosen the "way" of wisdom and
embodies the piety that is at the heart of the search for wisdom in
Proverbs. In fact, it might be said that the Job of 1:1-5 is the hero of a
sapiential success story.

Two short chapters later, however, the window to wisdom's house
has been shattered by chaos and unexplainable tragedy; the vision of
the "good" life promised by traditional pedagogy to those who choose
the "right" way is no longer clear, and Job curses the day of his birth:

"After this Job opened his mouth and cursed the day of his birth.
Job said:
'Let the day perish in which I was born,
    and the night that said,
    "A man-child is conceived."

[24] Job 1:1-5.

Let that day be darkness!
   May God above not seek it,
   or light shine upon it.'"[25]

The existential questions of life, the same questions that people bring
with them to the worship event, emerge, demanding answers. Where
is God? Does God care? How can faith make sense of my life?

Thus, Job's journey of conversion begins. The development of his
journey contains several elements that are important to the proposed
wisdom foundation for liturgical theology.[26]

First, as Carol Newsom suggests, the story, taken as a whole, juxtaposes two different ways of seeing the world; Job represents two disparate linguistic worlds, two different ways of talking.[27] This is reflected
in the different ways of talking that emerge in the narrative—Job's
language, the language of Job's friends, God's language, and the discursive language that frames the poetic dialogue (1–2; 42:7-17)—each
of which have a particular moral vision and understanding of the
world embedded within their structure.[28]

The question of language, as emphasized earlier, is of central importance to liturgical renewal.[29] Clifford Geertz explains that language is
what a community uses to describe its faith and justify its identity.

[25] Job 3:1-4.
[26] William Brown, *Character in Crisis: A Fresh Approach to the Wisdom Literature of the Old Testament* (Grand Rapids, Mich.: Eerdmans, 1996) 51, argues that
the focus of Job is not on suffering as a universal problem but rather on the
"journey or development of a person's character in response to an instance of
seemingly inexplicable suffering."
[27] Carol Newsom, "The Moral Sense of Nature: Ethics in Light of God's
Speech to Job," *Princeton Seminary Bulletin* 15 (1994) 9–27.
[28] Leo Perdue, *Wisdom and Creation: The Theology of Wisdom Literature* (Nashville:
Abingdon Press, 1994) 124–5, similarly suggests that there are a variety of literary forms in Job. There is the didactic narrative frame of the book (1–2; 42:7-
17), the lament in Job's two soliloquies in chapters 3 and 29–31, and sapiential
disputation in 4–27 and 38:1–42:6, in which Job enters into debate, in a sense,
with YHWH or perhaps more correctly, with his tradition's perception of YHWH.
Important to the integration of these three forms in Job is that together they
compose a kind of critical reflection and engagement that "leads to the reshaping of the tradition and even offers the possibility of the redescription of reality."
[29] Mark Searle, "The Uses of Liturgical Language," *The Landscape of Praise:
Readings in Liturgical Renewal*, ed. Blair Gilmer Meeks (Valley Forge, Pa.:
Trinity Press International, 1996) 105–10, discusses how liturgical discourse is

However, it is not only the actual spoken words that carry the meaning of language but also the "way" they are spoken and how hearers perceive them.[30]

This is of particular importance to the faith community; as Farley contends, ecclesia has a constitutive history, a collective memory and a distinctive ritual practice, all of which are mediated into consciousness linguistically. Not only does the distinct language of ecclesia "spill over" into the operative languages of the social world, but the languages of the social world influence the language of ecclesia.[31]

What this implies, as Irwin and other liturgical theologians have argued concerning liturgical texts and language, is that the context of a worship event becomes part of the text, part of the mediating structure.[32] Each community is historically particular; its language and actions have certain moral norms and principles built into them that determine the decisions people make in given situations. In other words, as Geertz explains, communities have a particular world view, a moral vision, embedded in their way of talking.[33] Because of this, transformation involves a redescription of reality, a redescription that happens in worship when the community's way of defining itself is juxtaposed to God's discourse of redemption.

Such a redescription or redefining of reality is what happens in Job, a fact that is exemplified perhaps most clearly on a linguistic level.[34] As Job 1:1 begins, the voice of a narrator relates the story in concise

---

performative; the sacraments are social actions of a community, and sacramental discourse is how we actively "think about" that action.

[30] Clifford Geertz, "Thick Description: Toward an Interpretive Theory of Culture," *The Interpretation of Cultures: Selected Essays,* ed. Clifford Geertz (New York: Basic Books, 1973) 145.

[31] Farley, *Ecclesial Man,* 118–20, argues that there is a "linguistic stratum which carries the community's meant-content without raising the question as to the bearing of that content on truth or reality." What this means is that there is a stratum of language that correlates the enduring features of a community; this stratum is made up of the community's story and imagery. In conjunction with this, however, there is also the language of creeds, doctrine, and apologetics. Often this second form of language dominates the first, suppressing the community's more essential and enduring images.

[32] Kevin Irwin, *Context and Text: Method in Liturgical Theology* (Collegeville: The Liturgical Press, 1994) iii–ix.

[33] Geertz, "Thick Description," 151.

[34] Perdue, *Wisdom and Creation,* 128.

discursive language, implying that the hearers are members of a "community of shared values." As Newsom suggests, however, the relationship established between hearer and narrator by these initial words is not really one of equality. The "tidy" prose language masks an inequality that is inherent in Job's traditional world view.[35]

For example, Job 1:1-5 establishes the narrator as a source of moral judgement. First, the narrator informs readers of who Job is and describes his integrity. Then, in 1:8, God's authoritative voice appears in the form of a rhetorical question to confirm what the narrator has described: "The LORD said to Satan, 'Have you considered my servant Job? There is no one like him on the earth, a blameless and upright man who fears God and turns away from evil.'"[36] Newsom observes that "first the narrator tells us explicitly what we are to know about Job; then we are invited to confirm."[37]

The deductive course of events in these opening verses, expressed in discursive authoritative language, invites readers to participate in the narrative, but only to the extent that they affirm what the narrator has told them. Thus, the readers' participation is not dialogical; the invitation is to participate only within the parameters of that tradition's authoritative and hierarchical framework.[38]

What is happening in this prose framework is evident in many institutional structures. Lather describes the process in her work in critical education theory. The dominant or authoritative class, she explains, secures hegemony by portraying symbols and guidelines for social practice in such a way that the unequal relations of power and privilege remain hidden.[39] Within such a hegemonic structure, the dominant culture or tradition tries to "fix" the meaning of signs and symbols in such a way that to challenge them would seem unnatural.[40]

---

[35] Carol Newsom, "Cultural Politics and the Reading of Job," *Biblical Interpretation: A Journal of Contemporary Approaches* 1 (July 1993) 120–4, suggests that Job 1–2 and 42 is "the product of an elite author who has chosen to write in a calculated, folktale style. The style is an invitation to its audience to participate in a certain type of reading community that is also a type of moral community."

[36] Job 1:8.

[37] Newsom, "Cultural Politics and the Reading of Job," 121.

[38] Ibid., 122.

[39] Patti Lather, "Critical Theory, Curricular Transformation, and Feminist Main-streaming," *Journal of Education* 166 (1982) 55–6.

[40] McLaren, *Life in Schools*, 174. Newsom, "Cultural Politics and the Reading of Job," 122–3, notes that even the language of the dialogue between God and

In the prose narrative that begins Job's story, with its stabilizing linguistic form, the moral world view established in Proverbs, one in which there is a compatibility between integrity and success, is confirmed, and a religiously and socially conservative vision of reality is stabilized. It is not until Job 3:1 that a process of practical wisdom, of critical reflection, similar to that outlined in the previous chapter, is begun.

To read Job 3 is to enter a different linguistic world, one where the logical deductive language of Job 1–2 is replaced by the dissonant language of metaphor. This transition from prose to poetic dialogue introduces a shift in moral world view. Job recognizes that traditional understandings, those things that were established by his communal pedagogical foundations, are not adequate for the tragic circumstance of suffering in which he finds himself. Therefore, instead of compliance with his destiny, he resists, cursing his own and creation's existence.[41]

Newsom suggests that the metaphorical quality of Job's speech reflects his struggle with how to appropriate the received wisdom of his tradition. Perdue carries this assessment even further: "Job seeks by the power of his spoken word, formulated in lament and curse, to obliterate all existence. . . . Job seeks to subvert not only creation and blessing, but all life-giving traditions of salvation in the Israelite faith."[42]

Job, in effect, poses a direct challenge to the tradition of redemption history:

"With God are wisdom and strength;
    God has counsel and understanding.
If God tears down, no one can rebuild;
    if God shuts someone in, no one can open up. . . .
God leads priests away stripped,
    and overthrows the mighty.
God deprives of speech those who are trusted
    and takes away the discernment of the elders.

---

hasatan doesn't have the tensive quality that invites the reader to question whether *hasatan* is just or fair in challenging Job's integrity. Rather, the linguistic form in 1–2 is such that "motives for piety and the relation between wealth and behavior" are not questioned or challenged. The dominant understanding of God and faith are reinforced.

[41] Perdue, *Wisdom and Creation*, 131, Newsom, "Cultural Politics and the Reading of Job," 124–5.

[42] Newsom, "Cultural Politics and the Reading of Job," 133.

God pours contempt on princes,
    and looses the belt of the strong. . . .
God makes nations great, then destroys them;
    God enlarges nations, then leads them away."[43]

As Perdue demonstrates, in this doxology, Job destabilizes the language of redemption history, making clear his skepticism regarding divine providence in directing human history. The Hebrew tradition is clearly under assault.

Throughout the poetic dialogue, the struggle with traditional understandings is evident, particularly in the way Job treats inherited authoritative language in a non-authoritarian way. An example of this is in Job 7:

"What are human beings, that you make so much of them,
    that you set your mind on them,
visit them every morning,
    test them every moment?
Will you not look away from me for a while,
    let me alone until I swallow my spittle?"[44]

Newsom argues that Job's words in this passage reflect a reversal of the language of creation in Psalm 8. In effect, Job "establishes a subversive relationship to the authoritative language of tradition."[45]

Finally, in an effort to counter Job's destabilizing attack on their tradition, Job's friends, silent until now, enter the dialogue. Adopting the common pedagogical form of sapiential instruction found in Proverbs, their speeches function to defend tradition, to defend the moral and pedagogical school out of which they and Job have come.

In addition, the voice of the narrator is now gone, and the reader is compelled to engage in the story, as a subject. The poetic or metaphorical language, begun in Job 3, challenges readers to listen, discern, and participate.

From the perspective of critical theory, what happens in Job 3 is that a framework for discourse emerges within which transformation of

[43] Job 12:13-14, 19-21, 23. The NRSV has been altered to reflect inclusive language for God.
[44] Job 7:17-19.
[45] Newsom, "Cultural Politics and the Reading of Job," 126.

oppressive structures is possible. This characteristic is one of the elements of Job that makes it so compelling a conversation partner in contemporary liturgical discussions, particularly regarding justice issues.

As Lather explains, transformation of hegemonic structures becomes possible when individuals become aware that the vision of truth mediated by dominant systems is contradictory to or inadequate for what they experience in their daily lives. This awareness and the reflection it initiates make equality of dialogue possible. Thus, reconciliation and transformation are also possible.[46]

The ensuing dialogues between Job and his friends do not result in transformation. In fact, the arguments and responses build to an almost frustrating level as rival images are exchanged.[47] This also is not uncommon to hegemonic structures.

Freire provides insight into this through his work in liberation theology. As he explains, the only way authentic transformation of communal structures can happen is if the "oppressed" group becomes the restorer of the humanity of both, or if all participants become "subjects" in a mutually influencing dialogue. Because the friends' discourse is reactionary, defending the established tradition, its transformative potential is lost.

At first, William Brown explains, there appears to be a relationship of equality between Job and his friends; they all enjoy an honored position in the community, and, as a result of that position, they have until now shared the same understandings of God and the world. However, in the face of Job's suffering and questioning of his tradition, the friends stalwartly "attempt to press the dynamics of the discourse back into the traditional hierarchical setting of conventional wisdom teaching, which Job regards now as nothing else than a pedagogy for the oppressed."[48] The friends are determined to find an "answer" to Job's problem in the teachings and ethos of ancient wisdom, establishing themselves in a position of authority over him.[49]

---

[46] James G. Williams, "Job and the God of Victims," *The Voice from the Whirlwind,* ed. Leo Perdue and W. Clark Gilpin (Nashville: Abingdon Press, 1992) 208–10.

[47] Newsom, "Cultural Politics and the Reading of Job," 129–30.

[48] Brown, *Character in Crisis,* 64–5.

[49] Newsom, "Cultural Politics and the Reading of Job," 128–9, demonstrates that the friends' speeches are primarily restatements of what persons in the community would know to be true as part of a shared communal knowledge.

When Job refuses to accept the assumptions of tradition, he becomes a "stranger," an outsider, amongst those with whom he was once equal:

"[God] has put my family far from me,
   and my acquaintances are wholly estranged from me.
My relatives and close friends have failed me;
   the guests in my house have forgotten me;
my serving girls count me as a stranger;
   I have become an alien in their eyes."[50]

Brown notes that the words for "alien" and "stranger" in these verses are used in Proverbs 1–9 to refer to the "strange woman." Unlike Proverbs, however, the book of Job ultimately affirms Job's "dissenting voice of pathos, a voice that conventional wisdom would rather muffle."[51]

This movement within Job to embrace the voice of the "stranger," the voice of pathos, is foundational to similar efforts to establish liturgical structures that are more inclusive. We turn now to examine how Job's passionate conviction to vindicate himself leads to reconciliation with God and transformation of his world view.

RESTRUCTURING A FAITH WORLD

As noted above, Job's dialogues with his friends do not result in healing or transformation. Job does not experience healing until his world view is reoriented by his encounter with God in Job 38–41. As the narrative has progressed, Job has challenged God, defended his integrity, and pleaded with God to vindicate him. God's ultimate response? A panoramic view of the cosmos:

"Then the LORD answered Job out of the whirlwind:
'Who is this that darkens counsel by words without knowledge?
Gird up your loins like a man,
   I will question you, and you shall declare to me. . . .

See also Tryggve Mettinger, "The God of Job: Avenger, Tyrant, or Victor?" *The Voice from the Whirlwind,* ed. Leo Perdue and W. Clark Gilpin (Nashville: Abingdon Press, 1992) 41.

[50] Job 19:13-15.
[51] Brown, *Character in Crisis,* 68–9.

"'Have you entered into the springs of the sea
    or walked in the recesses of the deep?
Have you comprehended the expanse of the earth?
    Declare, if you know all this. . . .

"'Who has cut a channel for the torrents of rain,
    and a way for the thunderbolt,
to bring rain on a land where no one lives,
    on the desert, which is empty of human life,
to satisfy the waste and desolate land,
    and to make the ground put forth grass. . . .

"'Look at Behemoth,
    which I made just as I made you;
    it eats grass like an ox. . . .

"'It is the first of the great acts of God—
    only its Maker can approach it with the sword.
For the mountains yield food for it
    where all the wild animals play.'"[52]

In these speeches from the whirlwind, yet another linguistic form
emerges, that of redemptive discourse.

In the divine speeches, God rebukes Job but does not silence him;
much as Job appeals to insights gained from his personal experience
and integrity over against the insights of traditional wisdom, so God
appeals to Job's experience and character. Another authority is
asserted, one that is different from the non-dialogical one in Job 1–2.

Unexpectedly, Brown explains, "Yahweh does not . . . admonish
Job for questioning the ethos of traditional wisdom as represented by
his friends. . . . What Yahweh has to say also breaks with the long-
held principles and boundaries set by traditional wisdom."[53] God
urges Job to a deeper contemplation of the world around him. God
challenges Job, through the dazzling portrayals of creatures on the
margins of Job's universe, to see creation not as mere scenery to a
picture of which Job and his tradition are the center, but as having
intrinsic worth and value.[54]

[52] Job 38:1-3, 16-18, 25-27; 40:15, 19-20.
[53] Brown, *Character in Crisis*, 90.
[54] Newsom, "The Moral Sense of Nature," 9–14.

As Newsom argues, Job's identity as a patriarch operated within a moral field of inequality. The norms and values of his society urged him toward moral actions such as praying for the needy and feeding the hungry; what Job did not recognize was that these moral actions were based on a dominant/subordinate hierarchy, one which maintained classes of persons and did nothing to transform the structures that perpetuated the suffering.

Job's deep rootedeness in the moral world of biblical patriarchy, Newsom continues, "shapes his sense of self and other, his expectations about the world and his place in it, his sense of obligation, the particular way in which he experiences loss and suffering, and of course, his image of God."[55] God's response to Job challenges his tradition's moral world view, a tradition whose structures for mediating truth uphold positions of "honor" by maintaining a subordinate class of "contemptible" people. Ironically, because of his suffering, Job, once a respected sage, finds himself in that subordinate class:

"But now they make sport of me,
   those who are younger than I,
whose fathers I would have disdained
   to set with the dogs of my flock. . . .
Through want and hard hunger
   they gnaw the dry and desolate ground. . . .
They are driven out from society;
   people shout after them as after a thief. . . .
A senseless, disreputable brood,
   they have been whipped out of the land.

"And now they mock me in song;
   I am a byword to them.
They abhor me, they keep aloof from me;
   they do not hesitate to spit at the sight of me."[56]

In part because Job becomes identified with this "senseless disreputable brood," he develops the ability to understand a deeper truth about God and the world.

In response rather than answering Job in the expected language of patriarchy, thus reinforcing the hierarchy, God offers Job a metaphorical

[55] Ibid., 12.
[56] Job 30:1-9.

picture of the world that is radically different from the one to which Job is accustomed. In fact, the divine speeches create a paradigm shift from an anthropocentric world view to a moral framework that has its starting point in creation.[57] Thus, the restructuring of Job's faith world begins with contemplation of the goodness of the natural world. Once Job begins to view his own integrity in relation to the whole of creation, his faith identity is also reshaped.

Several important connections can be made at this point between the dialectic of conversion in Job and contemporary liturgical concerns. First, the restructuring of Job's faith world occurs as God fills Job's vision with beings that he never had considered as genuine "others." After the divine speeches, Job encounters creation as it exists in relations of interdependence.

This connects with the earlier discussions of the intersubjectivity of human existence. Lathrop points out that Church "gatherings" thrive even in this age of the demise of most community gatherings. This is because people in the faith community are connected in ways that transcend human autonomy and secularity.[58]

A similar understanding is developed at some length in Farley's work on the interhuman. He argues that several spheres of human reality are interconnected—"individual agents, face-to-face relations, and social institutions." Human daily experience involves encounter with each of these spheres. Human reality, he contends, depends on the interdependence of all of these spheres.[59]

One reason for the diminishment of faith's deep symbols, says Lathrop, is that the Church seems to have forgotten that it exists within this larger world of interconnection. Trapped within collapsing denominational and institutional structures, the Church seems to have forgotten that the world is a "mutually sustaining web of interdependence."[60]

Contemporary liturgical theologians seek to rediscover or create worship patterns that will engage this web of interdependence and bring to the surface yet again the deep meanings of faith, meanings also mediated in the divine speeches in Job. Humans live in the world with other creatures and with each other, all of whom are valued by

[57] Newsom, "The Moral Sense of Nature," 13.
[58] Lathrop, *Holy Things*, 1–2.
[59] Farley, *Good and Evil*, 283.
[60] Joseph C. Hough and John B. Cobb Jr., *Christian Identity and Theological Education* (Chico, Calif.: Scholars Press, 1985) 56.

God as part of a "good" creation; the true "virtue" or goodness of creation actually lies in the beauty and holiness of its interrelationships, in its juxtapositions.

This is central to the connection between liturgy and justice developed by the liturgical movement. James White explains that "justice" means to attribute to all persons their full human worth; injustice is to deny others their inherent worth as part of God's creation. For Christians, justice is one form in which love is expressed.[61] In order authentically to make determinations of agapic praxis or justice requires a world view that welcomes the "stranger" as an equal participant in ecclesia. The Eucharist, says White, is that focused event in which the community acts out the agapic base of its life together. How the community conceives of self, others, and God is envisioned and formed in its eucharistic practice.

This transformative potential of eucharistic celebration has been distorted by a materialistic world view in which liturgical structures and moral thinking are grounded in donor/recipient or dominant/subordinate relationships similar to those in Job's traditional world.[62] Too often, the structures and practices around the Lord's table do not adequately model egalitarian and dialogical relationships; liturgical practices and images fail to interpret our relationship with God in a way that supports human responsibility for and connectedness to all of creation.

The language of the divine speeches in Job exemplifies from within Scripture the language of balance and ecumenism that is the aim of much liturgical renewal. It is a language in which, "each thing, each person, has a place, a purpose, and a limit . . . there are places where I must not tread, places where the energy and vitality and indeed the violence of my being must meet its own limit."[63] As God lifts up before Job pictures of wild and mythical animals over which Job has no control and which do not fit any of Job's moral constructs, Job is challenged to rethink his own moral system, a system that insists on dependent social relationships.

A faith understanding that begins in contemplation of the "other" as an equal and valued part of God's creation is inherent in Edward

[61] James White, *Christian Worship in North America: A Retrospective: 1955–1995* (Collegeville: The Liturgical Press, 1997) 175–6.

[62] Ibid.

[63] Newsom, "The Moral Sense of Nature," 20.

Farley's understanding of "god-terms." As Wendy Farley emphasizes, god-terms are a theme in Edward Farley's work because he recognizes that concepts such as obligation, beauty, the sacred, and dignity have been rendered meaningless by post-Enlightenment ways of knowing.[64]

These ways of knowing house a logic of domination that perpetuates patriarchy and oppression. As a result, all reality in an industrial society is viewed in terms of its value as a commodity:

"The flattening out of reality into numbers creates ideal conditions for its domination. The complexity of beings is rendered invisible so that they can be mastered by thought; the integrity and intrinsic value of beings is dismissed as mere sentiment, freeing us from the ethical resistance beings exert against their own domination."[65]

Farley's reflective ontology combats this tendency of contemporary epistemological models to quantify knowledge and to see human reality merely as "an object that occupies this or that causal system of its environment."[66]

Farley does this by arguing that the power of evil and alienation in the world is not broken by the "pseudo securing of goods at hand." Such efforts at overcoming evil only result in turning external frameworks, such as ethnic traditions, religious traditions, or nations, into idolatrous substitutes for God's presence. The only way to disrupt evil is by existing within life's tragic structure in a stance of faithfulness toward that which transcends humanity. Then, says Farley, human perception of the world is reoriented such that beauty and holiness become apparent in all creation.[67]

---

[64] In this society, it is not easy to express what sort of "reality" obligation is since it cannot be subjected to laboratory experiments or empirical research. Thus, it becomes relegated to a prevailing human paradigm that is therapeutic. What this means is that ethics, disconnected from the god-term "obligation," becomes tied to "right behavior" that is adopted in order to avoid going to prison or losing one's job. Trapped within self-generated, individually expressed "shoulds" and "oughts," ethics becomes a series of contractual negotiations rather than a communal pattern based on mutual compassion and respect. See Farley, *Deep Symbols*, 42–4.

[65] Farley, "Eros and the Truth," 24–5.

[66] Farley, *Good and Evil*, 11.

[67] Ibid., 166.

In Job 38–41, the language of contemplation depicts those creatures on the margins of the cosmos as "subjects" instead of as "flat" characters or objects that are subordinate to Job.[68] In the same way, Farley's delineation of the variegated spheres of human existence underlines the perspective inherent in wisdom that the whole of life, the whole of the cosmos, is beautiful; reducing any aspect of it to a commodity is a violation of God's truth and of God's creative presence.[69]

Such an understanding is related to the faith community's expressions of gratitude to God. True gratitude, Don Saliers argues, is not an individualistic experience. It involves becoming attuned to the created world "in all of its beauty, terror and mystery."[70] It involves plunging the depths of creation to discover the mysteries of God's enduring presence.

As such, gratitude is not only personal thanksgiving for a successful life; authentic gratitude is recognition of God as the source of all life. When, in liturgy, the community sees the world as Job did in 38–41, the capacity for true gratitude and thus for moral praxis is deepened.[71]

Through its experiences of God's presence and expressions of gratitude, the faith community also becomes more aware of the pain and suffering in the world. This shift from an anthropocentric world view to a cosmological one, from individualistic perceptions to communal ones, is reflected in the conclusion of Job.

As stated earlier, Freire contends that real transformation of institutional forms occurs only when the oppressed group becomes the restorer of the humanity of both, if both parties become "subjects" in an open and liberating dialogue.[72] What is involved in this is establishing a framework of discourse that allows each "subject" to maintain

---

[68] Brown, *Character in Crisis*, 131.

[69] Farley, "Eros and the Truth," 28.

[70] Don Saliers, *Worship as Theology: Foretaste of Glory Divine* (Nashville: Abingdon Press, 1994) 100–5, suggests that the wonder of "being" is the origin of human gratitude. In the background of such gratitude lies the tragic structuring of human existence that is always there in the liturgy as we juxtapose light with dark, joy with sadness, water with thirst, and bread with hunger. Redemption occurs as we begin to refer all these things to God. Liturgy forms human capacities to live thankfully within the structures of the world.

[71] Hough and Cobb, *Christian Identity and Theological Education*, 62.

[72] Paulo Freire, *Pedagogy of the Oppressed*, trans. Myra Bergman Ramos, rev. ed. (New York: Continuum, 1995).

integrity and particularity without becoming so exclusive and dogmatic that dialogue with other traditions is impossible.

To revisit the discussion in Chapter 3, such an intersubjective approach to faith requires a theological method that is ontologically grounded, one that insists that the ultimate reality of faith does not depend on its existence within the parameters of particular vehicles of duration.[73] In a similar vein, Lather suggests that the development of a transformative counter-hegemony entails exposing structural contradictions, articulating ideological alternatives, and establishing an altered ethos that moves in the direction of communal unity.

It can be argued that such a transformative element is present at the end of Job's story. Job reenters his traditional community, not condemning his friends but praying for them and thus restoring them.[74] Evidence also emerges that Job's prior independence has become interdependence. That he has become aware of the intrinsic value of all creation is hinted in the fact that, against the norm of his tradition, Job's daughters are named and "given an inheritance along with their brothers."[75] On at least one level, Job appears to have broken with tradition and begun the process of severing the oppressive bonds of patriarchy.

At the end of the narratives, Job returns to his community as a more fully human character because he has a more mature, more authentic, sense of gratitude. He has learned that true "virtue" exists in recognition of human interconnectedness with all of creation. As Carole Fontaine expresses it, Job awakens from the "dogmatic slumber of his former piety" with a new awareness of the suffering of others.[76]

CONCLUSION

"The shaman has journeyed far and wide, up and down, through and beyond. He has considered the stars and stones, the birds of prey and the dead tree that scents the waters of life, the ways of humanity and the way of wisdom, and he is content. In the knowledge derived from

---

[73] Edward Farley, "Thinking Toward the World: A Case for Philosophical Pluralism in Theology," *American Journal of Theology and Philosophy* 14 (January 1993) 55.

[74] Carole Fontaine, "Wounded Hero on a Shaman's Quest," *The Voice from the Whirlwind*, ed. Leo Perdue and W. Clark Gilpin (Nashville: Abingdon Press, 1992) 70.

[75] Job 42:15. See also Brown, *Character in Crisis*, 116–9.

[76] Fontaine, "Wounded Hero," 81.

his travels, the human community is built up and broken down and built up yet again. We, the audience, have come to know ourselves, the world, and God better by means of the journey into which the author of Job has catapulted us, so that in the end we too can affirm with Job, the wounded healer, 'We had heard by the hearing of the ear, but now our eyes have seen.'"[77]

The challenge facing contemporary liturgical renewal is not unlike that faced by Job, namely to reappropriate the themes and structures of tradition for circumstances that don't seem to "fit" those structures. Linked to this challenge is a moral concern; as we noted at the outset of this chapter, the discovery of faith's deep structures involves continually pushing beyond tradition's vehicles of duration in order to grasp the ultimate reality at the center of tradition. It means uncovering those aspects of tradition and its institutions that ideologically conceal faith's essence and thus limit its transformative potential.

While Proverbs images normative character and suggests how that character leads to the "good" life, this normativity is challenged in Job by existential realities in which virtue and integrity do not achieve the expected results. As such, the development of the wisdom corpus from Proverbs to Job, as well as the internal framework of Job, provides for the Judeo-Christian tradition a model (1) for engaging and transformatively reappropriating tradition and (2) for an ongoing dialectic of critical reflection.

Central to this project's thesis, Proverbs and Job set forth this model from a perspective quite different from that of redemption history. In fact, as the preceding paragraphs have demonstrated, Job challenges the assumptions of redemption history. This aspect of the critical-reflective process in Job is of particular importance to renewal of liturgical structures that are rooted in a biblical matrix dominated almost exclusively by redemption history.

As Farley explains, ecclesia's witness to the "redemptive alteration of human existence" points to a redeemer and certain events that happened in space and time. Ecclesia and its "truth" are historical in this sense. In Israel's redemption history, salvation is the story of YHWH and YHWH's people. With Christ, ecclesia appears; the story of Jesus "shatters" Israel's story of salvation. In this process of destabilization, similar to the metaphorical process, some traditional imagery is

[77] Ibid., 85.

retained and modified. What is most radically changed, however, is the meaning and imagery of "Yʜwʜ's people." Often, Farley explains, in the attempt to make tradition and its images understandable for particular historical circumstances, tradition is integrated into prevailing world views or frameworks; the risk is ever-present that in this process of integration or "translation," the liberating truth of Christ's redemptive presence will be lost.

In historical treatments of biblical theology, examined in Chapter 4, the cosmological element of ecclesia, the way in which Christ blurs provincial boundaries, is not adequately emphasized. One reason for this, as Taylor illuminates, may be that the historical-critical method is primarily diachronic and as such tends to privilege tradition. In this process, he explains, normativity is a "matter of faithfulness of commitment to a tradition unfolding through past horizons." What often happens is that the focus is on bringing present developments into accord with authoritative tradition. Such approaches, not unlike that of Job's friends, often strive primarily to demonstrate that the privileged tradition is "credible" or "intelligible."[78]

Whether made explicit or not, however, synchronic strategies of interpretation are also present when the community seeks to appropriate classic texts and tradition:

"Synchronic movement is not from past texts to present ones, or a movement occurring between horizons and boundaries encounterable primarily in the present period. It requires navigating the interpretive complexities arising when a presently received text's meanings are refracted, in any given present, into particular cultural forms or into diverse strata of political power."[79]

Such a synchronic interpretation of tradition is how Job "reads" his tradition in the midst of circumstances of tragic suffering and alienation. It is a process inherent in the metaphorical foundation of wisdom, and it is a way of "reading" biblical texts that correlates with Farley's notion of theology as habitus.

Such critical reflection is necessary if the faith community and its liturgical structures are to become a horizon of redemption where the discourse of grace and agapic love disrupts the tragic structure of existence, revealing the deeper reality and mystery of God's presence.

[78] Taylor, "Celebrating Difference," 263.
[79] Ibid., 264.

Chapter 8

Implications of a Wisdom Liturgical Method

"The Almighty—we cannot find;
   God is great in power and justice,
   and abundant righteousness God will not violate.
Therefore, mortals fear God;
   God does not regard any who are wise in their own conceit."[1]

One thing that can be observed about human living in this contemporary age is that "knowing" God, experiencing God's presence, is a difficult thing to do. Having a cognitive or affective certainty of God's presence is a rare commodity. There are those times in our lives when God seems near, times when we experience the exuberant joy of being in God's presence, a joy spoken of in Proverbs 8:

"When God marked out the foundations of the earth,
   then I was beside God, like a master worker;
and I was daily God's delight,
   rejoicing in God's inhabited world
   and delighting in the human race."[2]

Always, however, the world's brokenness touches our delight, often turning our exuberance into lament and shadowing our joy with doubt and uncertainty.

Even as the contemporary faith community remains committed to being God's "delight" and "rejoicing before God always," the world is

---

[1] Job 37:23-24. The NRSV has been altered to reflect inclusive language for God.

[2] Prov 8:29-30. The NRSV has been altered to reflect inclusive language for God.

bombarded by circumstances that make people doubt God's presence and God's justice—the threat of biological warfare, economic insecurities, the continued existence of hunger, racism, and violence. In the face of these uncertainties about the "goodness" of life and of God, traditional proclamations of faith, traditional "words" of promise and hope, often sound like only hollow optimism to some and are offensive to the intellectual biases of others. Some in our society suspect that the Church exists only as a place of escape from a troubled world. Others are frustrated that the faith community not only is unreliable as a fortress against life's existential storms but is, in fact, as entangled in brokenness as the world outside its doors.

Efforts have been made and continue to be made to restore the Church's vitality and integrity. A multiplicity of interpretive approaches, theological methods, and liturgical practices have risen to the occasion of contemporary fragmentation and pluralism. In the face of shifting cultural assumptions and new contextual realities, these responses have proposed alternative methods and have suggested new ways of understanding faith, the Church, and God.

The argument in this project joins that of others in the theological community who seek the renewal of the Church against the backdrop of these present circumstances. It invites an interdisciplinary gathering of diverse literature for a central focus on contemporary liturgical concerns. The project has offered a correlation of three perspectives—liturgical theology, Edward Farley's philosophical theology, and wisdom theology—as a prolegomenon to a wisdom liturgical method.

This chapter sketches some ways that a wisdom liturgical method might be reflected in liturgical practice. The following implicatory forays into the instrumental potential of this prolegomenon are not intended to be exhaustive. They are offered in the form of conclusions to be critically tested in the liturgical praxis of the community and are suggested as the foundation for future work.

CONTRIBUTION TO LITURGICAL THEOLOGY

The questions directed to Christian worship by the current context are multiple and were raised in Chapter 1. When incoherence and the absence of God are dominant cultural themes, how do the juxtapositions inherent in worship mediate God's presence? What is the role of the Church's discourse in the broader, increasingly more pluralistic arena of public discourse? How can traditional patterns be renewed or reconstructed without diminishing the enduring wisdom they contain? How can liturgy mediate truth in the current sociopolitical interpretive situation so that the community is challenged more closely to correlate its divine immanent essence?

Various liturgical scholars, as seen in Chapter 2, have dealt with one or more of these issues, but no method has emerged that addresses them in an integrative fashion. Wisdom provides a biblical foundation for such an integrative method.

Some of wisdom's general tenets have been examined in detail and are revisited in summary form here:

1. Wisdom's epistemology intersects with the epistemological shifts of this contemporary age.

2. A wisdom perspective fosters an understanding of tradition that is not dogmatic or exclusive of other traditions.

3. Wisdom respects creation as interconnected; thus, its model for relating to God, self, and the world is not hierarchical as dominant theological models have been. There is a non-hierarchical ethical dimension to wisdom's focus on cosmology and anthropology.

4. Wisdom insists on the centrality of community and encourages critical reflection on communal tradition and understandings.

5. A wisdom perspective locates the foundation of theological knowing in individual and communal experience of God's presence. The "data for theology is lived experience that, for the most part, is not overridden by imposed interpretive categories or constructs."[3]

6. Through metaphorical connections and juxtapositions of ordinary objects, actions, and words with language about God, wisdom seeks the deeper structures or meanings of faith, community, and the divine.

7. The structural and historical development of Proverbs and Job models from within the biblical corpus the critical-reflective interaction operative between present concerns and the wisdom of tradition.

These tenets, as they developed historically and are reflected in Proverbs and Job, engage some of the growing edges of liturgical

[3] Walter Brueggemann, *Theology of the Old Testament: Testimony, Dispute, Advocacy* (Minneapolis: Fortress Press, 1997) 680.

theology, suggesting a corrective to those liturgical methods that have maintained too close a reliance on biblical redemption history.

Walter Brueggemann shows how the current epistemological situation has "unsettled" the consensus of biblical scholarship that existed at mid-century. A positive outcome of this unsettlement, he says, is that it reminds us of the inherently unsettled nature of the Old Testament. Thus, the new pluralism in Old Testament studies points to a "pluralism of faith affirmations and articulations of Yahweh in the text itself."[4]

It is not possible, Brueggemann continues, to return to "older assured hegemonies" or to arguments in favor of a "singular coherent faith articulation in the text." Any new method that speaks to the current context must allow for the plurality of voices that constitutes the substance of the Old Testament, recognizing that the various texts contain a rich diversity of testimonies concerning God and the community's relationship to God.

Because of this, the wisdom liturgical method proposed here does not claim dominance or superiority over other methods that might be generated as a result of dialogue with different biblical voices, voices that also make legitimate claims about God. This project does suggest, however, that wisdom's primary tenets, its response to the cultural challenges of its own historical context, and its method of appropriating tradition make it a viable conversation partner for liturgical theology at the end of the twentieth century. A wisdom liturgical method also offers a corrective to liturgical methods that have allowed particular biblical voices or perspectives, such as redemption history, to dominate.

PARAMETERS OF A WISDOM LITURGICAL METHOD

Chapter 1 suggested that "an understanding of *leitourgia* as transformative . . . operates out of the belief that in Christ the whole world and all of humanity's actions in the world are redeemed." This project has demonstrated that such an understanding of liturgy (1) engages Farley's argument for a return to the notion of theology as habitus and (2) can be expanded upon through dialogue with the methodological framework of Old Testament wisdom.

Several questions arise: Where can a wisdom influence be discerned in current liturgical practice, and how can a wisdom liturgical method

---

[4] Ibid., xv.

make those influences more explicit? How can an ongoing self-critique, such as that inherent in the structural development of Proverbs and Job, become a part of "fixed" liturgical structures? How does a wisdom liturgical method influence the shape and function of liturgical praxis?

On one level, how a wisdom influence and framework are implicit to authentic liturgy has already been examined in detail. Chapter 6, for example, explored the journey of conversion that is implied in the metanarrative of Proverbs.[5] Several of the tenets of wisdom summarized above were highlighted as constituting the landscape of that journey. For instance, faith, in wisdom theology, does not consist of mastering empirical data; rather, it is a hermeneutical journey of discovery, a habitus wherein hearts and minds become oriented toward God.

Wisdom's journey of faith—from praxis to theory to praxis, from communal tradition or actions to critical reflection on those actions to renewed communal action—is also reflected in the liturgical journey. This insight was discussed earlier in connection with the faith community's role in character formation.

A primary goal of the journey of conversion is to enable the faith community to enter into the tragic structure of human existence with a new understanding of what is ultimate and with a new understanding of the relationship between God, self, others, and the world. By analogy, as the community encounters God in authentic liturgy, participants are enabled to look at the world and their existence in the world in a new way.[6] As reflected in Job's story, this ultimately means that the community's moral world view and praxis are transformed; the connection between cosmos and ethos and between pathos and

---

[5] William Brown, *Character in Crisis: A Fresh Approach to the Wisdom Literature of the Old Testament* (Grand Rapids, Mich.: Eerdmans, 1996) 151–63, concludes that the "way of wisdom is the prescribed way of the community."

[6] Mark Searle, "Journey of Conversion," *Worship* 54 (January 1980) 47, notes that the stages of ritual, the sense of journey implicit to ritual, reflects the more basic pattern of human transition or change. Thus, while the stages of the "journey" may be more focused or explicit in ritual, the actual distinction between the performed rite and the daily circumstance is a blurred one. Crisis breaks into a person's life and in the consequent "confrontation with mystery," transformation occurs. Rite and symbols, Searle suggests, have the unique purpose of "naming the experience and offering the assurance of meaning to an experience which otherwise threatens to overwhelm."

ethos is made explicit, resulting in agapic praxis.[7] In liturgy, this transformation is enacted ritually as the community responds to the ordo's proclamations of the gospel with a greater awareness of the interconnectedness of all creation and by "welcoming the stranger" to its banquet table in a mutually influencing relationship.

A semblance of this sense of journey, implicit to ritual, can be seen in the basic movement of the "Service for the Lord's Day" in the *Book of Common Worship:*[8]

Gathering

The Word

The Eucharist

Sending

As people gather to worship, they bring with them the questions and entanglements of their daily praxis and look to the wisdom of the Christian tradition for answers to these existential problems. Two elements of this "gathering" are vital. One is to praise God. The other is to be reminded of the need for God's grace. A function of the prayer of confession in this first part of the worship event is to make explicit the brokenness of the world, the fragile nature of human relationships, and the human struggle to live within the tragic structure of existence without insisting upon idolatrous self-securing.

Even as the community names the world's evils, it also names the promises of God in the face of that evil. This is a function of the second part of this worship pattern's movement, "proclaiming the Word." The hope of Christ proclaimed in the word disrupts the tragic structure of the world and enables the community to become a transformative presence in the world.[9]

[7] Edward Farley, *Good and Evil: Interpreting a Human Condition* (Minneapolis: Fortress Press, 1990) 190–3, argues that according to the Christian paradigm of redemption, the presence of the sacred breaks the hold of idolatry and enables a stance of courage within tragic circumstances. Beyond this, as people encounter the sacred, they are also drawn outside of self toward the other. "Courage" reduces the dominance of egocentrism and awakens a passion for the mystery of the "face." In other words, transformation results in a renewed awareness of and stance of agape toward the other's well-being and need.

[8] *Book of Common Worship* (Louisville: Westminster/John Knox Press, 1993) 46.

[9] Edward Farley, "Toward a New Paradigm for Preaching," *Preaching as a Theological Task: World, Gospel, Scripture,* ed. Thomas G. Long and Edward

Hearing God's word of hope in the face of the world's brokenness invites response. The juxtaposition of the contemporary context with tradition and with God's word enables transformation both of traditional understandings and of the contemporary context. Renewed by the experience of God's love and forgiveness, the response of the community breaks forth in several forms of thanksgiving: affirmations of faith, commissioning and ordination services, prayers of intercession, and passing of the peace, to mention a few.

The "Eucharist" embodies both the proclamation of the word and communal response. In this meal, as discussed in Chapter 3, the community does not merely remember or reenact a past event. Rather, it enacts and images a transformed world, a world infused with the grace proclaimed in the word, in which all people are welcomed and included as participants in the riches of God's reign.

The final movement of the Service for the Lord's Day is the "sending." The journey in search of knowledge of God now sends people into the world, back to the "lived" experience from which they came. Similar to Job as he returns to his community, however, participants are transformed; through worship, their intentions and actions have been formed.[10] They have been empowered to live within the tragic circumstances of human existence in courage and freedom.[11] In the juxtapositions of the ordo, as all the details of daily existence are gathered together with God's word, participants are enabled to envision the world redeemed.[12]

The metaphor of journey is not found exclusively in the wisdom corpus, although as discussed in Chapter 6, the symbol of the "way" is central to Proverbs. However, one aspect of faith's journey of

---

Farley (Louisville: Westminster/John Knox Press, 1996) 165–6, discusses liturgy as the locus of proclamation and argues that preaching is a discourse of redemption.

[10] Don Saliers, *Worship as Theology: Foretaste of Glory Divine* (Nashville: Abingdon Press, 1994) 148.

[11] Farley, *Good and Evil*, 128.

[12] Douglas Ottati, *Reforming Protestantism: Christian Commitment in Today's World* (Louisville: Westminster/John Knox Press, 1995) 73–4, emphasizes that "if sin means a world of fragmentation and conflict, then grace means the realignment of our partial cities and partial goods within God's all-inclusive city. Grace means re-generation, the re-turning of persons and communities toward abundant life, toward true communion with God in community with others."

discovery made clear in the wisdom corpus in particular is that the journey is ongoing; a community's faith world view is always "in-process." This ongoing critical-reflective interaction between contemporary horizons and tradition, vital to liturgical renewal, is inherent in the framework of wisdom.

As Brueggemann argues, "practitioners of wisdom" in the wisdom corpus are exemplary practical theologians. They are engaged daily in "faith praxis." This means that "they are constantly facing new experience that must not only be integrated into the deposit of learning, but must be permitted to revise the deposit of learning in light of new data."[13]

Such ongoing critical reflection is inherent in authentic liturgy as well. To see liturgy as a journey can help to remind us that liturgy is not "instrumental."[14] As Alexander Schmemann emphasizes, Christian liturgy is not cultic; it does not exist to provide a place of isolation or escape from the world. Rather, through worship's juxtapositions, people are reminded that all of life, and thus all of the world, is created by God and is filled with meaning and purpose.[15] The mission of the Church is to enact and embody a vision of a transformed world; this mission overflows the parameters of particular liturgical events as the people of the community make ethical decisions and exist in relation with one another, God, and the world in their daily lives.

On one level, then, a wisdom framework is implicit to liturgy. However, as stated earlier, wisdom cannot claim sole ownership of the journey motif in biblical literature. It is also important, therefore, to

[13] Brueggemann, *Theology of the Old Testament*, 685.

[14] Horace T. Allen, "Liturgy as the Form of Faith," *The Landscape of Praise: Readings in Liturgical Renewal*, ed. Blair Gilmer Meeks (Valley Forge, Pa.: Trinity Press International, 1996) 7–10, points to Calvin's emphasis that faith is an experience of commitment nurtured in the community by word and sacrament. In Proverbs, as seen earlier, the centrality of community is evident as teaching occurs in a family setting. The gender-specific references in both Proverbs and in Calvin's model are to be noted as problematic; however, an important point made by the family focus is that the locus of faith is not in individual piety but in a communal social setting. See also Brian Gerrish, *Grace and Gratitude: The Eucharistic Theology of John Calvin* (Minneapolis: Fortress Press, 1993) 36–41.

[15] Alexander Schmemann, *For the Life of the World: Sacraments and Orthodoxy* (New York: St. Vladimir's Seminary Press, 1973) 123.

examine some ways that a wisdom liturgical method influences the actual words, actions, and rituals of the ordo.

Eucharistic Prayers

As Gordon Lathrop argues, a twofold communal action brings to expression the primary meaning of the ordo:

"The Gospel tradition makes clear that the Christian continuation of meal-keeping has deep roots in the many layers of the Jesus tradition. To eat this meal in the community is to continue what began in the life of Jesus, who came eating and drinking, held meals with sinners, spoke of the dominion of God as a wedding feast, and interpreted his own death as a meal. For the community the meal is the very presence of Christ himself. Word service and the meal of the Jesus tradition . . . here again is the way liturgical meaning occurs."[16]

The Eucharist is central to Christian worship; because of this, the liturgical movement has devoted much attention to the form of Eucharistic Prayers. A wisdom liturgical method can contribute to those efforts on several levels.

First, wisdom's linguistic patterns can influence the use of language in Eucharistic Prayers. As suggested in Chapter 1, it is the structure of language that enables past events to change present horizons. Because remembering is central to eucharistic practice, an examination of the language used in liturgical remembering of the paschal mystery is crucial to renewal. Wisdom can contribute in several ways.

In the Eucharist, David Power argues, the community names or addresses God using memorial discourse. This language has a metaphorical structure and invites the community into relation with God through Christ and into the eschatological hope to which the juxtaposition of language and symbol points. The importance of correlating wisdom theology with this process has already been examined in Chapters 3 and 5. Several aspects of this discussion can be mentioned here in reference to the Eucharistic Prayer in particular.

As Farley argues, redemptive ecclesial presence centers on how the sacred is known and interpreted in the community and on how communal mediations of the sacred break the hold of ideological dynamics both in

---

[16] Gordon Lathrop, *Holy Things: A Liturgical Theology* (Minneapolis: Fortress Press, 1993) 44.

the Church and in the world.[17] In terms of how the sacred is known and expressed in Eucharistic Prayer, the ability of wisdom's metaphorical language to remain rooted in concrete historical experience while pointing to the mysterious and ineffable aspects of God's presence is of central importance. Wisdom helps to restore a balance between the metaphorical discourse of blessing and memorial and ontological discourse, both of which, Power argues, are important to eucharistic theology.

In Western methodologies centered on redemption history, "hegemonic discourses" have dominated in expressing God's presence.[18] Monarchical and male metaphors for God historically have gained primary attention. Farley argues that in authentic ecclesial existence, primary metaphors for God's relation to human beings are more interpersonal, growing out of the sphere of the interhuman and reflecting the compassionate action of God in creation and ultimately in Christ.[19] Wisdom offers alternative images or metaphors for the community's expressions of God's presence, images that could be utilized in the language of Eucharistic Prayer.

Not only does wisdom offer different metaphors for God, such as "Sophia" as discussed in Chapter 5, an overall structure of doxology within wisdom stands in juxtaposition to and disrupts ideological or tragic structures.[20] This is reflected in the language of creation in Proverbs 8:

"Ages ago I was set up,
    at the first, before the beginning of the earth.
When there were no depths I was brought forth,
    when there were no springs abounding with water.

[17] Edward Farley, *Ecclesial Man: A Social Phenomenology of Faith and Reality* (Philadelphia: Fortress Press, 1975) 146.

[18] Elisabeth Schüssler Fiorenza, *Jesus: Miriam's Child, Sophia's Prophet* (New York: Continuum, 1994) 5–8. See also Marjorie Proctor-Smith, *Praying with Our Eyes Open: Engendering Feminist Liturgical Prayer* (Nashville: Abingdon Press, 1995) 17–40.

[19] Farley, *Good and Evil*, 143–4.

[20] Leo Perdue, *Wisdom and Creation: The Theology of Wisdom Literature* (Nashville: Abingdon Press, 1994) 330–42, highlights the numerous metaphors used in wisdom in relation to creation, reality, humanity, and the world: fertility (Proverbs 8), artistry (Job 9:6; 37:18), birth and nurture (Prov 8:22-31), household (Proverbs 31), city (Proverbs 1; 8; and 9), and garden (Prov 3:13-20), to mention a few.

Before the mountains had been shaped,
before the hills, I was brought forth."[21]

The language in this hymn of praise both describes the origins of the cosmos and metaphorically points to the enduring presence of wisdom, of Sophia, in creation.

In the final part of Proverbs 8, Sophia invites hearers to enter into a relationship with her, to take up the study of wisdom:

"And now, my children, listen to me:
  happy are those who keep my ways.
Hear instruction and be wise,
  and do not neglect it.
Happy is the one who listens to me,
  watching daily at my gates,
  waiting beside my doors.
For whoever finds me finds life
  and obtains favor from the LORD."[22]

As Leo Perdue suggests, Sophia,

"the firstborn of creation, perhaps active in the shaping of the cosmos . . . now issues once more the call to life that she had offered in the first section of the poem (8:1-11). This closure, where the end returns to the beginning, gives the invitation of Woman Wisdom even greater authority."[23]

As noted earlier, Sophia's invitation is inclusive; she stands at the intersection of public discourse, disrupting human structures with the language of inviting and creation and calling all of humanity to gather around her banquet table (9:1-5).

In this wisdom hymn and in Job, a multiplicity of variegated symbols and images of God's creative presence in the universe emerge as central:

"Have you entered the storehouses of the snow,
  or have you seen the storehouses of the hail,

---

[21] Prov 8:23-25.
[22] Prov 8:32-35.
[23] Perdue, *Wisdom and Creation*, 91.

which I have reserved for the time of trouble,
    for the day of battle and war?
What is the way to the place where light is distributed,
    or where the east wind is scattered upon the earth?

"Can you bind the chains of Pleiades,
    or loose the cords of Orion?
Can you lead forth the Mazzaroth in their season,
    or can you guide the Bear with its children?
Do you know the ordinances of the heavens?
    Can you establish their rule on the earth?"[24]

As seen in this language from the YHWH speeches, wisdom does not produce a unified linguistic discourse but rather a "reflective linguistic-symbolic discourse."[25] Such language reminds us that according to Jewish and Christian tradition, language about God must always be understood as metaphorical. God language is "symbolic, metaphoric, and analogous because human language can never speak adequately about divine reality."[26]

To use aspects of the hymnic imagery in Proverbs or doxological language from Job in Eucharistic Prayers, particularly in that part of the prayer focused on thanksgiving and praise, can renew the community's appreciation for God's work in creation; it can also establish metaphorical language for naming God that speaks to the elusive quality of God's presence. Such language reminds the community of its interrelation with and responsibility for the created world, thus making more explicit the link between cosmos and ethos in liturgical forms.

Wisdom can also contribute to discussions regarding the shape of Eucharistic Prayers. This contribution is of particular importance when the structure of the Eucharistic Prayer and the structure of faith are seen as interconnected.[27] As Marjorie Proctor-Smith notes, contemporary renewal of Eucharistic Prayers has sought to recover ancient patterns. One thing that has been emphasized in this retrieval

[24] Job 38:22-24, 31-33.
[25] Schüssler Fiorenza, *Jesus: Miriam's Child, Sophia's Prophet*, 161.
[26] Ibid.
[27] David Power, *Eucharistic Mystery: Revitalizing the Tradition* (New York: Crossroad, 1995) 135.

is the impossibility and inadequacy of establishing a unitary Eucharistic Prayer.[28]

A major change initiated by the liturgical reform in relation to this has been the adoption of the "Antiochene" pattern for the prayer. In this pattern, the general movement is "from thanksgiving and praise to the institution narrative, followed by an explicit statement of remembrance of Christ, an invocation of the Spirit, intercession (sometimes), and a concluding doxology."[29] This pattern allows for multiformity even as it provides a common framework. It focuses on the life and ministry of Jesus as well as on the passion, and emphasizes "meal" over "sacrifice." In addition, in its focus on thanksgiving for creation, the pattern engages contemporary cosmological concerns.

Wisdom's metaphorical structure and theological content contain similar emphases. For example, sacrificial language is not common to wisdom theology. In addition, its metaphors for God and dialogical structure make it possible to follow this pattern while engaging cosmological concerns and drawing attention away from the traditional focus on redemption history. One reason that using wisdom's language of creation accomplishes this is that wisdom focuses on creation as the context for redemption history.[30]

[28] Howard Hageman, "The Eucharistic Prayer in Reformed Tradition," *Reformed Liturgy and Music* 22 (Fall 1988) 187–9, emphasizes this development within the Reformed Tradition. In the 1946 *Book of Common Worship,* there are only three Eucharistic Prayers; the 1970 *Worshipbook* has only two. The most recent *Book of Common Worship* (1993) contains twenty-six Eucharistic Prayers.

[29] Proctor-Smith, *Praying with Our Eyes Open,* 128–9. Power, *Eucharistic Mystery,* 82, explains that the idea of a unitary prayer, "either in the form of an original text or of an original structure, was at one stage important because of the attempt to discover the Semitic roots of the prayer." This focus no longer dominates eucharistic study. Emphasis is now placed on the diversity of Christian prayers, seeking to understand how they are related to Jewish texts. A comparative approach, says Power, helps to uncover the "flexibility of structure and meaning within a common tradition of memorial."

[30] It must be noted here again that wisdom is not the only part of Scripture that can claim such a centrality for creation. Such an emphasis is found in Genesis and the Psalms, just to mention two. Brueggemann, *Theology of the Old Testament,* 528–51, examines a wealth of Old Testament texts that speak to "creation as Yahweh's partner." I submit that it is the combination of form and content in wisdom and its unique ability to engage contemporary theology and liturgical theology that give it such visibility and credibility for the purposes of this project. In addition, wisdom's personification of wisdom and

Fred Craddock has discussed this in relation to preaching by delineating what he calls a "theocentric christology." Creation, argues Craddock, is the context for God's mighty acts in history. In a theocentric christology with this focus, Christ is seen as the decisive content of the gospel but not as the origin of it; God's relationship with the entire world becomes the larger context of Christ's story. Beginning with God as Creator, Craddock continues, provides a broad and inclusive context of meaning in which historical events from the Exodus to Christ's death and resurrection find their most authentic truth.[31]

Another contribution a wisdom liturgical method can make to Eucharistic Prayer is in relation to intercession. As Lathrop argues, prayer at the eucharistic table is held together by a dialectic of praise and petition, doxology and lament. This juxtaposition of thanksgiving and beseeching is central to the prayer. It urges the community to recognize God's presence in the midst of tragedy.[32] As discussed at length in Chapter 7, the dialectic of praise and lament is clearly operative in Job. Job's contemplation of the created universe leads to his recognition of God's presence in the entirety of his life and transforms his moral world view. In Job, the connection between pathos and ethos is made explicit; it is a connection that can also be made more explicit in Eucharistic Prayer as the community is encouraged through the prayer's language and structure to "remember" the suffering of those not present either historically or currently.

The Eucharistic Prayer draws participants into a deeper gratitude for God's gifts of life and grace, shaping a piety in which human hearts and minds become more attuned to the "world in all its beauty, terror, and mystery."[33] Wisdom, too, invites hearers to be more attentive to God and to God's world, thus reorienting their lives within a framework of continuous gratitude. More work can certainly be done in juxtaposing wisdom understandings and structure with Eucharistic Prayer as it has developed historically, particularly as regards its Jewish roots, and as it is practiced in liturgy today.

---

of folly give it a unique quality. See James Crenshaw, *Old Testament Wisdom: An Introduction* (Atlanta: John Knox Press, 1981) 96.

[31] Fred Craddock, "The Gospel of God," *Preaching as a Theological Task*, ed. Thomas G. Long and Edward Farley (Louisville: Westminster/John Knox Press, 1996) 73–81.

[32] Lathrop, *Holy Things*, 57–8.

[33] Saliers, *Worship as Theology*, 88.

One very practical way of making the influence of wisdom more explicit in Eucharistic Prayer is exemplified in Power's example of how the basis for the prayer could be the lectionary texts for a given Sunday. He composed the following Eucharistic Prayer for the Twenty-fifth Sunday of the Year, Cycle B, when the readings are: Wis 2:12, 17-20; Ps 54:3-4, 5, 6-8; Jas 3:16–4:3; Mark 9:30-37:

"In the peace of the Spirit, O God, we are bidden by your grace to come to the table set by Christ and to give you praise and thanksgiving for the work which you have wrought in him for the world.

We come to find a wisdom which reveals your presence even in the midst of a time troubled by discrimination, jealousy and strife, of a time wherein death knows no bounds, and we thank you for the just one in whose death your love prevailed."[34]

The prayer continues, but this excerpt demonstrates Power's effort to incorporate the ethical orientation found in the readings from Wisdom, Psalm 54, and James. This use of lectionary texts as a source for Eucharistic Prayer suggests that greater inclusion of the wisdom corpus in the lectionary might lead to a more explicit influence of wisdom on liturgy as a whole.[35]

Other examples of specific uses of a wisdom method in liturgical praxis could be offered, but the intent of this dissertation is not to delineate the method but to lay groundwork for it. The preceding discussion demonstrates, however, some ways a wisdom liturgical method can influence liturgical practice. A final word can be said in that regard.

A concern of liturgical renewal has been to lessen the gap between clergy and laity, between theory and practice. A more intentional focus on wisdom theology's structure and content can aid in this, particularly as its discourse is participatory. This was demonstrated in

[34] Power, *Eucharistic Mystery*, 330.

[35] Marjorie Proctor-Smith, *In Her Own Rite: Constructing Feminist Liturgical Tradition* (Nashville: Abingdon Press, 1990) 125–7, argues that "an androcentric hermeneutic has influenced both the choice of texts to be included and the way in which the three readings and psalm for each Sunday are related to one another." Alyce McKenzie, *Preaching Proverbs: Wisdom for the Pulpit* (Louisville: Westminster/John Knox Press, 1996) xi, notes that in general most lectionaries avoid Proverbs.

Chapter 5's discussion of the interactional nature of proverbial wisdom; as seen there, the use of wisdom, or the retrieval of tradition and the appropriation of it for the present, depends on the "wisdom of the theologizing community." This focus on the participatory nature of wisdom is also reflected in Job as in the shift from the prologue to the poetic dialogues beginning in Job 3, hearers are invited to engage the story as subjects.

When this happens, when hearers are invited into a mutually influencing dialogue, reconciliation and transformation are made possible, particularly transformation of oppressive structures. In addition, to invite communal participation in the appropriation and reconstruction of tradition roots theology firmly in the faith community, which is a foremost aim of liturgical theology.

CONCLUSION

> "What we call the beginning is often the end.
> And to make an end is to make a beginning.
> The end is where we start from.
>
> "We shall not cease from exploration
> And the end of all our exploring
> Will be to arrive where we started
> And to know the place for the first time."[36]

Theology as habitus is a wisdom that orients all the experiences, thoughts, and actions of people's lives toward God. Living within this hermeneutic orientation, says Douglas Ottati, those "who would respond to God find themselves called to relate all things both critically and constructively to God and God's purposes. They are called to participate fully in the full field of natural and cultural interrelations."[37]

By gathering the diverse voices of wisdom, liturgical theology, and philosophical theology around a common contemporary discussion table, this project has attempted to mirror such an integrative approach and to restore to liturgical method a clearer connection to theology as habitus.

As Brueggemann notes, this contemporary era is marked by (1) a pluralism of faith affirmations evident in the text, (2) a pluralism of

---

[36] T. S. Eliot, "Little Gidding," *Scrutiny* 11 (Spring 1943) 216–29.
[37] Ottati, *Reforming Protestantism*, 65.

methods for interpreting the text, and (3) a pluralism of interpretive communities.[38] This pluralism and the various sociocultural shifts at the end of the twentieth century have brought with them numerous challenges, precipitating crisis and change in the Church. This contemporary era can nevertheless be an exciting time of growth and renewal within the faith community as it struggles yet again to appropriate the wisdom of tradition for present circumstances.

Wisdom theology can be a dynamic partner in that struggle. In some sense, Sophia's voice calls the faith community today to a new journey of instruction, to the critical-reflective task of rethinking faith's deep symbols, of "remembering the mystery and giving it expression in the face of what appear to be overwhelming discreditations and displacements."[39] Through its language, structure, and dialogical movement between the horizons of everyday reality and tradition, wisdom models from within and for the Judeo-Christian tradition a method for undertaking this process of "rethinking." Wisdom provides a model for "setting the problem" of liturgical method from a perspective appropriate to this contemporary age.

The reality of human living is that there are those times when God is with us and we can "taste and see" that truth. There are also those times when God is with us but we are unable to see or hear God. The faith community, both historically and in the present, stands in the tension between God's elusiveness and God's immanence. This tension is inevitable within the tragic and broken reality of human existence.

It is at this horizon, in the intersection of the "already" and the "not yet" of the faith, that authentic worship happens.[40] To engage in contemplative piety at this fusion of horizons, as Job did, is to experience the beauty and holiness of God and God's creation and to become aware of the interrelationship of all things. It is also to live within the human circumstance of tragedy and suffering in a stance of courage and praise, always journeying toward a wisdom of heart and mind that can proclaim:

"O that my words were written down!
   O that they were inscribed in a book!

[38] Brueggemann, *Theology of the Old Testament*, xv.
[39] Edward Farley, *Deep Symbols: Their Postmodern Effacement and Reclamation* (Valley Forge, Pa.: Trinity Press International, 1996) 26.
[40] Saliers, *Worship as Theology*, 190.

O that with an iron pen and with lead
   they were engraved on a rock forever!
For I know that my Redeemer lives,
   and at the last will stand upon the earth;
and after my skin has been destroyed,
   then in my flesh I shall see God,
whom I shall see on my side,
   and my eyes shall behold, and not another.
   My heart faints within me!"[41]

---

[41] Job 19:23-27. The NRSV has been altered here to reflect inclusive language for God.

Bibliography

Ackoff, Russell. "The Future of Operational Research Is Past." *Journal of Operational Research Society* 30 (1979) 93–104.

Agnew, Mary Barbara. "Liturgy and Christian Social Action." *The Landscape of Praise: Readings in Liturgical Renewal.* Ed. Blair Gilmer Meeks, 44–52. Valley Forge, Pa.: Trinity Press International, 1996.

Aleshire, Daniel. "Introduction: The Good Theological School." *Theological Education* 30 (Spring 1994) 5–16.

Alexander, J. Neil, ed. *Time and Community.* Washington, D.C.: Pastoral Press, 1990.

Allen, Horace T. "Liturgy as the Form of Faith." *The Landscape of Praise: Readings in Liturgical Renewal.* Ed. Blair Gilmer Meeks, 7–10. Valley Forge, Pa.: Trinity Press International, 1996.

Anderson, Bernhard. *From Creation to New Creation: Old Testament Perspectives.* Minneapolis: Augsburg Press, 1994.

Aristotle. *Nichomachean Ethics.* Trans. Martin Ostwald. Indianapolis: Bobbs-Merrill, 1962.

Aune, Michael B. "Worship in an Age of Subjectivism Revisited." *Worship* 65 (May 1991) 224–38.

Baker, John. "Epistemological and Historical Remarks on a Present Conflict." *Perspectives in Religious Studies* 15 (Summer 1989) 121–31.

Baldovin, John. *Worship: City, Church, and Renewal.* Washington, D.C.: Pastoral Press, 1991.

Baumer, Franklin. *Religion and the Rise of Skepticism.* New York: Harcourt, Brace, and World, 1960.

Baumstark, Anton. *Comparative Liturgy.* Westminster, Md.: Newman Press, 1958.

Bell, Catherine. *Ritual Theory, Ritual Practice*. New York: Oxford University Press, 1992.

Benjamin, Jessica. *The Bonds of Love: Psychoanalysis, Feminism, and the Problem of Domination*. New York: Pantheon Books, 1988.

Bergant, Dianne. *What Are They Saying about Wisdom Literature?* New York: Paulist Press, 1984.

Birch, Bruce. "Biblical Preaching as Moral Reflection." *Journal for Preachers* 5 (1982) 13–17.

Birch, Bruce, and Larry Rasmussen. *Bible and Ethics in Christian Life*. Minneapolis: Augsburg Press, 1989.

Black, Max. *Models and Metaphors*. Ithaca, N.Y.: Cornell University Press, 1962.

Bondi, Richard. "The Elements of Character." *The Journal of Religious Ethics* 12 (1984) 201–18.

Book of Common Worship. Louisville: Westminster/John Knox Press, 1993.

The Book of Services. Nashville: The United Methodist Publishing House, 1984.

Bradshaw, Paul. *The Search for the Origins of Christian Worship: Sources and Methods for the Study of Early Liturgy*. New York: Oxford University Press, 1992.

Brown, William. *Character in Crisis: A Fresh Approach to the Wisdom Literature of the Old Testament*. Grand Rapids, Mich.: Eerdmans, 1996.

Browning, Don. *A Fundamental Practical Theology*. Minneapolis: Fortress Press, 1991.

Brueggemann, Walter. "A Convergence in Recent Old Testament Theologies." *Old Testament Theology: Essays on Structure, Theme and Text*. Ed. Patrick Miller, 95–110. Minneapolis: Fortress Press, 1992.

_____. *Finally Comes the Poet*. Minneapolis: Fortress Press, 1989.

_____. Foreword to *From Creation to New Creation: Old Testament Perspectives*, by Bernhard Anderson. Minneapolis: Fortress Press, 1994.

_____. "Hope and Despair as Seasons of Faith." *The Landscape of Praise: Readings in Liturgical Renewal*. Ed. Blair Gilmer Meeks, 172–9. Valley Forge, Pa.: Trinity Press International, 1996.

_____. *In Man We Trust: The Neglected Side of Biblical Faith*. Atlanta: John Knox Press, 1972.

_____. *The Prophetic Imagination.* Philadelphia: Fortress Press, 1978.

_____. "A Shape for Old Testament Theology, I: Structure Legitimation." *Old Testament Theology: Essays on Structure, Theme and Text.* Ed. Patrick Miller. Minneapolis: Fortress Press, 1992.

_____. "A Shape for Old Testament Theology, II: Embrace of Pain." *Old Testament Theology: Essays on Structure, Theme and Text.* Ed. Patrick Miller. Minneapolis: Fortress Press, 1992.

_____. "The Social Significance of Solomon as a Patron of Wisdom." *The Sage in Israel and the Ancient Near East.* Ed. John G. Gammie and Leo Perdue, 129–32. Winona Lake, Ind.: Eisenbrauns, 1990.

_____. *Theology of the Old Testament: Testimony, Dispute, Advocacy.* Minneapolis: Fortress Press, 1997.

Burghardt, Walter J. "A Theologian's Challenge to Liturgy." *Theological Studies* 35 (June 1974) 233–48.

Burkhart, John. *Worship.* Philadelphia: Westminster Press, 1982.

Buttrick, David. "The Praise of Ordinary People." *The Landscape of Praise: Readings in Liturgical Renewal.* Ed. Blair Gilmer Meeks, 256–61. Valley Forge, Pa.: Trinity Press International, 1996.

_____. "Speaking Between the Times." *Theology and the Interhuman.* Ed. Robert R. Williams, 147–59. Valley Forge, Pa.: Trinity Press International, 1995.

Camp, Claudia. *Wisdom and the Feminine in the Book of Proverbs.* Sheffield, England: Almond Press, 1985.

_____. "Woman Wisdom as Root Metaphor: A Theological Consideration." *The Listening Heart: Essays in Wisdom and the Psalms in Honor of R. E. Murphy.* Ed. K. G. Hoglud et al., 45–76. JSOTSS. Sheffield: JSOT Press, 1987.

Childs, Brevard. *Biblical Theology in Crisis.* Philadelphia: Westminster Press, 1970.

Chopp, Rebecca. *Saving Work: Feminist Practices of Theological Education.* Louisville: Westminster/John Knox Press, 1989.

Cobb, John. "*Good and Evil* in Process Perspective." *Theology and the Interhuman.* Ed. Robert R. Williams, 3–20. Valley Forge, Pa.: Trinity Press International, 1995.

_____. *The Structure of Christian Existence.* New York: Seabury Press, 1975.

Collins, J. J. "Proverbial Wisdom and the Yahwist Vision." *Gnomic Wisdom.* Ed. J. D. Crossan, 1–18. Chico, Calif.: Scholars Press, 1980.

Collins, John. "New Testament Cosmology." *Cosmology and Theology.* Ed. David Tracy and Nicholas Lash. New York: Seabury Press, 1983.

Collins, Mary. "Critical Questions for Liturgical Theology." *Worship* 53 (July 1979) 302–17.

_____. "The Public Language of Ministry." *The Jurist* 41 (1981) 292.

_____. *Worship: Renewal to Practice.* Washington, D.C.: Pastoral Press, 1987.

Craddock, Fred. "The Gospel of God." *Preaching as a Theological Task.* Ed. Thomas G. Long and Edward Farley. Louisville: Westminster/John Knox Press, 1996.

Crenshaw, James. "Method for Determining Wisdom Influence upon 'Historical Literature.'" *Journal of Biblical Literature* 88 (1969) 129–42.

_____. *Old Testament Wisdom: An Introduction.* Atlanta: John Knox Press, 1981.

_____. "Popular Questioning of the Justice of God." *Zeitschrift für die alttestamentliche Wissenschaft* 82 (1970) 380–95.

_____. "Prolegomenon." *Studies in Ancient Israelite Wisdom.* Ed. H. M. Orlinsky. New York: KTAV Publishing House, 1976.

Dallen, James. "Liturgy and Justice for All." *Worship* 65 (July 1991) 290–306.

Delbanco, Andrew. *The Death of Satan: How Americans Have Lost the Sense of Evil.* New York: Farrar, Strauss, and Giroux, 1995.

Dix, Gregory. *The Shape of the Liturgy.* New York: Seabury Press, 1983.

Duba, Arlo. "Why a Eucharistic Prayer?" *Reformed Liturgy and Music* 22 (Fall 1988) 187–9.

Duke, James. "Farley's Prolegomena to Any Future Historical Theology." *Theology and the Interhuman.* Ed. Robert R. Williams, 105–24. Valley Forge, Pa.: Trinity Press International, 1995.

Dykstra, Craig. "The Formative Power of the Congregation." *Religious Education* 82 (Fall 1987) 530–46.

Edwards, Jonathan. "Treatise Concerning Religious Affections." *The Works of Jonathan Edwards,* vol. 1. Ed. Edward Hickman. Edinburgh: The Banner of Truth Trust, 1974.

Eliade, Mircea. *The Sacred and the Profane: The Nature of Religion—The Signifi-cance of Religious Myth, Symbolism and Ritual within Life and Culture.* New York: Harper and Row, 1957.

Eliot, T. S. "Little Gidding." *Scrutiny* 11 (Spring 1943) 216–29.

Empereur, James. *Exploring the Sacred.* Washington, D.C.: Pastoral Press, 1987.

Fagerberg, David. *What Is Liturgical Theology? A Study in Methodology.* College-ville: The Liturgical Press, 1992.

Farley, Edward. *Deep Symbols: Their Postmodern Effacement and Reclamation.* Val-ley Forge, Pa.: Trinity Press International, 1996.

_____. *Divine Empathy: A Theology of God.* Minneapolis: Fortress Press, 1996.

_____. *Ecclesial Man: A Social Phenomenology of Faith and Reality.* Philadelphia: Fortress Press, 1975.

_____. *Ecclesial Reflection: An Anatomy of Theological Method.* Philadelphia: Fortress Press, 1982.

_____. *The Fragility of Knowledge: Theological Education in the Church and Uni-versity.* Philadelphia: Fortress Press, 1988.

_____. *Good and Evil: Interpreting a Human Condition.* Minneapolis: Fortress Press, 1990.

_____. "Response." *Theology and the Interhuman.* Ed. Robert R. Williams, 247–62. Valley Forge, Pa.: Trinity Press International, 1995.

_____. "Re-thinking the God-Terms—Tradition: The God-Term of Social Remembering." *Toronto Journal of Theology* 9 (Spring 1993) 67–77.

_____. *Theologia: The Fragmentation and Unity of Theological Education.* Philadelphia: Fortress Press, 1983.

_____. "Thinking Toward the World: A Case for Philosophical Pluralism in Theology." *American Journal of Theology and Philosophy* 14 (January 1993) 51–63.

_____. "Toward a New Paradigm for Preaching." *Preaching as a Theological Task: World, Gospel, Scripture.* Ed. Thomas G. Long and Edward Farley, 165–75. Louisville: Westminster/John Knox Press, 1996.

_____. "Truth and the Wisdom of Enduring." *Phenomenology of the Truth Proper to Religion.* Ed. Daniel Guerriere. Albany: State University of New York Press, 1990.

Farley, Wendy. "Eros and the Truth: Feminist Theory and the Claims of Reality." *Theology and the Interhuman*. Ed. Robert R. Williams, 21–39. Valley Forge, Pa.: Trinity Press International, 1995.

Farmer, K. A. *Proverbs and Ecclesiastes: Who Knows What Is Good?* Grand Rapids, Mich.: Eerdmans, 1991.

Fontaine, Carole. *Traditional Sayings in the Old Testament*. Sheffield, England: Almond Press, 1982.

————. "Wounded Hero on a Shaman's Quest." *The Voice from the Whirlwind*. Ed. Leo Perdue and W. Clark Gilpin. Nashville: Abingdon Press, 1992.

Forstman, Jack. "A Historical Theologian in Ed Farley's Court." *Theology and the Interhuman*. Ed. Robert R. Williams, 125–46. Valley Forge, Pa.: Trinity Press International, 1995.

Freire, Paulo. *Pedagogy of the Oppressed*. Trans. Myra Bergman Ramos. Rev. ed. New York: Continuum, 1995.

Fulkerson, Mary McClintock. "*Theologia* as a Liberation *Habitus*: Thoughts toward Christian Formation for Resistance." *Theology and the Interhuman*. Ed. Robert R. Williams, 160–80. Valley Forge, Pa.: Trinity Press International, 1995.

Gadamer, Hans-Georg. "The Exemplary Significance of Legal Hermeneutics." *Primary Readings in Philosophy for Understanding Theology*. Ed. Diogenes Allen and Eric O. Springsted, 263–80. Louisville: Westminster/John Knox Press, 1992.

————. *Truth and Method*. New York: Crossroad, 1982.

Geertz, Clifford. *The Interpretation of Cultures: Selected Essays*. New York: Basic Books, 1973.

————. *Local Knowledge: Further Essays in Interpretive Anthropology*. New York: Basic Books, 1983.

————. *Myth, Symbol and Culture*. New York: Norton, 1971.

Gerrish, Brian. *Grace and Gratitude: The Eucharistic Theology of John Calvin*. Minneapolis: Fortress Press, 1993.

Gilkey, Langdon. *Naming the Whirlwind: The Renewal of God-Language*. New York: Bobbs-Merrill Company, 1969.

————. "Power, Order, Justice and Redemption: Theological Comments on Job." *The Voice from the Whirlwind: Interpreting the Book of Job*. Ed. Leo Perdue and W. Clark Gilpin, 159–71. Nashville: Abingdon Press, 1992.

_____. *Society and the Sacred.* New York: Crossroad, 1981.

Gnuse, Robert. *Heilgeschichte as a Model for Biblical Theology: The Debate Concerning the Uniqueness and Significance of Israel's Worldview.* New York: College Theology Society University Press of America, 1989.

Gottwald, Norman. *The Hebrew Bible: A Socio-Literary Introduction.* Philadelphia: Fortress Press, 1985.

_____. *The Tribes of Yahweh.* Maryknoll, N.Y.: Orbis Books, 1979.

Grimes, Ronald. *Beginnings in Ritual Studies.* Rev. ed. Columbia: University of South Carolina Press, 1995.

_____. *Ritual Criticism.* Columbia: University of South Carolina Press, 1990.

Guerriere, Daniel, ed. *Phenomenology of the Truth Proper to Religion.* Albany: State University of New York Press, 1990.

Gustafson, James. "A Response to the Book of Job." *The Voice from the Whirlwind: Interpreting the Book of Job.* Ed. Leo Perdue and W. Clark Gilpin, 172–84. Nashville: Abingdon Press, 1992.

Habel, Norman. "The Symbolism of Wisdom in Proverbs 1–9." *Interpretation* 26 (1972) 131–57.

Hageman, Howard. "The Eucharistic Prayer in Reformed Tradition." *Reformed Liturgy and Music* 22 (Fall 1988) 190–3.

Halberstam, David. *The Best and the Brightest.* New York: Random House, 1972.

Hart, James G. "Divine Truth in Husserl and Kant: Some Issues in Phenomenological Theology." *Phenomenology of the Truth Proper to Religion.* Ed. Daniel Guerriere, 21–46. Albany: State University of New York Press, 1990.

Hauerwas, Stanley. *Character and the Christian Life: A Study in Theological Ethics.* San Antonio, Tex.: Trinity University Press, 1975.

_____. *A Community of Character.* Notre Dame, Ind.: University of Notre Dame Press, 1981.

Heidegger, Martin. "The Way Back into the Ground of Metaphysics." *Primary Readings in Philosophy for Understanding Theology.* Ed. Diogenes Allen and Eric O. Springsted, 248–62. Louisville: Westminster/John Knox Press, 1992.

Henderson, J. Frank. "The Names and Images of God." *Landscape of Praise: Readings in Liturgical Renewal.* Ed. Blair Gilmer Meeks, 263–7. Valley Forge, Pa.: Trinity Press International, 1996.

Hermisson, Hans-Jurgen. "Observations on the Creation Theology in Wisdom." *Israelite Wisdom.* Ed. J. G. Gammie, W. A. Brueggemann, J. M. Ward. Philadelphia: Fortress Press, 1984.

Hilkert, Mary Catherine. *Naming Grace: Preaching and the Sacramental Imagination.* New York: Continuum, 1997.

Hodgson, Peter. "The Face and the Spirit." *Theology and the Interhuman.* Ed. Robert R. Williams, 40–50. Valley Forge, Pa.: Trinity Press International, 1995.

_____. *New Birth of Freedom.* Philadelphia: Fortress Press, 1976.

Hoffman, Lawrence. *Beyond the Text: A Holistic Approach to Liturgy.* Bloomington: Indiana University Press, 1989.

Hoffman, Lawrence, and Paul Bradshaw, eds. *The Making of Jewish and Christian Worship.* Notre Dame, Ind.: University of Notre Dame Press, 1991.

Hough, Joseph C., and John B. Cobb Jr. *Christian Identity and Theological Education.* Chico, Calif.: Scholars Press, 1985.

Huffman, Walter. "The Concept of Sacred Space." *The Landscape of Praise: Readings in Liturgical Renewal.* Ed. Blair Gilmer Meeks, 127–30. Valley Forge, Pa.: Trinity Press International, 1996.

Husserl, Edmund. *Ideas: General Introduction to Pure Phenomenology.* London: Allen and Unwin, 1931.

Irwin, Kevin. *Context and Text: Method in Liturgical Theology.* Collegeville: The Liturgical Press, 1994.

_____. *Liturgical Theology: A Primer.* Collegeville: The Liturgical Press, 1990.

Jones, Cheslyn, Geoffrey Wainwright, and Edward Yarnold, eds. *The Study of Liturgy.* New York: Oxford University Press, 1983.

Kaufmann, Gordon D. *God the Problem.* Cambridge, Mass.: Harvard University Press, 1979.

_____. *In the Face of Mystery: A Constructive Theology.* Cambridge, Mass.: Harvard University Press, 1993.

_____. "Nuclear Eschatology and the Study of Religion." *Journal of the American Academy of Religion* 51 (1983) 13–24.

Kavanagh, Aidan. *On Liturgical Theology.* New York: Pueblo, 1984.

Kelleher, Margaret Mary. "Liturgical Theology: A Task and a Method." *Worship* 62 (January 1988) 2–24.

Kelsey, David. *Between Athens and Berlin: The Theological Education Debate.* Grand Rapids, Mich.: Eerdmans, 1993.

_____. *To Understand God Truly: What's Theological about a Theological School?* Louisville: Westminster/John Knox Press, 1992.

_____. *The Uses of Scripture in Recent Theology.* Philadelphia: Fortress Press, 1975.

Koernke, Teresa. "An Ethics of Religious Behavior." *Worship* 66 (January 1992) 25–38.

Kohak, Erazim. *The Embers and the Stars.* Chicago: University of Chicago Press, 1984. (Quoted in Farley, Edward. *Deep Symbols: Their Postmodern Efface-ment and Reclamation.* Valley Forge, Pa.: Trinity Press International, 1996.)

Kraftchick, Steven J., Charles D. Myers, and Ben Ollenburger, eds. *Biblical Theology: Problems and Perspectives—In Honor of J. Christiaan Beker.* Nashville: Abingdon Press, 1995.

Kung, Hans. "A New Basic Model for Theology: Divergencies and Convergen-cies." *Paradigm Change in Theology: Symposium for the Future.* Ed. Hans Kung and David Tracy, 439–52. New York: Crossroad, 1991.

Kung, Hans, and David Tracy, eds. *Paradigm Change in Theology: Symposium for the Future.* New York: Crossroad, 1991.

Lang, Bernhard. *Wisdom and the Book of Proverbs: An Israelite Goddess Redefined.* New York: Pilgrim Press, 1986.

Lather, Patti. "Critical Theory, Curricular Transformation, and Feminist Main-streaming." *Journal of Education* 166 (1982) 55–66.

Lathrop, Gordon. "At Least Two Words: The Liturgy as Proclamation." *The Landscape of Praise: Readings in Liturgical Renewal.* Ed. Blair Gilmer Meeks, 183–5. Valley Forge, Pa.: Trinity Press International, 1996.

_____. *Holy Things: A Liturgical Theology.* Minneapolis: Fortress Press, 1993.

Levinson, Daniel, et al. *The Seasons of a Man's Life.* New York: A. A. Knopf, 1977.

Lewin, Kurt. *Field in Social Science.* New York: Harper and Row, 1951.

Lindbeck, George A. *The Nature of Doctrine: Religion and Theology in a Postliberal Age.* Philadelphia: Westminster Press, 1984.

Loder, James. *Religious Pathology and the Christian Faith.* Philadelphia: West-minster Press, 1966.

Lonergan, Bernard. *Insight: A Study of Human Understanding*. New York: Philosophical Library, Inc., 1957.

Lovin, Robin, and Frank Reynolds, eds. *Cosmogony and Ethical Order*. Chicago: University of Chicago Press, 1985.

Lowe, Walter. "Issues of *Good and Evil*." *Theology and the Interhuman*. Ed. Robert R. Williams, 51–64. Valley Forge, Pa.: Trinity Press International, 1995.

MacIntyre, Alasdair. *After Virtue: A Study in Moral Theory*. Notre Dame, Ind.: University of Notre Dame Press, 1981.

Macy, Gary. *The Banquet's Wisdom: A Short History of the Theologies of the Lord's Supper*. New York: Paulist Press, 1983.

McFague, Sallie. *Metaphorical Theology: Models of God in Religious Language*. Philadelphia: Fortress Press, 1982.

McKane, William. *Proverbs: A New Approach*. Philadelphia: Westminster Press, 1970.

McKenzie, Alyce. "Different Strokes for Different Folks: America's Quintessential Postmodern Proverb." *Theology Today* (July 1996) 201–12.

_____. *Preaching Proverbs: Wisdom for the Pulpit*. Louisville: Westminster/ John Knox Press, 1996.

McLaren, Peter. *Life in Schools: An Introduction to Critical Pedagogy in the Foundations of Education*. Miami: Longman, Inc., 1989.

Miller, Patrick J. "Introduction." *Old Testament Theology: Essays on Structure, Theme and Text*. Minneapolis: Fortress Press, 1995.

Mitchell, Nathan. *Cult and Controversy: The Worship of the Eucharist Outside Mass*. New York: Pueblo, 1974.

Morrill, Bruce T. "Anamnesis as Dangerous Memory: A Dialogue between Political and Liberation Theology." Ph.D. diss., Boston College, 1995.

Murphy, Roland. *The Forms of the Old Testament Literature*. Volume 13: *Wisdom Literature: Job, Proverbs, Ruth, Canticles, Ecclesiastes, Esther*. Grand Rapids, Mich.: Eerdmans, 1981.

_____. *The Tree of Life: An Exploration of Biblical Wisdom*. New York: Doubleday, 1990.

_____. "Wisdom and Creation." *Journal of Biblical Literature* 104 (1985) 3–11.

Newbigin, Lesslie. *Truth to Tell: The Gospel as Public Truth*. Grand Rapids, Mich.: Eerdmans, 1991.

Newsom, Carol. "The Moral Sense of Nature: Ethics in Light of God's Speech to Job." *Princeton Seminary Bulletin* 15 (1994) 9–27.

_____. "Woman and the Discourse of Patriarchal Wisdom: A Study of Proverbs 1–9." *Gender and Difference in Ancient Israel.* Ed. Peggy L. Day, 142–60. Minneapolis: Augsburg Fortress, 1989.

O'Connor, Kathleen. "The City Square and the Home: Wisdom's World." *Journal for Preachers* (March 1996) 10–15.

_____. "Wisdom Literature and Experience of the Divine." *Biblical Theology: Problems and Perspectives.* Ed. Steven J. Kraftchick, Charles D. Meyers, Ben C. Ollenburger. Nashville: Abingdon Press, 1995.

Ogletree, Thomas. "Christian Social Ethics as a Theological Discipline." *Shifting Boundaries: Contextual Approaches to the Structure of Theological Education.* Ed. Barbara Wheeler and Edward Farley, 201–40. Louisville: Westminster/John Knox Press, 1991.

Ollenburger, Ben. "Biblical Theology: Situating the Discipline." *Understanding the Word: Essays in Honor of Bernhard W. Anderson.* Ed. James Butler et al. Sheffield: JSOT Press, 1985.

O'Malley, J. W. "Reform, Historical Consciousness and Vatican II's *Aggiornamento.*" *Theological Studies* 32 (1971) 573–601.

Ottati, Douglas. *Reforming Protestantism: Christian Commitment in Today's World.* Louisville: Westminster/John Knox Press, 1995.

Perdue, Leo. *The Collapse of History: Reconstructing Old Testament Theology.* Minneapolis: Fortress Press, 1994.

_____. *Wisdom and Cult.* Missoula, Mont.: Scholars Press, 1977.

_____. *Wisdom and Creation: The Theology of Wisdom Literature.* Nashville: Abingdon Press, 1994.

_____. *Wisdom in Revolt: Creation Theology in the Book of Job.* Sheffield, England: Almond Press, 1991.

Poling, James N., and Donald E. Miller. *Foundations for a Practical Theology of Ministry.* Nashville: Abingdon Press, 1985.

Power, David. "Cult to Culture: The Liturgical Foundation of Theology." *Worship* 54 (November 1980) 482–94.

_____. *Eucharistic Mystery: Revitalizing the Tradition.* New York: Crossroad, 1995.

_____. "Liturgical Praxis: New Consciousness at the Eye of Worship." *Worship* 61 (July 1987) 292–305.

_____. "People at Liturgy." *Twenty Years of Concilium—Retrospect and Prospect.* Edinburgh: T. & T. Clark, 1983.

_____. *Unsearchable Riches: The Symbolic Nature of Liturgy.* New York: Pueblo, 1984.

Priest, John F. "Where Is Wisdom to Be Placed?" *Studies in Ancient Israelite Wisdom.* Ed. H. M. Orlinsky, 281–8. New York: KTAV Publishing House, 1976.

Proctor-Smith, Marjorie. *In Her Own Rite: Constructing Feminist Liturgical Tradition.* Nashville: Abingdon Press, 1990.

Reeder, Rachel. "Art of Our Own Making." *The Landscape of Praise: Readings in Liturgical Renewal.* Ed. Blair Gilmer Meeks, 11–13. Valley Forge, Pa.: Trinity Press International, 1996.

Ricoeur, Paul. *Figuring the Sacred: Religion, Narrative, and the Imagination.* Ed. Mark I. Wallace. Minneapolis: Fortress Press, 1995.

_____. *The Rule of Metaphor: Multi-disciplinary Studies of the Creation of Meaning in Language.* Trans. Robert Czerny et al. Toronto: University of Toronto Press, 1977.

Rieff, Philip. *The Triumph of the Therapeutic: The Uses of Faith after Freud.* New York: Harper and Row, 1968.

Roberts, J.J.M. "Historical-Critical Method, Theology and Contemporary Exegesis." *Biblical Theology: Problems and Perspectives.* Ed. Steven Kraftchick, Charles Myers, and Ben Ollenburger. Nashville: Abingdon Press, 1995.

Saliers, Don. *Worship as Theology: Foretaste of Glory Divine.* Nashville: Abingdon Press, 1994.

Sasse, Herman. *This Is My Body.* Minneapolis: Augsburg Press, 1959.

Schillebeeckx, Edward. *Christ the Sacrament of the Encounter with God.* New York: Sheed and Ward, 1963.

Schmemann, Alexander. *The Eucharist.* New York: St. Vladimir's Seminary Press, 1986.

_____. *For the Life of the World: Sacraments and Orthodoxy.* New York: St. Vladimir's Seminary Press, 1973.

_____. *Introduction to Liturgical Theology.* New York: St. Vladimir's Seminary Press, 1986.

_____. "Liturgy and Theology." *The Greek Orthodox Theological Review* 17 (1972) 86–100.

_____. *Sacraments and Orthodoxy.* New York: Herder and Herder, 1965.

_____. "Theology and Liturgical Tradition." *Worship in Scripture and Tradition.* Ed. Massey Shepherd. New York: Oxford University Press, 1963.

Schmidt, H. H. "Creation, Righteousness, and Salvation: 'Creation Theology' as the Broad Horizon of Biblical Theology." *Creation in the Old Testament.* Ed. Bernhard Anderson. Philadelphia: Fortress Press, 1984.

Schon, Donald. "The New Scholarship Requires a New Epistemology." *Change* (November/December 1995) 27–33.

_____. *The Reflective Practitioner: How Professionals Think in Action.* New York: Basic Books, 1983.

Schreiter, Robert. *Constructing Local Theologies.* Maryknoll, N.Y.: Orbis Books, 1985.

Schüssler Fiorenza, Elisabeth. *In Memory of Her: A Feminist Theological Reconstruction of Christian Origins.* New York: Crossroad, 1992.

_____. *Jesus: Miriam's Child, Sophia's Prophet.* New York: Continuum, 1994.

Scott, R.B.Y. "Solomon and the Beginnings of Wisdom in Israel." *Supplements to Vetus Testamentum* 3 (1955) 262–71.

_____. "Wisdom and Creation: The AMON of Proverbs 8:30." *Vetus Testamentum* 10 (1960) 213–23.

Searle, Mark. "Journey of Conversion." *Worship* 54 (January 1980) 35–55.

_____. "Liturgy as Metaphor." *Worship* 55 (March 1981) 98–120.

_____. "Renewing the Liturgy—Again." *Commonweal* (18 November 1988) 617–22.

_____. "The Uses of Liturgical Language." *The Landscape of Praise: Readings in Liturgical Renewal.* Ed. Blair Gilmer Meeks, 105–10. Valley Forge, Pa.: Trinity Press International, 1996.

Soskice, Janet Martin. *Metaphor and Religious Language.* Oxford: Clarendon Press, 1985.

Taylor, Barbara Brown. *The Preaching Life.* Boston: Cowley Publications, 1993.

Taylor, Mark K. "Celebrating Difference, Resisting Domination: The Need for Synchronic Strategies in Theological Education." *Shifting Boundaries: Contextual Approaches to the Structure of Theological Education.* Ed. Barbara Wheeler and Edward Farley. Louisville: Westminster/John Knox Press, 1991.

Terrien, Samuel. *The Elusive Presence: Toward a New Biblical Theology.* New York: Harper and Row, 1978.

_____. "The Play of Wisdom: Turning Point in Biblical Theology." *Horizons in Biblical Theology* 3 (1981) 125–53.

Towner, W. Sibley. "The Renewed Authority of Old Testament Wisdom for Contemporary Faith." *Canon and Authority: Essays in Old Testament Religion and Theology.* Ed. George W. Coats and Burke O. Long. Philadelphia: Fortress Press, 1977.

Tracy, David. *Analogical Imagination: Christian Theology and the Culture of Pluralism.* New York: Crossroad, 1981.

_____. "The Analogical Imagination in Catholic Theology." *Talking about God: Doing Theology in the Context of Modern Pluralism.* Ed. David Tracy and John B. Cobb Jr. New York: Seabury Press, 1983.

_____. "Analogy and Dialectic: God-Language." *Talking about God: Doing Theology in the Context of Modern Pluralism.* Ed. David Tracy and John B. Cobb Jr. New York: Seabury Press, 1983.

_____. *Blessed Rage for Order: The New Pluralism in Theology.* New York: Seabury Press, 1975.

_____. "Religious Values after the Holocaust: A Catholic View." *Jews and Christians after the Holocaust.* Ed. Abraham Peck. Philadelphia: Fortress Press, 1982.

Tracy, David, and Nicholas Lash, eds. *Cosmology and Theology.* New York: Seabury Press, 1983.

Trulear, Harold. "The Sacramentality of Preaching." *The Landscape of Praise: Readings in Liturgical Renewal.* Ed. Blair Gilmer Meeks, 202–10. Valley Forge, Pa.: Trinity Press International, 1996.

Van Gennep, Arnold. *The Rites of Passage.* Chicago: University of Chicago Press, 1960.

Vincie, Catherine. "Tension and Transformation in Public Prayer." *The Landscape of Praise: Readings in Liturgical Renewal.* Ed. Blair Gilmer Meeks, 97–104. Valley Forge, Pa.: Trinity Press International, 1996.

Von Allman, Jean-Jacques. *Worship: Its Theology and Practice*. New York: Oxford University Press, 1965.

Von Rad, Gerhard. *Wisdom in Israel*. Nashville: Abingdon Press, 1972.

Wainwright, Geoffrey. *Doxology: The Praise of God in Worship, Doctrine, and Life*. New York: Oxford University Press, 1980.

_____. *Eucharist and Eschatology*. London: Epworth Press, 1971.

Wasserman, Marney. "The Shape of Eucharistic Thanksgiving." *Reformed Liturgy and Music* 29 (1995) 139–45.

Weiler, Kathleen. *Women Teaching for Change: Gender, Class and Power*. New York: Bergin and Garvey Publishers, 1988.

Westermann, Claus. *Blessing in the Bible and the Life of the Church*. Philadelphia: Fortress Press, 1978.

_____. *Creation*. Philadelphia: Fortress Press, 1974.

_____. *Roots of Wisdom: The Oldest Proverbs of Israel and Other Peoples*. Louisville: Westminster/John Knox Press, 1990.

Wheeler, Barbara G. "Uncharted Territory: Congregational Identity and Mainline Protestantism." *The Presbyterian Predicament: Six Perspectives*. Ed. Milton J. Coalter, John M. Mulder, and Louis B. Weeks. Louisville: Westminster/John Knox Press, 1990.

Wheeler, Barbara, and Edward Farley, eds. *Shifting Boundaries: Contextual Approaches to the Structure of Theological Education*. Louisville: Westminster/John Knox Press, 1991.

Wheelwright, Philip. *Metaphor and Reality*. Bloomington: Indiana University Press, 1962.

White, James. *A Brief History of Christian Worship*. Nashville: Abingdon Press, 1993.

_____. *Christian Worship in North America—A Retrospective: 1955–1995*. Collegeville: The Liturgical Press, 1997.

Williams, James G. "Job and the God of Victims." *The Voice from the Whirlwind*. Ed. Leo Perdue and W. Clark Gilpin, 208–10. Nashville: Abingdon Press, 1992.

Williams Robert R. "Tragedy, Totality, and the Face." *Theology and the Interhuman*. Ed. Robert R. Williams, 80–104. Valley Forge, Pa.: Trinity Press International, 1995.

Wink, Walter. *Transformation: Toward a New Paradigm for Biblical Study.* Philadelphia: Fortress Press, 1973. (Quoted in Roberts, J.J.M. "Historical-Critical Method, Theology and Contemporary Exegesis." *Biblical Theology: Problems and Perspective.* Ed. Steven Kraftchick, Charles Myers, and Ben Ollenburger. Nashville: Abingdon Press 1995.)

Witherington, Ben. *Jesus the Sage: Pilgrimage of Wisdom.* Minneapolis: Fortress Press, 1994.

Wolsterstorff, Nicholas. "Liturgy, Justice, and Tears." *Worship* 62 (September 1988) 386–403.

Zimmerli, Walther. "The Place and Limit of Wisdom in the Framework of the Old Testament." *Studies in Ancient Israelite Wisdom.* Ed. H. M. Orlinsky. New York: KTAV Publishing House, 1976.

Index

being-founded, 112
faith community as redemptive
    horizon, 69, 105–6, 159, 218
reality-apprehension and the faith
    community, 74, 76, 87
theological portraiture, 68, 98ff, 140
tragic structure of human existence,
    109ff, 132, 158, 228
universal face, 114, 115n
Fontaine, Carole, 169–75, 244–5
foundational theology, 53

Geertz, Clifford, 181–2
Gilkey, Langdon, 13, 18, 78, 175–6

Habel, Norman, 179–80, 213–6
habitus, 12, 81ff, 101, 105, 116–7, 162,
    197, 201–3, 217–8, 262
    as hermeneutic orientation, 54
Heidegger, Martin, 90–1
Hilkert, Mary Catherine, 57ff, 156
historical positivism, 98, 139–40
historical theology, 68, 98
Holocaust, 151

idolatry, 110–1, 135, 219
imagination, 194–6
interhuman, 8–9, 33, 109, 228, 240
intersubjectivity, 95, 98, 106ff, 124,
    201, 240
    and biblical theology, 136–7

Job
    1–2; 42:7-17, 231
    1:1, 232
    1:1-5, 230
    1:8, 233
    3, 234
    3:1-4, 231
    7:17-19, 235
    12:13-14, 235
    12:19-21, 235

12:23, 235
19:13-15, 237
19:23-27, 264
30:1-9, 239
34:1-3, 171
37:23-24, 247
38:22-33, 258
38–41, 237
and skepticism, 145
and contractual theology, 158
journey of conversion, 213–6, 231, 251

Kavanagh, Aidan, 102–3, 134
Kelleher, Margaret Mary, 84ff
Kelsey, David, 81ff
knowing-in-action, 25–6
knowledge
    empirical, 10, 31, 170
    and liberation, 27
    as art, 72
    professional knowledge, 71–2
    tacit, 25, 170

Lathrop, Gordon, 1, 10, 24, 76, 83–4,
    88, 91, 118–9, 148, 173–4, 184–5,
    189, 225, 240
legem credendi lex statuat supplicandi,
    4–5, 28
leitourgia, 23, 52
lex agendi, 198
lex credendi, 28, 35, 40, 139, 198
lex orandi, 28, 35, 40, 44, 139, 198
liberation theology, 146
Lindbeck, George, 138–9
liturgical movement, 3–7, 14, 24–5, 58,
    65–6, 75–6, 78, 87, 161–6, 168, 222–3
    and biblical theology, 101, 124, 146
liturgical theology, 22, 28, 29, 35, 46ff,
    50, 87, 148, 151–2, 161
    method, 85ff
    v. theologies from worship, 35ff,
        82n, 85, 92, 139
    v. theologies of worship, 29–35, 92

liturgy
   agapic dimension of, 118
   and Christian identity, 5
   and conversion, 69–70, 86–7, 119
   and epistemology, 48ff
   and juxtaposition, 2, 24, 76, 91–2
   and justice, 131ff, 148, 236, 241
   and language, 91–2, 94–5, 166–7, 173
   androcentric nature of, 61–2
   as communal activity, 50ff, 106
   as horizon of truth, 67–8, 84ff
   as ontological condition of theology,
      53
   cultic categories of, 52–3, 134, 218
   eschatological dimension, 202

metaphor, 172, 234
metaphorical language
   and eucharistic narrative, 133, 185–6
   and liturgy, 166–7
   and the wisdom corpus, 167ff
   for God, 154–5, 163
   monarchical metaphors, 113
   interpersonal metaphors, 113–4
metaphorical process, 2, 179ff, 213–6
metaphysics, 90–1
Mitchell, Nathan, 33ff
modern historical consciousness, 44
Murphy, Roland, 150–1, 172

Newsom, Carol, 231, 233n, 239

O'Connor, Kathleen, 126, 211–2, 217
ontology, 68n, 87, 88ff, 152, 176
   of symbols, 176–8
ordo, 3, 7, 10, 75–8, 92, 102, 148, 173–4,
   225
Ottati, Douglas, 83n

paideia, 81n
paroemiology, 169
paschal mystery, 8n
pathos, 47

Perdue, Leo, 15ff, 101n, 137ff, 163–4,
   172–3, 182–4
phenomenology, 49, 53ff, 75, 77n
philosophical theology, 73
pluralism, 262–3
Power, David, 32, 89ff, 92–6, 117,
   151–3, 186
   ontology, 89ff, 176–8
   anamnesis, 133, 255
Proctor-Smith, Marjorie, 19, 57n, 61–2,
   108, 258–9
profane, 13n, 51, 54, 218
proverb performance, 169–72
proverbial sayings, 168ff
Proverbs
   1–9, 203–4, 216, 237
   1:1-7, 205
   1:20-21, 193
   4–6, 216
   4:10-19, 213
   4:10-15, 179
   4:16-19, 213
   7:6, 204, 214
   8:1, 207
   8:9, 207
   8:1-9, 193
   8:22-31, 208
   8:23-25, 257
   8:29-30, 247
   8:32-35, 257
   9:1-6, 216
   9:1-9, 183
   as example of sapiential imagina-
      tion, 163
   sacramental aspects, 211ff

redemption, 112, 220
redemption history, 5, 15–6, 79, 102,
   111, 147, 234–5, 245–6
redemptive discourse, 105, 238
reflective ontology, 68, 97ff, 228, 242–3
reflective thinking, 165
reflective transfer, 170

sacramental imagination, 58n, 156
sacramental language, 103
sacramental theology, 56
  mysterion, 57n
  sacramentum, 57n
  and Proverbs, 217
sacraments
  eucharist, 34, 47, 89, 133, 217, 241,
    253
sacred, 13n, 51, 54, 88, 134, 255–6
Saliers, Don, 23, 56–7, 69, 86–7, 201–3
salvation history, 135, 145
sapientia, 73
sapiential imagination, 60, 155n, 161ff,
  182, 195
Schmemann, Alexander, 22, 50ff, 102,
  199, 211, 217–8
Schon, Donald, 25ff, 35–6, 47, 71ff,
  169
scientia, 73
Searle, Mark, 14, 173, 186–7, 213–6
Seitel, Peter, 170–2
skepticism, 144–5, 150
Sophia, 198, 204, 207ff, 256–8
subjectivism, 106ff
systematic theology, 38

Taylor, Barbara Brown, 1n, 194
technical rationality, 36, 72, 83

Terrien, Samuel, 121, 188, 207–10
  theology of presence, 122–3
theocentric piety, 67
theologia, 37n, 59–60, 81–2, 210
theological education, 36, 47n, 66, 101,
  162n, 227
theological method
  as criteriology, 73–4, 88
  problem setting in, 72, 88, 128, 170
thick description, 31n
Tracy, David, 155–6
tradition, 129ff, 142–3
  as constructed, 108
  and Christianity's house of author-
    ity, 129ff, 134, 220
  and proverbial sayings, 168
  in the wisdom corpus, 143
  vehicles of social duration, 68

virtue, 198, 200–2

Wainwright, Geoffrey, 38–9, 41ff
Westermann, Claus, 148–9
wisdom theology
  social-scientific approach to, 142ff
  and creation theology, 149ff
words of power, 8, 33, 34–5, 79, 153,
  225

Zimmerli, Walther, 149–50